RACE AND SPORT

RACE AND SPORT

The Struggle for Equality on and off the Field

Essays by
SCOTT BROOKS
JOHN M. CARROLL
GERALD R. GEMS
C. KEITH HARRISON
RITA LIBERTI
MICHAEL E. LOMAX
PATRICK B. MILLER
KENNETH L. SHROPSHIRE
EARL SMITH
ALICIA VALDEZ

Edited by
CHARLES K. ROSS

UNIVERSITY PRESS OF MISSISSIPPI
Jackson

www.upress.state.ms.us

The University Press of Mississippi is a member of the Association of American University Presses.

Print-on-Demand Edition

Library of Congress Cataloging-in-Publication Data

Race and sport : the struggle for equality on and off the field / essays by Scott Brooks . . . [et al.] ; edited by Charles K. Ross.
    p. cm.
  Includes bibliographical references and index.
  ISBN 1-57806-657-3 (cloth : alk. paper)
  1. Racism in sports—United States—History. 2. African American athletes—History. I. Brooks, Scott. II. Ross, Charles Kenyatta, 1964–
  GV706.32.R28 2004
  796'.0989—dc22   2004013284

British Library Cataloging-in-Publication Data available

CONTENTS

ACKNOWLEDGMENTS

The Porter L. Fortune Jr. History Symposium began as an annual conference on Southern history in 1975. Over the years symposia topics have ranged from the slave experience in America to the environment and Southern history. The twenty-seventh symposium, held September 25–27, 2002, focused on "Race and Sport" and the difficult struggle for racial equality on and off the playing fields of the United States. My colleagues in the history department were extremely helpful in planning this symposium and offering words of advice and encouragement. Bob Haws's leadership and support was constant and Joe Ward offered valuable advice on logistics. Kees Gispen, Nancy Bercaw, Mark Healy, Bob Haws, Brett Shadle, James Payne, Win Jordan, and Joe Ward helped introduce presenters and facilitated thought-provoking dialogue; I thank them. Special thanks to Pro Football Hall of Famer Kellen Winslow who was gracious enough to open the symposium with stimulating and challenging remarks.

Betty Harness and Michelle Palmertree were invaluable in helping to plan and complete numerous tasks, as were numerous graduate students in the history department who made trips to the airport and helped distribute programs. Shirley Joiner helped in revising papers for this volume, along with copying papers. Various resources from the African American Studies Program were also helpful in editing this volume. Herman Payton was instrumental in designing the symposium programs.

An irreplaceable debt is owed to my family, and I would like to thank my wife Valeria whose never-ending support included running errands behind the scenes, which helped make my responsibilities much easier. Once again she put aside her own work to plow through mine. Errors that remain are no one's fault but my own.

INTRODUCTION

CHARLES K. ROSS

The analysis of American sport history is a relatively new area of scholarly inquiry. Intellectuals in general, including historians, all but ignored sport as a suitable field of study. The first major scholarly article on American sport history was Frederick L. Paxson's "The Rise of Sport," published in 1917 in the *Mississippi Valley Historical Review*. A student of the renowned Western historian Frederick Jackson Turner, Paxson argued that the rise of sport in the late nineteenth century was a response to the rise of cities where Americans were deprived of a rigorous rural and frontier life. It would be thirty-six years before another essay on sport appeared in the prestigious *Journal of American History* (the former *MVHR*).[1]

Paxson must be given credit for facilitating the study of sport history in general; however, Edward Bancroft Henderson is credited with initiating the examination of African Americans in sport specifically. An educator in the segregated school system in Washington, D.C., in the 1920s, where he taught physical education and helped organize several black sports organizations, Henderson was also a prolific writer. Popular writers, academicians from various disciplines, and scholars of different philosophies have all depended on Henderson's work for source material, analysis, and clues in the designing of their own publications dealing with African American athletes. Nearly every article, book chapter, and survey text written over the last half-century that includes information on the history of African American athletes has seemingly been influenced by his work in one way or another. Henderson rightfully deserves to be called the "Father of Black Sport History." His writings were intended to foster pride among African Americans and alter white racial beliefs. In 1939, Henderson published *The Negro in Sports*, the first survey ever completed on African American involvement in sport and arguably the one work that has had the most influence on subsequent research dealing with the history of the black athlete in American sport.[2]

Henderson's research and writings focused on African American athletes in both segregated and white organized sports during the late nineteenth and twentieth centuries. African Americans participated in baseball, horse racing, bicycling, and boxing after the Civil War but were systematically forced out of these sports as America embraced legalized segregation. The painful limitations of segregation helped make Jack Johnson and Jackie Robinson mythical figures among African Americans during the first half of the twentieth century. The sacrifices and struggles of Johnson, Robinson, and many other black athletes have completely changed how mainstream America views black participation on the field today. Several athletes, such as Michael Jordan and Tiger Woods, have even been given credit with "transcending race," and black athletes now dominate various team sports widely supported by white fans. However, although the playing fields of the United States were integrated in the late nineteenth and early twentieth centuries, institutional racism continues to prevent African Americans from rising to various coaching, administrative, and ownership positions in sports.

Although this volume of essays is connected by the central themes of race and equality, by no means is it an exhaustive examination of the struggle for racial equality in sports. Instead, it is a thematic collection of papers and essays, beginning with early black participation in football and ending with contemporary images of black athletes in the media. In the first essay, John Carroll argues that Fritz Pollard's contributions to professional football, both on the field and off, demand that he be placed in the Pro Football Hall of Fame. Pollard was not the first African American to play in the NFL, but he was the dominant force advocating integration of pro football. Carroll points out that during the NFL's thirteen-year color barrier, Pollard was instrumental in coaching and organizing all-black pro football teams. He helped organize the first interracial all-star game in Chicago in 1922 and was the first pro coach to showcase black players from historically black colleges.

The second paper by Kenneth Shropshire examines the business legacy of boxing great Sugar Ray Robinson. Shropshire discusses the successful business career of Robinson and how several modern day athletes have emulated themselves after the great middleweight champion. Robinson consciously reinvested in the African American community—specifically Harlem, where his Sugar Ray's Café was located and frequented by numerous celebrities both black and white. According to Shropshire, Robinson must be credited for facilitating the notion that black athletes can be successful in the business arena, and points to several current-day examples that include Magic Johnson, Dave Bing, Keyshawn Johnson, Willie Davis, Julius Erving, and others who have benefited from Robinson's business legacy.

Rita Liberti explores black women's basketball in North Carolina during the 1930s and 1940s, and how ideas of womanhood meshed with athletic competition. Liberti credits African American faculty members and administrators with a more "expansive conceptualization of womanhood" than their white counterparts who limited women's sports on most white colleges to intramurals. Historically black institutions of higher education were seen as the single most important avenue in the development of black leaders in general; for young black women, these institutions sought to instill a sense of community responsibility. Traveling across the segregated South was difficult and challenging but in a team sport where collective reliance was vital, racism underscored the necessity for group improvement.

In his paper on the challenges that legal segregation presented to both African American and Latino major league baseball players during spring training, Michael Lomax argues that during the initial phase of integration accommodation was the prevalent strategy used by these players, but by the early 1960s that had dramatically changed: players that experienced racial barriers became increasingly less tolerant and more outspoken against racial indignities. Segregated Florida forced teams to find separate housing for African American and Latino players away from their white teammates. Lomax points out that this policy began to change as a result of local NAACP chapters that organized protests; black and brown players who spoke out against segregation; and some team owners who sought hotels willing to house all players regardless of race. According to Lomax, Hank Aaron was one of the most outspoken opponents of segregated housing for black players in Florida. Aaron was aware that black players were key components of all teams by the early 1960s, and also that segregation was being attacked all over the United States, and he felt strongly that spring training sites should be no different.

In his survey of race, religion, and sport in the Pacific during the late nineteenth and early twentieth centuries, Gerald Gems contends that sport was a tool used to advocate American democracy. However, within the ideas of democratic teamwork were notions of racial and religious stigmas that "often determined who played, how they played, and the values projected." Gems argues that American sporting influences could be clearly seen in Japan and the Philippines in particular. Baseball was introduced in Japan by American teachers in the 1870s along with their ideas of racial superiority. Whites instructed native Japanese on the rules of the game but dared not play with them or allow them to observe games as spectators at social clubs. By the 1930s professional teams had been formed that were highly competitive; this was made clear when a Japanese team traveled to the United States, played various teams, and won the majority of the games. This allowed the Japanese to challenge "Anglo perceptions of superiority, western colonialism, and notions of Asian leadership." Baseball was the chosen sport in the Philippines, too, introduced by American soldiers as early as 1898. According to Gems, native Filipinos were also subjugated by Protestant missionaries seeking religious conversion, educators who introduced English to replace their native dialect, and U.S. bureaucrats who employed men and women as servants and prostitutes. Complete assimilation did not happen in the Philippines; Gems argues that instead cultural adaptation won out.

In his overview of today's African American student athletes, Earl Smith points to societal problems such as HIV/AIDS, homicide rates, poverty, educational levels, and overall socioeconomic background as having profound effects on their ability to successfully navigate through the academy. Smith contends that the business of college athletics creates individual casualties because of exploitation that manifests itself via low graduation rates, particularly among African American males. Compensation for student athletes is not embraced by Smith as a trade-off for diplomas, but he does advocate stipends or increases in scholarship aid. This could be easily done based on the billions of dollars generated by NCAA athletic programs. The African American student athlete must face the stark reality that assuming he or she will reach the professional ranks is unrealistic. These students must begin to assert themselves academically, otherwise the "games African American males play will continue to look like the racial apartheid system that was dominant in the early social history of this country as it developed into the United States of America."

In his essay on muscular assimilationism and the paradoxes of racial reform, Patrick Miller attests that "black athletic success offered a measure of hope to those who sought the best means to soften racial prejudice and advance the cause of social justice." Those few black athletes allowed to participate with and against white athletes in various sports during the heyday of segregation were provided the opportunity to challenge and break down prevalent racial stereotypes. Miller contends this was vital in providing a ray of hope on a very dismal racial landscape, that these few accomplishments provided aspirations that other societal barriers might one day be challenged as well. Miller points to the historic accomplishments of Fritz Pollard, Jesse Owens, Joe Louis, and Jackie Robinson as fundamental in changing the racial landscape in sports. These athletes performed "interracial education" on the psyche of mainstream America, which began to prepare white Americans for new challenges to old societal barriers. Miller states, however, that the success of black athletes on the field has not led to opportunities off it. It was easier to allow African Americans to participate as key players of various sports than to grant leadership roles in other occupations.

The final paper by C. Keith Harrison examines the images of African American student athletes and male athletes in the media. Harrison argues that identity for many black males in general and athletes in particular is shaped by popular culture, the influence of various media outlets, and the lack of media exposure to alternative role models. According to Harrison, the slang term *baller* exemplifies success and credibility among African American youth as it relates to sports, entertainment, and, at times, unlawful activities. The term can be used as a noun, adjective, or verb. This type of modification of the English language historically can be seen as both a survival mechanism and act of rebellion. Harrison would like to see the negative connotations of the term baller replaced by more positive images of African Americans being successful—for example as doctors, lawyers, educators, or entrepreneurs. There is very little balance in terms of media images for what is supposedly attainable, specifically for black males. The constant coverage of black athletes like LeBron James, Michael Vick, Sammy Sosa, and entertainers such as Sean "P-Diddy" Combs, Jay-Z, and Snoop Doggy Dogg is not counteracted by the same coverage of black male Ph.D.'s, businessmen, and trained professionals.

C.K.R.

Notes
1. Steven A. Riess, *Major Problems in American Sport History* (Boston: Houghton Mifflin Company, 1997), 2.
2. David K. Wiggins, *Glory Bound Black Athletes in a White America* (New York: Syracuse University Press, 1997), 221–222, 230–231.

RACE AND SPORT

FRITZ POLLARD AND INTEGRATION IN EARLY PROFESSIONAL FOOTBALL

JOHN M. CARROLL

Frederick Douglass "Fritz" Pollard was not the first African American to play professional football or the first of his race to play in the National Football League (NFL), but he was the dominant force in the struggle to keep the NFL integrated. From 1919, when he first played pro football, until after World War II, when a decade-long ban on blacks participating in the NFL ended, Pollard was a major champion of integrated play. He was not always successful in his efforts, but Pollard kept alive a dream for many black athletes: to play at the highest level of pro football. For a variety of reasons, Pollard's efforts and accomplishments have not been widely acknowledged. Pollard deserves recognition for his pioneering struggle to integrate the game by induction in the Pro Football Hall of Fame.

Pollard was raised in a family that, by the time of his birth in 1894, was several generations removed from slavery and might best be described as middle, to upper-middle-class. His parents and his older brothers and sisters had established high standards of achievement in academics as well as athletics before Pollard donned his first football uniform. The Pollard brothers were gifted athletes and worked diligently to hone their skills, recognizing that sport was one of the few avenues to advancement, status, and financial reward for black Americans in the repressive racial climate of turn-of-the-century America. Pollard was different from most African Americans of his generation in that he grew up in a previously all-white neighborhood, Rogers Park, in northern Chicago. From childhood, Pollard was not only schooled in athletics, but in how to get along with whites without debasing his dignity and pride.[1]

Following in the footsteps of his older brothers Luther, Leslie, and Hughes, Pollard became a three-sports star at the overwhelmingly white Lane Tech High School on Chicago's North Side. Unlike his more robust brothers, Pollard was small and wiry even by the standards of the day (five-foot-six and 140 pounds as a senior halfback), and relied on speed, agility, and guile, skills he and his brothers refined in games in their backyard. Deflecting racial taunts and physical abuse in Chicago's rough-and-tumble scholastic league, Pollard made All-Cook County in baseball, track, and football in his senior year. He decided to focus on football, reasoning that an aspiring black athlete had greater opportunities in that sport. Big-time football meant the college game, and with that in mind Pollard reported for freshman football practice at nearby Northwestern University in the fall of 1912.[2]

Although a better than average student, Pollard had little interest in academics at the time and saw his mission at Northwestern purely in terms of football. As a youth, he had developed a tough outer shell of assertiveness and confidence often described as cockiness by those who knew him—likely a by-product of his small stature and his intense desire to compete with and live up to the expectations of his brothers. If he acted assertively and exuded confidence, he usually got to play in games his brothers organized in Rogers Park. The traits of overconfidence and bravado, Pollard trademarks throughout his life, only got him into trouble at Northwestern. When preliminary practice sessions ended, the dean summoned Pollard to inquire about his intentions of registering at the Evanston school. Pollard told him that he would like to register, but that his main goal at Northwestern was to play football. The dean found Pollard's objective unacceptable and sent him packing.

After playing that fall for an Evanston team in a loosely organized professional league, Pollard decided to go east, where his brother Leslie had made his mark as a football player at Dartmouth. At the request of his mother, Pollard agreed to stop off in Providence and visit Brown University. He liked what he saw and registered as a special student to make up deficiencies in foreign languages. When he failed to accomplish that objective by the fall of 1914, Pollard set out for Dartmouth to try out for the football squad. Dartmouth coach Frank Cavanaugh welcomed Pollard, but the college dean refused to register him once he found out that Fritz had already attended Brown.

Embarrassed and ashamed, Pollard consulted with William Henry Lewis, a Harvard graduate and the first African American All-American football player. Lewis arranged for Pollard to enroll at Harvard and play for the school's iron-fisted coach, Percy Haughton. While waiting to register, Pollard watched one game in street clothes from the Harvard bench as Haughton sent in waves of players against hapless Bates College. After the game, Fritz was enticed by a Bates coach who he had known in Chicago to forget Harvard and attend the Lewiston, Maine school.

Pollard sat out the fall football season due to his frequent change of schools and grew despondent during the long Maine winter. He dropped out of Bates and returned to Boston, where Lewis gave him a stern lecture about becoming a "tramp athlete." Lewis made arrangements for Pollard to attend high school as a special student in Springfield, Massachusetts, where the now Boston attorney had many contacts. After his language deficiency was remedied, Lewis urged, Pollard should re-apply to Brown. He was accepted at the Providence school and started on his way to football stardom.[3]

Pollard's successful football career at Brown did not come easy. Initially shunned by his white teammates and singled out as a target on the practice field, Pollard summoned every ounce of resolve and applied what he had learned in Chicago about confronting racism, and somehow endured. Ultimately, it was his sheer athletic ability that won him a sometimes grudging acceptance from his teammates. After leading Brown to a stunning victory over the Mighty Blue of Yale in November 1915, Pollard established himself as one of the premier halfbacks in the East. On New Year's Day 1916, Pollard became the first African American to play in what would become the prestigious Rose Bowl game. The following season was even more spectacular for Pollard as he led the once lightly regarded Bruin eleven to consecutive victories over Yale and Harvard. Walter Camp, who watched both games, remarked that Pollard was "the greatest halfback these eyes have seen." At the end of the season, Camp named Pollard to his first-team All-American team, making Fritz the second black to be so honored and the first African American selected to a backfield position.[4]

The future looked bright for Pollard, but neglect of his college studies and America's entrance into World War I would alter his future. During the winter of 1916–17, Pollard became something of a celebrity in both white and black America: John D. Rockefeller, Jr., a Brown alumnus, appeared on campus and offered to pay for Pollard's expenses. With the approval of the university president, Pollard gladly accepted. Over the next few months, Fritz traveled frequently to East Coast cities to accept accolades from civil rights groups and black fraternal organizations. He later admitted that "I was young and foolish and crazy." He was Fritz Pollard, All-American, and "my head was getting a little bit big then." As a result, Pollard neglected his studies and by the end of the spring semester he was academically ineligible to compete in athletics. The nation was also at war.[5]

Unlike some eastern colleges, Brown played a full schedule in 1917 including some games with military teams, but Pollard was forced to observe from the sideline. When he failed to improve his grades during the fall semester, Fritz joined an army program as a physical director for the Young Men's Christian Association. He was assigned to Camp Meade, Maryland, where elements of the 92nd Negro Division were training. After the African American regiments left for Europe in the summer of 1918, Pollard was reassigned to Lincoln University, a black college near Philadelphia, where he directed physical training for the Lincoln Student Army Training Corps. Among his duties was coach of the Lincoln football team. After the Armistice, Pollard continued as coach at Lincoln through the 1920 season. With two years of college eligibility remaining, Pollard enrolled at the University of Pennsylvania Dental School in 1919 and tried out for the Penn football team. When he realized he was not welcome despite his All-American credentials, Pollard abruptly quit and played in a number of games with a pro team in the Philadelphia area.[6]

During the 1919 football season, Frank Nied, owner of the Akron Indians of the informal Ohio League, recruited Pollard to play several pivotal games. For the next two seasons, Fritz coached the Lincoln Lions on Saturday afternoons and then took a late train to the Midwest for the Sunday pro contests. Pollard became an immediate sensation in the so-called Ohio League, which became part of the American Professional

Football Association (APFA) in 1920. As a running back and gate attraction Fritz was second only to Jim Thorpe, who played for Canton. During the 1920 season, Pollard took over some of the coaching responsibilities at Akron and introduced the eastern formations he had learned at Brown. The following year he assumed head coaching duties in conjunction with Elgin Tobin. Under Tobin and Pollard, Akron—renamed the Pros—won the 1920 APFA championship.[7]

When Pollard played his first game for Akron in October 1919, there was only one other black player in pro football: former University of Minnesota second team All-American end Robert "Rube" Marshall, nearly forty years old, played for the Rock Island Independents. Life in professional football was anything but easy for young Pollard. He was a marked man on and off the field. "Nied and Ranney [the Akron owners] befriended me," Pollard recalled, "because I was a Negro and they were afraid *for* me." Even Akron fans had mixed feelings about Pollard. Some came to the Rubber City's League Park to see his sensational runs; others turned out to verbally and/or physically abuse the diminutive Pollard. "Akron was just like Mississippi in those days," Pollard explained. "A lot of Southerners came there after the war." And they were very prejudiced. In Akron, when Pollard, known as the "dusky shifter," scored, "the hometown jazz band struck up its 'coon song,' 'The Dark Boy Blues.'"

"You had to be tough as nails to play in that league," Pollard recalled. "And that went double if you were black because they really came after us." The excitable Pollard sometimes retaliated "by taunting spectators and players, alike. They would scream from the sidelines, 'We're going to get you on that playing field, nigger, and kill you,' and I would yell back, 'If you can catch me.'" For his protection, Pollard dressed for home games at Frank Nied's cigar store, was driven to the park just before game time, and sprinted on the field as the teams lined up for the kickoff.[8]

It is difficult to determine the extent to which the opposition was out to "get" Pollard, because the early pro game was characterized by extremely rough and sometimes unethical play. Pollard's teammate Scotty Bierce remembered that "anything short of murder went without penalty. We just lined up against each other, face to face, and it was nothing short of war." But Pollard was keenly aware that some opponents singled him out for extra harsh treatment. "The white players were always trying to hurt me," he recalled, "and I had to be able to protect myself if I was going to stay in the game." He responded to the threat in a restrained but direct manner. When players roughed him up or called him foul names, he said, "I'd pay them no mind, but I would notice who the player was, and the first opportunity that presented itself I'd kick them right in the guts or hit my knee against their knee, knocking it out of joint. And then I'd let them know, quietly, why I did it."

Pollard and other early black players faced Jim Crow wherever they went. Jay Mayo "Ink" Williams, Fritz's college and later pro teammate, recalled that in a Green Bay hotel they were "paged out of the dining room" and escorted to the office where they were told, "We don't allow colored people to eat in our hotel." In Canton, Ohio, Williams, who was seated with white players, "was allowed to go on eating—the management simply put a screen around the table." In the 1970s, Pollard calmly reflected on how he dealt with the racial barriers he faced in pro football. "My father had taught me that I was too big to be humiliated by prejudiced whites. If I figured a hotel or restaurant didn't want me, I'd stay away. I didn't go sniffing around hoping they'd accept me. I was never interested in socializing with whites. I was there to play football and make money."[9]

From the beginning, Pollard recognized the tenuous position of African American players in the APFA (which would change its name to the National Football League two years later). In the 1940s, he alleged that at the organizational meeting of the APFA in 1920, some owners attempted to raise the race issue. According to his account, Alva "Doc" Young, owner of the Hammond Pros, and Nied and Art Ranney of Akron "protested loudly the bringing up of the race question. They couldn't understand why a football player couldn't be considered a football player without the question of his color coming into the discussion." For the moment the issue of racial restrictions in the APFA was put on hold. Over time, Pollard came to believe that George Halas, coach and owner of the Decatur Staleys, later to be known as the Chicago Bears, was one of the owners who had raised the color ban issue at the organizational meeting in Canton.[10]

During the 1921 season, Pollard recruited two prominent African American players who had been stars at predominantly white colleges to play in the APFA. Paul Robeson, a close friend of Pollard's and a former All-American end at Rutgers, played under Pollard's direction at Akron and helped lead the Pros to a fast start with a 7–0 record. Pollard's former teammate at Brown University, end Jay Mayo "Ink" Williams, was signed, at Pollard's suggestion, by Doc Young of the Hammond Pros. The following year Pollard recruited African American John Shelbourne, a former Dartmouth College star fullback who had taken over as coach of Lincoln University, to play for Hammond. Pros owner Doc Young was one of only a few APFA owners who were willing to hire African American players. Unfortunately, Hammond did not draw well at home and beginning in 1921 essentially became a road team. "The three or four or five games they [road teams] filled in the schedules of the ruling clubs," according to Louisville Brecks owner Aaron Hertzman, "enabled the league to keep going." Of the eight African American players who participated in the APFA/NFL between 1920 and 1926, five of them played at one point with the Hammond Pros. This meant that they played perhaps a third as many games as players who competed for the so-called "ruling clubs." Thus, it is unfair to measure the merits and contributions of early African American players in the NFL on the basis of statistics alone as the Pro Football Hall of Fame apparently does.[11]

During the 1921 season, Pollard became convinced that George Halas, coach of the Chicago Staleys, canceled a scheduled game with Akron—which might have given the Rubber City team a chance at the championship—because the Pros had two African Americans in their lineup. Pollard maintained that Halas had used him to get recognized in 1920 when Fritz, as coach of Akron, agreed to play against the Staleys in Chicago at the end of the season, giving Decatur a chance to win the APFA championship. He remained convinced that the race issue was behind the canceled game in 1921 and Halas's refusal to schedule Milwaukee the following year when Pollard was a player/coach for the Badgers. It is unclear what Halas's views on race were in the 1920s, but it was not uncommon for coaches at the time to alter schedules at the close of seasons to increase their chances to win the championship, which was based on the best winning percentage. The evidence suggests that Halas canceled the 1921 Akron game to increase his team's chances to win the APFA title, which it did. Pollard, however, never forgave Halas, and maintained for the rest of his life that Papa Bear in those days "was as prejudiced as hell." Halas fiercely denied the charges.[12]

After a fast start in 1921, Akron slumped badly toward the end of the season due, in part, to injuries sustained by Robeson and Pollard. After the season Pollard was dismissed as a player and head coach and Robeson was released as well. Management blamed the team's downfall on "several members [of the team who] failed to keep in condition toward the lag end of the season." The reason given for firing Pollard, according to a Cleveland newspaper, was "promoters of the team charge Pollard played indifferent football last fall." It seems clear that Pollard and Robeson were the scapegoats for the team's collapse, their injuries were not taken seriously, and that "indifferent football" and not being in condition could be read as "lazy Negroes" or worse. Despite the setback, Pollard landed on his feet in 1922 when he was recruited by two Chicago promoters as a player/coach of a new franchise in Milwaukee in what was now called the NFL. Pollard brought in Robeson to fill an end position and a number of former eastern college players to form the nucleus of the Milwaukee Badgers. Almost from the start, the Badgers were a team plagued by internal turmoil. Pollard shared head coaching duties with Al "Budge" Garrett, an American Indian and former Rutgers star. Midway through a lackluster season (2–4–3), Garrett and Pollard were fired as coaches and replaced by Jimmy Conzelman. Pollard never commented directly on what caused his dismissal by the Badgers. A reporter who interviewed him about his problems in Milwaukee, however, wrote that "interference from some of the owners as to the team's operation, and resentment that a Black man was running the show, curtailed Fritz' tenure in Milwaukee.[13]

After the season ended, Pollard helped organize an interracial all-star game in Chicago featuring the finest black players in the area against a white team organized by Dick King, a former Harvard running back who played for the Milwaukee Badgers. The event was sponsored by Chicago *Defender* publisher Robert Abbott and café owner Bill Bottom. Its purpose was to showcase some of the finest African American football players in the nation and underscore the desirability of integrated competition in sport. "Fritz Pollard and his All-Stars," as the black team was called, boasted NFL players Robeson, John Shelbourne, Ink Williams, and Fred "Duke" Slater (Iowa-Rock Island). The team was augmented by members of the Lincoln Athletic Club eleven of Chicago and included future NFL players Sol Butler and Dick Hudson. Initially scheduled for American Giants Park, the game was moved to Scherling Park due to poor weather and less than anticipated interest. A small, shivering crowd braved sub-zero weather to watch Pollard connect with Robeson on a twenty-yard touchdown pass and a 6–0 victory for the black all-stars. Although little noted at the time or since, the game was the first of its kind and emphasized the pride of the African American players who were participating in integrated professional football.[14]

The following summer Pollard received an offer from Doc Young of Hammond to play for the Indiana team. He accepted, and also took on head coaching duties at the request of the players. As a "road team" in the NFL, Hammond played an attenuated schedule against league opponents. This meant that paydays were fewer and less lucrative than with many NFL franchises. Pollard, always interested in making as much money as possible, moonlighted as a player in the rough-and-tumble Pennsylvania "Coal League" during 1923–24. Charles Copley, a former teammate in Akron and Milwaukee, recruited Pollard to play for the Gilberton Catamounts in the anthracite coal region of Pennsylvania. With President Joe Carr attempting to impose a salary cap on players' salaries in the NFL, a number of league players opted to play in the Coal League, or like Pollard, participate in both leagues. As a result of a significant number of NFL and former NFL players, the quality of football in the Coal League was excellent. Pollard commuted between Chicago and eastern Pennsylvania during the 1923–24 seasons. He played for Gilberton on Sundays and coached the Hammond Pros during the week. Among a long list of "firsts" associated with Pollard, he was the first African American to play football in the Coal League or the Coal Region. His moonlighting venture proved to be lucrative until the Coal League collapsed after the 1924 season under the weight of escalating player salaries and a miners' strike.[15]

Pollard began the 1925 season as player/coach of the Hammond Pros. He brought in Dick Hudson, who had played in the 1922 black all-star game, and re-acquired Sol Butler, who had been sold to Akron the previous season. These players, in addition to Pollard and Ink Williams, made Hammond the most integrated team in the early NFL. It was not necessarily a good sign, because Doc Young and the Pros were struggling financially. His son, Colonel H. N. Young, recalled that "Mother washed the uniforms" and "we lost our butts." After playing only one game, Akron owner Frank Nied wanted Pollard to return as player/coach of the Rubber City team. Doc Young agreed to sell Pollard along with backs Guil Falcon and Dunc Annan to Akron. Now thirty-three, Pollard showed he had not lost much of his old form as he led the Pros to the top of the NFL standings with a 4–0–2 record. However, an early November road trip to Pennsylvania that required Akron to play games on consecutive days against Frankford and Pottsville ended the Pros' season. The twin losses virtually eliminated Akron from the title chase, and Nied, who was also struggling financially, decided to cancel the remainder of his scheduled games.

Pollard returned to Chicago, but soon learned that he might still have an opportunity to play more football that season. The reason was that the University of Illinois' spectacular halfback, Harold "Red" Grange, had signed a contract to play for the Chicago Bears. Bears player/coach Halas scheduled a number of league and exhibition games to take advantage of Grange's phenomenal popularity. Grange's debut in the NFL would have a far-reaching impact on the professional game and directly affect the small number of African American players who continued to participate.[16]

When the Bears' revised schedule was released, Pollard called Providence Steam Roller general manager, Charles Coppen, whom he had known from his college days at Brown, and offered his services for an early December game which Halas had scheduled against the Steam Roller. Coppen immediately signed Pollard to a contract for $500 to play against Grange at Boston's Braves Field. The clash between two of the finest open-field runners of the era turned out to be a bust. Grange, who had been hurt three days earlier in New York, played gingerly and was widely booed by the fans. Pollard struggled to maintain his footing on a frozen field and was ineffective. About the only thing that was normal for Pollard was that he became a special target for Chicago tacklers. The Providence *Journal* reported that "the Bears were so intent on squelching the dusky Fritz that five of the orange-jerseyed athletes piled on the former Brown star. The rough play cost Chicago 15 yards." Undoubtedly, Pollard blamed George Halas for the incident and it likely contributed to the feud between them, which ripened over the years.[17]

Pollard rejoined Akron as a player/coach for the 1926 season, his last in the NFL. Under the direction of Frank Nied, the Akron team was once again named the Indians, but like many NFL franchises that year it struggled at the gate. Unable to secure an NFL franchise in New York City, Charles C. "Cash and Carry" Pyle, Red Grange's agent and partner, organized a rival pro football circuit, the American Football League (AFL), with nine teams, and Grange of the New York Yankees as its featured attraction. In the key cities of New York, Chicago, Brooklyn, and Philadelphia there was head-to-head rivalry between the two leagues. The competition between the two leagues and extremely rainy fall weather in 1926 combined to create financial woes for many teams in both the NFL and AFL. With Pollard at quarterback, Akron's offense sputtered and the Indians got off to a disappointing 1–1–2 start. What was worse, very small crowds turned out at Akron's General Field to watch the Indian home games against Hammond and Canton. After a listless and disappointing scoreless tie with Canton on October 10, Nied gave Pollard his unconditional release as player and coach. An Akron news release stated that Indian management took the action because Pollard "failed to play up to the form expected of him." Pollard was quoted in the article as saying that he had intended to retire after the season, and that he wanted to end his pro career in an Akron uniform. He added that he had "never counted on being fired," and was heading home to Chicago.[18]

Pollard's last season at Akron in 1926 marked the height of black participation in big-time professional football in the pre-World War II era. In 1922, 1923, and 1925, five African Americans played in the NFL. Six blacks played big-time pro football in 1926, five in the NFL and one in the AFL. By 1927 only Duke Slater of the Chicago Cardinals remained on an NFL roster; he was joined by Harold Bradley in 1928. Only three other African Americans would play in the league before the color line was drawn in 1934. The AFL disbanded after the 1926 season, only one of its teams being absorbed by the NFL. One reason for the decline in the number of black players in the NFL was the withdrawal of many teams after the financially disastrous 1926 campaign. Twenty-two NFL teams began the 1926 season, but only twelve competed for the championship the following year. Ink Williams, Sol Butler, and Dick Hudson (players recruited by Pollard) played for teams that dropped out of the NFL and they were not signed by other franchises.

While there is no evidence that an organized racial barrier existed at the time, it is clear that some teams and their owners, such as the Hammond Pros, Rock Island Independents, and the Akron Pros, all of which folded in 1926, were more willing to hire African American players than other clubs. From 1920 to 1926 Hammond employed five different black players, Rock Island and Akron three each. There is also some evidence that racial tensions were rising in the NFL by the mid-1920s. Shortly after Pollard's retirement, New York Giants players refused to take the field in a Tuesday afternoon game against Canton at the Polo Grounds in New York. Giants management, which included Tim Mara and Harry "Doc" March, maintained that the large crowd might object to the presence of Canton quarterback Sol Butler on the field. The Chicago *Defender* linked the protest to a number of Southern players on the New York team including Steve Owen, "Cowboy" Hill, and Cecil "Tex" Grigg. After a ten-minute delay, Butler withdrew from the field voluntarily, advising his teammates to play and not disappoint the crowd.[19]

Aside from the prevailing racial climate, a number of factors made it difficult for many African Americans to find employment in the NFL. Most obvious is the small number of blacks who played football at white colleges, which were the recruiting grounds for pro teams. Beyond that, most African American players had to achieve All-American status just to be considered by NFL teams. There were no African American All-Americans in the 1920s. Pollard believed that the increasing acceptance of pro football by fans by the mid-1920s allowed owners to release black players who earlier were needed as drawing cards. Major African American newspapers, moreover, rarely covered the professional game, and its following in the black community was limited. Only occasionally did any number of African American fans turn out to see NFL games, such as the eight hundred (out of three thousand) who watched Ink Williams and Sol Butler perform for Hammond against the Cardinals in Chicago in 1924. As a rule, black fans, like their white brethren, did not have as much faith in pro football as they did in the college game. Under the circumstances, there was very little incentive for NFL owners to hire African American players unless they were clearly superior and could assure victories.[20]

After the 1926 season Pollard returned to Chicago, where he ran an investment business and during the fall helped out as a backfield coach under his friend Dick Hanley at Northwestern University. By 1928, however, his interest in Northwestern football became secondary to his concern about what he perceived to be an effort to eliminate African Americans from the NFL. That year only two African Americans, Duke Slater and Harold Bradley, played in the NFL, both with the Chicago Cardinals. It was increasingly clear to Pollard that a number of coaches and owners either refused or were reluctant to hire African American players. Among the owners, there were two infrequently stated reasons given for the paucity of blacks in the league. One was, as George Halas later rather lamely put it, that "probably the game didn't appeal to black players at the time." The other explanation was that the mixing of the races often led to ugly incidents on the gridiron.[21]

In 1928, Pollard organized an all-star black professional football team on Chicago's South Side with the expressed intention of showing that interracial football could be played without ugly incidents and that African Americans had the talent and interest in the pro game. The team, which became known as the Chicago Black Hawks the following season, scheduled games against white professional and semi-pro teams in the Chicago area. Pollard's South Side eleven was composed of aspiring young players from the area as well as NFL veterans Ink Williams, Sol Butler, and Pollard himself. Duke Slater also played for the team when he was not otherwise engaged with the Chicago Cardinals. While Pollard made his point that black and white teams and players could compete without serious incident, the Black Hawks drew poorly at the gate. As a result, Pollard and his general manager, Dr. Albert C. Johnson, took the team on the road during the late fall and winter months during the next three seasons. The Black Hawks played games mainly against white all-star teams in California, and a few exhibition contests against black teams in the upper South. But with the Depression worsening in the early 1930s, the Black Hawks, who sometimes played as the Fritz Pollard Stars, disbanded in California during the 1931–32 season due to poor attendance. Many of the players, nearly broke, were stranded in the West for some time. After failing to sell the rights to his life story to a Hollywood movie company, Pollard returned to Chicago nearly penni-less in the summer of 1932.[22]

Pollard's financial affairs were in a shambles as a result of the 1929 stock market crash and its aftermath. His investment firm was bankrupt and many investors held him responsible. Dispirited and barely able to avoid legal prosecution, Pollard left for New York City hoping for a fresh start. As was the case during a number of crises in his life, Pollard landed on his feet. He was able to secure a loan and set up a coal delivery busi-ness. Several years later, he entered the newspaper business, and estab-lished the nation's first black tabloid, the New York *Independent News*. While he struggled to make a living during the depths of the Depression, Pollard, like many African Americans interested in athletics, was con-cerned about ominous developments affecting black participation in the NFL. During the 1933 season, two African Americans played in the league, Joe Lillard of the Chicago Cardinals and Ray Kemp of the Pittsburgh Pirates. The following year no black players were signed to NFL contracts. Lillard, who was reputed to have a cocky demeanor, was not re-signed by the Cardinals. Kemp decided to attend graduate school at Bluefield State College in West Virginia rather than return to the Pirates. It is not clear if Kemp would have been allowed to play if he had returned to Pittsburgh. In 1934–35, few black sportswriters focused on the apparent problem in the NFL for fear of bringing attention to a "color barrier" which might or might not exist, and perhaps.worsen the situation. But Pollard was familiar with the racial views of some owners, and he was convinced that some sort of conspiracy against African Americans existed. He was determined to force the hand of NFL owners on the race issue.[23]

In February 1935, Pollard "planted" a story with Claude Barnett's Associated Negro Press which stated that Pollard's son, Fritz, Jr., a former high school All-American hurdler and All-Chicago halfback at Senn High School, who had recently dropped out of Brown University, "was undecided as to whether he will turn professional or wait until after the 1936 Olympics." The article reported "that young Pollard has been offered a swell contract to play professional football with the 1933 championship Chicago Bears." If the senior Pollard hoped to draw Bears owner George Halas out in the open on the color ban issue, his attempt failed. When contacted about the report, Halas denied that any offer had been made to Fritz, Jr., and cleverly pointed out that the NFL "has an unbreakable rule which forbids offers being made to any athlete until his class has graduated." Young Pollard had two years of college eligibility remaining, according to the story. Halas's response was somewhat ironic because he had been the last owner to break the so-called "Grange Rule" when he signed Joe Savoldi in 1930 before his class at Notre Dame had graduated. Pollard may have been foiled by Halas, but he was determined not to let matters rest.[24]

In the summer of 1935, Pollard accepted an offer to coach a professional, all-black Harlem football team organized and managed by Herschel "Rip" Day, an athletic promoter and Lincoln University alumnus. The team was named the Brown Bombers in honor of rising young heavyweight boxing contender, Joe Louis. There had been several black professional teams in Harlem of modest caliber in the past few years, but Day was determined to make the Brown Bombers the finest black pro eleven in the nation, on a par with Bob Douglas's famed New York Renaissance Big Five basketball team. Pollard was attracted to the offer to coach the Bombers, at least in part by his concern about the failure of NFL owners to sign African American players for the second consecutive season.

When he was asked in 1970 if he resented the fact that black athletes had it easier at that time than it had been for him decades before,

Pollard replied, "If someone has opened the doors for them, more power to them. I did everything I could to open doors and make it easier for them. When I organized that Brown Bomber team, and there weren't any black boys in the pro leagues, I did that deliberately to show them that these teams could play against a whole black team and not have any trouble or any prejudice, and could draw a good crowd." As he had earlier in Chicago with the Black Hawks, Pollard would try to showcase the best available black football talent in order to undermine the claim by some NFL owners and others that there was a scarcity of qualified African American players. He was further determined to schedule exhibition games with the local NFL teams, the Brooklyn Dodgers and the New York Giants, to underscore his points. New York *Amsterdam News* sportswriter Artie La Mar reported before the Bombers' 1935 season began that "negotiations for night games with the Brooklyn Dodgers and the New York Giants are under way." During the season, Lewis Dial of the New York *Age* printed a rumor, probably started by Pollard, that the Giants had challenged the Bombers to a game in late November. Dial quoted Pollard as saying that if the November date was not acceptable, "a post season game will be arranged."[25]

In fact, neither of New York's NFL teams was interested in playing the Brown Bombers or any other black team. Pollard's negotiations with New York Giants owner, Tim Mara, may have been outright unfriendly, in light of the fact that Fritz would later list Mara along with the Chicago Bears George Halas as mainly responsible for the ban on African Americans in the NFL after 1933. Despite his continuing and ultimately fruitless efforts in scheduling a game with either the Dodgers or Giants, Pollard and Day were pleased with their success in putting together a first-rate professional team. Pollard brought in former Chicago Cardinal halfback Joe Lillard as the centerpiece of the Bomber backfield, and signed former New York University and Brooklyn Dodger wingman Dave Myers and ex-Morgan College star, Thomas "Tank" Conrad to help provide potent offense. The Bomber line was anchored by former Providence Steam Roller end Howard "Dixie" Matthews and consisted of former African American standouts from both white and black colleges as well as a few non-college men. Pollard was a pioneer in tapping talent from the nation's black colleges.[26]

Scheduling only white professional teams from the northeast and playing their home games at Dyckman Oval in Manhattan, the Bombers got off to a fast start. In their opening game they humbled a much-touted team organized by former Army All-American, Chris Cagle (28–6), and then proceeded to demolish (27–0) an all-star eleven led by Cliff Montgomery, who had quarterbacked Columbia University to a Rose Bowl victory a few years before. As a gauge of the quality of the Bomber team, Cagle's all-stars had barely lost an exhibition game to the 1934 NFL champion New York Giants. Joe "Pop" Lillard provided a good part of the offense, but he was ably assisted by wingback Myers and the six-foot-three-inch, 240-pound Tank Conrad, who was dubbed the "Negro Nagurski" in the African American press. Although Myers and Lillard continued to show their previous NFL form, and the massive but quick Conrad was nearly unstoppable on line rushes, NFL owners showed no interest in the Bomber backfield trio. After five games the Brown Bombers were undefeated, racking up ninety-two points to their opponents' nine. The winning streak ended on the last day of the season when the New Rochelle Bulldogs, led by Edwin "Alabama" Pitts, defeated the Bombers, 7–6. Pitts, a legendary athlete of the 1930s who had played a number of years for New York's Sing Sing Prison team, the Blacksheep, and had been recently released by the NFL Philadelphia Eagles, scored the winning touchdown.[27]

Although the city's African American newspapers gave the Bombers ample coverage and duly praised Pollard and his players, the team struggled financially. The average attendance at Dyckman Oval, where the Bombers played most of their games, was about fifteen hundred per game—hardly enough to cover players' salaries. To create more excitement and help boost attendance, Pollard instituted a number of trick plays and unorthodox formations, including one called the "aeroplane shift," which the *Amsterdam News* claimed baffled opponents. Midway through the season, Pollard reluctantly agreed to allow the team to sing spirituals and "truck" from the huddle to the line of scrimmage. He told a reporter that he first opposed the singing and dancing routine, which the team sometimes used in practice drills, but "then it struck me all of a sudden that it might help them, and it might aid in selling the team to the public." In fact, Pollard anticipated some trends that would become part of the culture of the NFL by the late 1960s. Pollard stopped short of outright clowning antics, long part of African American professional sports, and then recently popularized by the black Cincinnati Clowns in baseball. The showmanship instituted by the Bombers was popular with the Harlem fans and did increase attendance, but Pollard admitted near the end of the season that "we've lost about $5,000 so far." He added that "we're getting new capital in next year and some new players and I'm sure we'll be a big financial success."[28]

In 1936, Pollard was once again unable to schedule an exhibition game with local NFL teams and was forced to start the season on the road with a series of warm-up games because Dyckman Oval, which was used by Negro League baseball teams, was unavailable until mid-October. Starting with a makeshift lineup, the Bombers lost their first four contests. But when the regulars arrived for the home opener against the Newark Bears of the newly organized American Professional Football League (APFL), it was apparent that Pollard had again put together one of the best minor-league teams in the country. In addition to Lillard and Conrad, the mainstays of the 1935 team, Pollard recruited former Morgan College triple-threat sensation Otis Thorpe, who would share season scoring honors with Lillard. The Bombers humbled the Bears, 41–0, before three thousand fans at Dyckman Oval, and proceeded to dominate the opposition for the rest of the season, posting a 6–0–1 record. Considering the rout of Newark of the upstart American League and a 29–0 whitewash of the highly regarded Frankford Yellowjackets, a former NFL team, Pollard could legitimately claim that he had demonstrated there were a good number of African American players capable of playing in the NFL. Yet, as before, the league owners showed no interest in either scheduling or recruiting players from the Brown Bombers.[29]

Pollard stayed on for another season as coach of the Bombers, but became increasingly pessimistic about the prospects of altering what was clearly a ban against African Americans playing in the NFL. The Bombers enjoyed another successful season in 1937 by posting a 5–2–1 record, including a 29–0 victory over the Jersey City Giants of the APFL. Pollard continued to showcase some of the best available black football talent from both black and white colleges. With Lillard and Conrad sidelined with injuries around midseason, Pollard inserted former Hampton

Institute wingback Charlie Paige into the backfield and he became one of the Bombers' running sensations of 1937. On the line, Pollard added former Brown University tackle Vernon Beaubien and center Al Harris, a recent Greensboro A&T standout. The Bombers played before relatively large home crowds in their third season, averaging more than three thousand per game and drawing more than nine thousand in Newark in a 28–14 loss to the Newark Tornadoes of the APFL. Pollard was prepared to coach the Bombers for another season before a challenge from a rival group of African American promoters caused him to change his mind.[30]

Prior to the opening of the 1938 Brown Bombers training camp at Verplank, New York, *Amsterdam News* sports columnist J. Wayne Burrell announced that James Semler, manager of the Black Yankees Negro National League baseball team, was organizing a "big time" black professional football team by the same name. In an interview with Burrell in which Semler conspicuously failed to mention the Brown Bombers, the Black Yankees manager remarked that "with the exception of one or two players appearing with white professional elevens, there is no place on [sic] the 'big time' for our stars of color." Semler said he was "appealing to the magnates in the two Negro [baseball] leagues and other sports-minded business men to cooperate with him in trying to create a place in the sun for these Negro gridiron heroes." The implication of Semler's remarks was clear: he was challenging Pollard's team for supremacy among New York's black fans and he obviously did not consider the Brown Bombers "big time." In a section devoted to notes and trivia following the interview, Burrell had "FRITZ POLLARD casting a watchful eye toward James Semler's Black Yankee Grid machine."[31]

Semler's remarks must have hurt Pollard, who had organized and coached black all-star teams beginning in the 1920s and whose Bombers were clearly the outstanding African American team in the country. Worse, it soon became apparent that Semler had made a deal with Alessandro "Alex" Pompez—owner of the Negro National League's Cuban Giants baseball team and a convicted numbers racketeer—to gain exclusive use of Dyckman Oval, which Pompez owned. When Pollard learned that the Bombers would not be allowed to use Dyckman Oval for their home games and realized that no suitable stadium close to Harlem was available, he promptly resigned as coach. He simply stated to the press that he was "no longer connected with the Brown Bomber football team nor any other in any capacity." The Brown Bombers carried on for several more years as a road team, but management could not afford to pay the best African American players, and the team never recaptured its past glory before wartime mobilization forced the franchise to fold. Pollard remained a vocal advocate of integration in the NFL mainly through his newspaper, the *Independent News*, but his on-field association with professional football as a player and coach came to an end.[32]

As the nation moved closer to war and the Brown Bombers struggled as a road team, fewer black New Yorkers remembered the pioneering integrationist efforts of Fritz Pollard. But in 1942, when rumors of an impending integration of big-time professional football and baseball were rife, and African American commentators praised the latest leaders in the movement, former Brown Bombers manager Rip Day paid Pollard a tribute in a testy letter to *Amsterdam News* columnist Dan Burley, who had been celebrating the recent efforts to integrate football as though the movement had begun yesterday. "I still say," Day wrote, "that Fritz Pollard did more to advance the idea of the best-against-the-best-regardless-of-color than any man in the business."[33]

Day might have added that Pollard had been a pioneer in breaking down racial barriers during his football career, both as a collegian and a professional. In 1916, he was the first African American to play in the Rose Bowl. That same year he became the first of his race to be named to a backfield position on Walter Camp's All-American team. He was the first widely known African American to participate in professional football, beginning in 1919, and one of the outstanding players and gate attractions in the early NFL.

Pollard is, or should be, remembered as the first black head coach and quarterback in the NFL. Few knew, however, that he was largely responsible for sustaining integration in the early NFL by recruiting fellow African Americans for his own team or other league teams. At the end of the 1922 season, Pollard helped organize the first interracial all-star game in Chicago in an effort to celebrate the accomplishments of black athletes and popularize the pro game in the black community. He later organized the Chicago Black Hawks and the Brown Bombers to try to maintain integration in the NFL and to attack the insidious color ban. He was the first professional coach to showcase football talent from the nation's traditionally black colleges, a source of players NFL teams failed to tap until the 1950s. The College Football Hall of Fame recognized Pollard's talent and extraordinary pioneering efforts by inducting him in 1954; the Pro Football Hall of Fame has yet to accord him a similar tribute.

Notes

1. The best sources on Pollard's family and background are Luther J. Pollard, "Memorandum on the Pollard Family" and John F. "Jay" Barry interview with Pollard, July 1970. Both are in the Brown University Archives, Providence, R.I. Also see Carl Nesfield, "Pride Against Prejudice: Fritz Pollard, Brown's All-American Pre-World War I Vintage," pt. 1, *Black Sports*, Nov. 1971, pp. 16–17, 20, 31. For a biography on Pollard that uses these sources and others listed below, see John M. Carroll, *Fritz Pollard: Pioneer in Racial Advancement* (Urbana: Univ. of Illinois Press, 1992).

2. Barry interview with Pollard, July 1970. On Pollard's high school career, see issues of the *Tech Prep*, Lane Technical High School's newspaper, for the years 1909–1912, in the Brown University Archives.

3. Barry interview with Pollard, July 1970; Jay Barry, "Fritz," *Brown Alumni Monthly*, October 1970, pp. 30–33.

4. Pollard's career at Brown can best be followed in the *Brown Daily Herald*, 1916–17. Camp is quoted in Jay Barry, "Memorandum on the 1916 Brown–Yale Game," in the Brown University Archives.

5. Pollard to Jay Barry, January 13, 1969, and Barry interview with Pollard, November 23, 1974, both in the Brown University Archives.

6. Nesfield, "Pride Against Prejudice," pt. 2, *Black Sports*, December 1971, p. 61; Barry interview with Pollard, July 1970.

7. Pollard's early career at Akron can best be followed in the Akron *Beacon Journal*, 1919–21. Also see Barry interview with Pollard, July 1970.

8. On African Americans in early professional football, see Joe Horrigan, "Follis Led Early Black Pioneers in Pro Football," *Game Day* program, National Football League, October 16, 1988. Seth H. Moseley, II, "Coach of a Different Color," *Game Day* program, vol. 14, no. 11, 1983, in the Pro Football Hall of Fame, Canton, Ohio; Sheila Tully and Andrew Bunie, *Paul Robeson: The Years of Promise and Achievement* (Amherst: University of Massachusetts Press, 2001), pp. 96–97; Ron Rapoport, "Fritz Pollard Remembers," Los Angeles *Times*, July 6, 1976.

9. Tully and Bunie, *Robeson*, 96; Nesfield, "Pride Against Prejudice," pt. 2, pp. 62, 77; Frank MacDonnell, "Gus Dorais Tells Story of Courage on the Gridiron," Detroit *Times*, November 29, 1933; Martin Bauml Duberman, *Paul Robeson* (New York: Alfred A. Knopf, 1988), p. 34.

10. Dan Burley, "Why No Negroes are Playing Pro Football," New York *Amsterdam News*, November 17, 1945; Barry interview with Pollard, July 1970.

11. Author interview with Colonel H. N. Young, December 2, 1988; Aaron Hertzman (letter) to Leo V. Lyons, February 24, 1961, in the Pro Football Hall of Fame; Carroll, *Fritz Pollard*, 14445.

12. Barry interview with Pollard, July 1970; Rapoport, "Fritz Pollard Remembers," Los Angeles *Times*, July 6, 1976. In the 1920s, NFL teams arranged their own schedules.

13. Tully and Bunie, *Robeson*, p. 97; Cleveland *Gazette*, April 1, 1922; Nesfield, "Pride Against Prejudice," pt. 2, p. 63; Barry interview with Pollard, July 1970. On Pollard's coaching and playing days in Milwaukee, see the Milwaukee *Journal*, September–December 1922.

14. Tully and Boyle, *Robeson*, pp. 109–10; Chicago *Defender*, December 16, 1922.

15. On Pollard's tenure with the Hammond Pros, see Brian S. Butler, "The Role of the Road Team in the N.F.L.: The Louisville Brecks," in Bob Braunwart, ed., *P.F.R.A. Annual, 1988*, pp. 29–47; Lance Trusty, "From Prairie Ball to the NFL: The Hammond, Indiana Pros, 1917–1926," a paper delivered at the North American Society of Sport Historians Convention, Clemson, South Carolina, May 28, 1989; author interview with Colonel H. N. Young, December 2, 1988. For an overview of Coal League football, see Joe Zagorski, "The Anthracite Football League," in Bob Braunwart, ed., *P.F.R.A. Annual, 1987*, pp. 31–38.

16. Barry interview with Pollard, July 1970. For Pollard's season with Akron, see the Akron *Beacon-Journal*, October–November 1925. On Red Grange's debut in the NFL, see John M. Carroll, *Red Grange and the Rise of Modern Football* (Urbana: University of Illinois Press, 1999), pp. 107–118.

17. Author interview with Pearce Johnson, June 13, 1988; Robert L. Wheeler, "That Old Steam Roller," Providence *Journal*, undated newspaper clipping, in the Brown University Archives; Providence *Journal*, December 10, 1925; Carroll, *Red Grange*, 114–15.

18. David S. Neft and Richard M. Cohen, *Pro Football: The Early Years, An Encyclopedic History, 1895–1959* (Ridgefield, CT: Sports Products, 1987), 54–57; Akron *Beacon-Journal*, September–October 1926; newspaper clipping dated October 24, 1926, in the Brown University Archives.

19. Horrigan, "Follis Led Early Black Pioneers"; Chicago *Defender*, November 6, 1926. The Giants–Canton game was held on Election Day and was preceded by two high school games. The event drew about forty thousand spectators. The New York *Times* made no mention of the Butler incident. See New York *Times*, November 3, 1926.

20. Frank Young, "A Few Words to the Sporting Editor of Chicago *American*," Chicago *Defender*, February 9, 1924.

21. Barry interview with Pollard, July 1970; Rapoport, "Fritz Pollard Remembers," Los Angeles *Times*, July 6, 1976.

22. Author interview with Fritz Pollard, Jr., June 12, 1987; Chicago *Defender*, September 10, 1927; June 11, 1932; January 28, 1933. Also see Ocania Chalk, *Black College Sport* (NY: Dodd, Mead, 1976), p. 315.

23. Nesfield, "Pride Against Prejudice," pt. 2, p. 80; author interview with Fritz Pollard, III, June 20, 1989. On the reorganization of the NFL and the question of

a ban against black players, see Gerald R. Gems, "Shooting Stars: The Rise and Fall of Blacks in Professional Football," in Bob Braunwart, ed., *P.F.R.A. Annual, 1988*, pp. 11–15 and Thomas G. Smith, "Outside the Pale: The Exclusion of Blacks from the National Football League, 1934–1946," *Journal of Sport History* 15 (Winter 1988), pp. 255–81, and especially p. 257 for statements by Halas and Rooney that there was no agreement to exclude African Americans. Also see Raymond Kemp interview, in the Pro Football Hall of Fame.

24. New York *Amsterdam News*, February 23, 1935. On the "Grange Rule" and Savoldi, see Carroll, *Red Grange*, pp. 104–05, 161.

25. Barry interview with Pollard, July 1970; New York *Amsterdam News*, August 31 and September 21, 28, 1935; New York *Age*, October 26, 1935.

26. Barry interview with Pollard, July 1970; New York *Amsterdam News*, September 21, 1935.

27. New York *Amsterdam News*, October 19, 26, November 2, 9, 16, 26, and December 7, 1935. On Pitts, see Dan Daly and Bob O'Donnell, eds., *Pro Football Chronicle* (NY: Collier Books, 1990), pp. 61–62.

28. New York *Amsterdam News*, November 9, 1935; Providence *Journal*, December 6, 1935.

29. New York *Amsterdam News*, September 26, October 10, 17, 24, 31, November 7, 14, 21, and December 5, 1936.

30. New York *Amsterdam News*, September–December 1937. See esp. September 25, October 9, and November 13 and 20.

31. J. Wayne Burrell, "Sports Whirl," New York *Amsterdam News*, July 30, 1938.

32. New York *Amsterdam News*, August 7, 1938; Barry interview with Pollard, July 1970. On Pompez and the connection between black professional sports and crime figures, see Donn Rogosin, *Invisible Men: Life in Baseball's Negro Leagues* (NY: Macmillan, 1983), pp. 105–08, 110–13.

33. Letter from Herschel "Rip" Day to Dan Burley, New York *Amsterdam News*, January 10, 1942. Also see New York *Amsterdam News*, December 6, 1941.

BEFORE MAGIC AND KEYSHAWN
Sugar Ray Robinson—The Businessman

KENNETH L. SHROPSHIRE AND SCOTT BROOKS

Business success on the part of professional athletes is a curious rarity. Akin to a movie star married to the same starlet for twenty-five years, that brand of success is the exception in the celebrity realm. "Traditionally, for some odd reason out there in the world, they think athletes aren't very smart. I want you to look at me as an athlete that's very smart, that has a very successful business. And whatever he touches, it does very well."[1] Those are not the words of Sugar Ray Robinson but of National Football League star wide receiver Keyshawn Johnson. On the business front, Johnson has been at times, a modern-day Sugar Ray.[2]

Robinson was a businessman who handled his ring career.[3] His activities as a businessman set a high standard for the role of athletes in this venue. His success in business while at the height of his athletic career is one of the qualities that raise Robinson above other athletes before or since. Other athletes generally hire someone—a sports agent or business manager—to handle their business while they compete. Full engagement may occur at or near the athlete's retirement, if ever. Robinson ignored the taboo of an athlete, particularly an African American athlete, going beyond entertaining on the field of play and actually making business investments—and more uniquely, investing in the African American community.

The scheme of reinvestment in the African American community has been problematically addressed from the time African Americans have legally had the opportunity to participate in American commerce. The ideas of African American self-help and bootstrapping are controversial. With the presence of racism as a barrier, some argue that there exists a limit as to how high one can pull oneself up, no matter how long the straps. Others argue, with regard to African American community rein-vestment: if it is such good business practice, why aren't rich white folks doing it? The African American athlete is presented with a conundrum, particularly when the prevailing business presumption is that investing in the African American community is not a good idea. Should he or she do something for the community he or she comes from, or do whatever appears to be most profitable from a business standpoint? Fears of being labeled an Uncle Tom or race traitor enter into the African American ath-lete's decision-making process. Their high profiles make them targets for those sometimes unjustified labels.

Robinson was the first athlete to fully explore the notion of commu-nity reinvestment. Robinson was his own man, and he relished that role; within that individuality he had the business savvy—and the desire—to invest in Harlem.

Athletes with business acumen are uncommon; African American athletes who exhibit or are given credit for having business acumen are rarer still. Unfortunately, African American athletes who invest in their own communities are virtually nonexistent.[4] By comparing him to two modern sports stars, Keyshawn Johnson and Earvin "Magic" Johnson, the singularity of Robinson is easier to grasp. References to other ath-letes provide insight as well, but Keyshawn and Magic come closest to the model Robinson established. On one hand, neither really meets the Robinson standard because they did not handle both their off- and on-the-field business as did Robinson. On the other, Keyshawn and Magic both conduct business in big cities, and their enterprises go beyond some of the traditional athlete business models (including Sugar Ray's) due primarily to the increased opportunities that all African Americans enjoy and the large salaries associated with professional sports today.

THE ATHLETE'S BUSINESS MODEL

The businesses athletes are involved in often carry with them some of the sports-industry flash they come from. The Everybody's All-American restaurant-bar setup, with a John Goodman-type old teammate behind the bar and sports memorabilia on display, is typical. The bar setting is an extension of the living room or the on-the-road hotel suite that athletes grow to be comfortable with and are used to entertaining in. From Sugar Ray's Café grew Mickey Mantle's, Joe Namath's Bachelors III, and Keyshawn's Reign along with others in between.

Dave Bing and the Bing Group is probably the best-known exception to this sports-themed post-playing career mode. The business of this former NBA star had annual sales of $300 million and employed over a thousand people in 2000. Bing's business is a multi-company organization located in the heart of Detroit, composed primarily of automotive suppliers.[5]

Roger Staubach leads the legion of former stars involved in various aspects of the real estate business. The former heavyweight champion of the world Larry Holmes made extensive real estate investments over the course of his boxing career, including a two-story office building on Larry Holmes Drive and the traditional Round One nightclub venture in his blue-collar home of Easton, Pennsylvania.[6]

The most elusive success story among athletes is the inner-city entrepreneur. More specifically, absent from athlete-turned-businessperson success stories is the one where the athlete invests in the African American community of major cities while at the height of his game. Larry Holmes and Easton do not qualify because of the size of the town. In the center of Easton there is a statue of a bugler; according to Holmes, "The joke around Easton was that some nights the city was so quiet you just waited for the damn bugler to blow."[7]

Rather than involvement in urban renewal, numerous athletes lend their names to a range of enterprises from bars to sneakers and warm-up suits to fragrances. Few have actually run these businesses. Michael Jordan gets credit for business success, but while not without boardroom savvy, he is far from being an entrepreneur. Jordan, for the most part, is selling his name. The success of the Jordan sneaker (which rescued the athletic apparel company Nike) and other endorsed products like underwear, sports drinks, and hot dogs is undeniable. Allen Iverson later pulled off a similar company-saving feat on Reebok's behalf with his own signature-model shoe. Recording studios and labels are part of the new mode, too. Michael Jordan has invested in Hidden Beach Records; Shaquille O'Neal has the Compton, California-based T.W.Is.M., The World is Mine.[8]

There have been a few apparel false starts, too. Shaquille O'Neal tried to ride the Internet wave with a design-your-own shoe and apparel website, Dunk.net. The bottom fell out of that venture when the rest of the new economy crumbled. Hakeem Olajuwon gave it a shot with a low-end athletic shoe. Neither was successful and neither was designed to have a particular impact on the African American community, other than Olajuwon's noble attempt at moving kids out of the $150-a-pair sneaker market.

Football hall-of-famer Willie Davis leads the list of athletes who are owners of beverage distributorships. The distributorship business is probably Julius Erving's biggest business foray, too. His Philadelphia Coca-Cola bottling partnership with African American businessman Bruce Llewellyn has been highly successful. Similarly, involvement in cookie-cutter fast-food franchises and automobile dealerships go slightly beyond the name-lending model.

THE ENTREPRENEURIAL SPIRIT

What was unique about Robinson's business style? In 1951 *Time* Magazine reported, "He now thoroughly enjoys his new personality as the responsible citizen. He is a big man in Harlem, a political power, who is often on the phone with his friend, the Mayor. Walter Winchell buzzes him often."[9] The breadth of Robinson's success is easy to see. Inside Sugar Ray's Café, patrons were liable to run into celebrities like Jackie Gleason, Frank Sinatra, or Nat King Cole, big-time boxers, and athletes from other sports. It was a place both to see and be seen.

For white celebrities and others, coming to Sugar Ray's exemplified what Norman Mailer wrote about in his essay *The White Negro* in 1957.[10] Mailer interpreted the embrace of things African American by whites in the middle of the last century as a way of fulfilling a desire to be a part of a culture that was vibrant enough to help them deal with death. In that era there was the need to cope with the real threat of the atomic bomb. This "embrace" was most evidenced in the white pursuit of jazz. Mailer viewed this as the embrace of things African American and hip or *cool*. Going to Harlem, being seen at Sugar Ray's Café, being seen with Sugar Ray were all *cool*. Sugar Ray's Café provided both literal and figurative soul food for those who ventured uptown.

Keyshawn Johnson makes it easier to indulge in this cooler world, by placing his restaurant Reign in Beverly Hills rather than in the Los Angeles Harlem equivalent, South Central. The food, however, and the clientele is genuine soul. The fried chicken, collard greens and macaroni and cheese all taste like Keyshawn's mother made them. That home-made quality does not come about by accident. Johnson insists that all of the cooks at Reign, no matter their previous culinary expertise, go through cooking school with his mother, Ms. Vivian Jessie. The menu contains two dozen of her recipes, only slightly tweaked for the broader palette. The name *Reign* is important to Johnson, too. "Me, I'd have named it anything other than my name. That's cheesy."[11]

Sugar Ray's biographer, Dave Anderson, wrote that Robinson had his business plan for a long time. "As a boy playing on a Harlem sidewalk, Sugar Ray Robinson liked to take in the whole street with a sweeping ges-ture and predict: 'I'm gonna own property around here some day.' "[12] He went on to own the entire block of Seventh Avenue between 123rd and 124th Streets.

Robinson's sister contends that his entrepreneurial aspirations and mind came naturally, carrying on a family tradition. "It's been a big thing for Ray, being a businessman. We've always had businesspeople in the family. Ray was strong for carrying on the tradition."[13]

In Robinson's day the images of a major league baseball player working in a sporting-goods store or learning the life insurance business in the off-season were not uncommon. No one was commanding the salaries that today allow the luxury of year-round workouts. Robinson recognized the rare financial opportunity he had as a highly compen-sated professional athlete.

SOCIAL CAPITAL: USING YOUR NAME TO MAKE A STATEMENT

Of athletes operating in major urban settings, Robinson had the fullest grasp of his business value; and, more than any other athlete, he understood the value was highest while his career was at its peak. That's where Sugar Ray was unique; of currently active athletes only Keyshawn comes close, with Shaquille O'Neal potentially on his heels.[14]

Magic Johnson is the paramount example today of an African American athlete investing in the African American community in the Robinson tradition. He is doing this not only in his adopted Los Angeles home but also in Harlem, Atlanta, Houston, and Cleveland.[15] But this is all the post-playing days of Johnson, not the middle of his career like Robinson. Magic Johnson is today's premier African American athlete investing in the community. The true entrepreneur in Johnson emerged after his retirement and after his announcement in 1991 that he was HIV positive. He did think about it. He saw "Cap'n," his teammate Kareem Abdul-Jabbar, declare bankruptcy in the mid-1980s. Jabbar's investments were largely of the hands-off, limited-partnership variety, including hotels, restaurants, and a jump rope. This prevailing model has the athlete investing cash and having little say in the business.

Magic Johnson has a say in the smallest of details in the businesses he owns. His intimate understanding of his clientele is telling. "See, you've got to understand African American people. I know my customer base, because I'm it. I told Loew's, African American people are going to eat dinner at the movies—those hot dogs are our dinner. Same with the drinks. Our soda sales were just O.K. I said African American people love our flavored drinks, because we were raised on Kool-Aid. So we put in punch and strawberry soda and orange and the numbers went through the roof."[16]

The active athlete most closely resembling the Robinson aura is Keyshawn Johnson. Reign for years has been one of the hottest restaurants in town. *Los Angeles Magazine* proclaimed it to have "the most elegant crowd in Los Angeles."[17] In that sense, he goes beyond Robinson. This is not South Central, this is Beverly Hills. Society would have had no part of an African American man owning a restaurant in Beverly Hills in the 1950s. But Keyshawn is also involved in real estate ventures based in South Central Los Angeles.

When Keyshawn opened Reign in June of 1999 he said, "I've never failed at anything and I don't expect to fail at this."[18] Robinson invested $100,000 to acquire the café property and $10,000 to fix it up. Contrast this with the $5 million investment by Keyshawn in Reign (including the purchase price of the building).[19] The dollars spent to put together these dreams illustrate the different times. The theme in Reign is I. M. Pei and marble, not sports posters, peanuts, and beer. The clientele of Reign is a Who's Who of Hollywood, including Denzel Washington, Dennis Hopper, Gary Busey, and Tyra Banks.[20] Johnson himself recognizes the statement he is making. "Here in this place in Los Angeles, for an upscale restaurant [to be] owned by an African American, not even an athlete, it's very very rare."[21]

Away from the glittering Hollywood night life, Keyshawn Johnson is part of Capital Visions Equities, a partnership investing between $50 and $75 million in a project in his old South Central neighborhood. This development is anchored by a Home Depot and includes a McDonalds, Hometown Buffet, a supermarket, and a drugstore. The Chesterfield Square development will offer long-term employment for more than six hundred people, many of them from the local community. The Western and Slauson Avenues address is just a few short blocks away from where the trucker Reginald Denny was beaten following the Rodney King verdict finding the Los Angeles police officers innocent.[22]

Keyshawn's investment is dwarfed by the $500 million in property owned by Magic Johnson and the more than three thousand people he employs. Magic's businesses include Starbucks, T.G.I. Fridays, and movie theaters and are situated in depressed inner-city neighborhoods.[23]

As did Sugar Ray, Keyshawn and Magic have rules of conduct in their places of business. The rules in these establishments were and are followed out of respect for the owners. There is a subtle understanding that these star owners could have placed their businesses elsewhere or selfishly squandered their earnings altogether. The message in the Beverly Hills portion of Keyshawn's portfolio is subtly different, a sort of "I'm giving you [blacks] this quality stuff in this quality neighbor-hood; now don't mess it up."

"No hats, no gang colors": the unique sign greets you at Magic Johnson Theatres in the Crenshaw District of South Central Los Angeles. You get a similar greeting before the previews begin inside the theatre. The projected, super-sized Magic Johnson grin lays down the rules regarding attire and silence during the screening.[24] Magic addressed the gang issue head-on when no one else seemed willing to do so. He essentially said: This property is off limits. Crips and Bloods and all other gangbangers, let this at least be a place where your mothers and sisters can go and see a movie.

Many in the audience can recall how long the neighborhood was without a theatre following the closing of the Baldwin several years before; real old heads remember when there was also the Leimert Theatre in the neighborhood, now a Jehovah's Witness Meeting Hall. James Hamilton is a process server and a nearly fifty-year resident of the Crenshaw District. He recalled the absence of a movie theater in the area after the closing of the Baldwin. "Look, if it wasn't for Magic, we'd still be driving all the way the hell out to Westwood to see a movie. Even when the Baldwin was on its last legs we had to go to Westwood to see anything that was made in the current decade. I'll take my hat off for and to Magic."[25]

Sugar Ray garnered the same respect. Robinson recounts that one night in his club he heard the hat-check girl call, "Sir, sir, you have to check your coat."

"Not me baby, I like to wear my hat and coat, I'll keep 'em on."

Sugar Ray approached the patron and simply said, "You wouldn't want to tread on the policy of the café, now would you?"

As he removed his hat and coat he simply replied, "No, sir, Champ." The response was less a response to intimidation than respect.[26]

Robinson's rules of decorum from the past mesh with those in both Keyshawn's and Magic's empires. In his autobiography Robinson writes, "Nothing makes a place look worse than for a man to be standing at a bar in his hat and coat, like someone waiting for a bus."[27] The rationale might have been explained differently, but at the heart was the concern about the perception of the business and its crossover capability.

Another connection among these three is their automobiles parked in front of their businesses. "Whenever my car was parked in front of my café, the grownups liked to drop in for a drink or for some fried chicken. They knew that if my car was out front, I was inside . . ."[28] Sugar Ray's Pink Cadillac had the same sandwich board effect as Keyshawn's candy apple red Ferrari does today. Patrons know Magic has arrived these days when he pulls up in his black Bentley convertible.

Robinson's view of the impact of his car in front of his restaurant was a bit extreme. "The car was the Hope Diamond of Harlem. Everybody had to see it or touch it or both to make sure it was real. And to most of them it literally was the *Hope* Diamond, because if skinny little Walker Smith could come off the streets to own a car like that, maybe they could too."[29]

Magic understood his potential for business clout, but he did not take real action until after his playing days were over. Robinson tried, but his personal spending habits and later problems prevented his ultimate success. Keyshawn Johnson may ultimately fulfill the dream. He's double dipping too, with the presence in Beverly Hills but with the commitment to invest in his community at the same time. "Because I've learned at a young age growing up in South Central Los Angeles, that things don't last forever. Football is great, it's a great financial benefit. You make a lot of money. But you burn up a lot of money."[30] Larry Holmes provides an explanation why some athletes work to excel in business outside of athletics. "I don't know an awful lot about psychology but I've noticed one thing about the smarter fighters. They always said and did things to convince themselves they didn't need boxing, that they could walk away whenever they wanted to."[31] His belief was that even greater success came in sport for those athletes that did not have the pressure of relying solely on their athletic ability for financial success.

SELF REPRESENTATION

The one feat Sugar Ray Robinson accomplished above other athletes involved in business is self-management. Sugar Ray gained management experience watching and serving as his trainer George Gainford's team captain and negotiating in his stead in his later amateur days. He recalled listening to Gainford deal with promoters. Robinson observed how Gainford manipulated and bargained with them, squeezing extra money out whenever he could. This was coupled with Sugar Ray's novel business sense based upon his experience hustling in the streets of Detroit and New York as a kid. Robinson did not trust anyone.

Robinson broke with the standard that had been set by the jazz musician Louis Armstrong. It was Armstrong who determined that for an African American artist to be successful he needed a white manager. According to cultural studies professor Todd Boyd, Armstrong's view was, "If you ever want to be rich in America, you got to be some white man's nigga."[32] The success Armstrong was referring to was the opportunity to perform. This carries on today, where in both entertainment and sports performers express the need not only to have managers but white managers. Although not as severe a trend as in earlier years, there are still African American athletes who prefer to be represented by a white agent over an African American one. The old belief is encapsulated in the often-quoted Malcolm X tale of the "White man's ice is colder."

It stands to reason that, if using an African American representative is the exception, then certainly self-representation is even more unlikely. Sugar Ray Robinson was the exception. It was not long into his professional career before Robinson bought out his first manager Kurt Hormann. He believed Hormann was taking advantage of him and that he was not earning what he should have been. Robinson borrowed $10,000 from promoter and manager Mike Jacobs to buy his way out of the Hormann deal. He also limited Gainford's responsibilities, giving him the authority to negotiate for him but not to accept any deals without his approval first. "No big decision is made without my knowledge. I must know what's going on. No one else is going to do the thinking for me. When something looks wrong to me, I open my mouth and sometimes make quite a lot of noise."[33]

Robinson knew that Gainford was not a bad man, and wanted the best for him—but he also knew that Gainford was out to get a higher cut. Sugar Ray's distrust compelled him to push harder for a fair wage and to refuse to play by the established rules of racial wage inequality. He gained a reputation for being shrewd, tough, even unreasonable. His often-quoted philosophy was simple and blunt: "I don't see why I should take 50 cents when I have a dollar coming."[34] However, Robinson's success threatened the white establishment. He received bad publicity as a boxer that reneged on deals and that whined and complained. His public image was not always a good one, as promoters and news reporters pinned him as being unreasonable, arrogant, and ungrateful. Robinson wrote in *Ebony* magazine in 1950, "I've said this before and I'll repeat it now; I think I'm the only fighter around who can account for every dollar he has earned from the first fight to the last. I've always kept a record of my ring earnings and what happened to them. It's a good habit, and [one] I wish more Negro fighters would acquire."[35]

Success and deep involvement in his own negotiations warranted Robinson an additional title: greedy. During the NBA lockout of players by owners in 1999, it was as though *USA Today* was primed by league ownership to publish the salaries of NBA players. This tactic of holding the athlete up as greedy is the standard in sports labor disputes today. Why are these athletes complaining when they make over $1 million per year to play a child's game? It is the athletes who are the employees and labeled as self-serving, ungrateful, spoiled, and greedy.

Robinson understood this negative imagery issue, but seemed relatively unconcerned. "I am a business person, a pretty good one I think, and I make no bones about it. That's another reason why I am unpopular in certain boxing and journalistic circles."[36]

CONCLUSION: SELF-REPRESENTATION TOWARD SELF-PRESERVATION

NBA All-Star Ray Allen is one modern-day athlete who approximates Sugar Ray with regards to career self-management and independence. He received a great deal of publicity when he fired his agent and negotiated his own deal, avoiding the need to pay someone three percent of his salary, opting instead to simply hire an attorney to review the contract. Allen Iverson is in a similar position, having fired his superstar agent David Falk. Others over the years who have represented themselves in contract negotiations in some form include former NBA star Danny Ainge and former Chicago Bear Mike Singletary.

But self-representation has long been the exception.[37] Robinson's self-management success was in stark contrast to previous fighters, including Joe Louis. Interestingly, Louis was asked by the IBC to approach Robinson and urge compromise. Ray was unreasonable, they felt, and out of place. Robinson blasted Louis. He inferred that Louis had sold out and was working with the IBC to do to him what they had done to Louis; shortchanging Louis on fight proceeds. Louis did not benefit financially from boxing. He died broke even though he had fought far beyond his desire and abilities, simply for compensation in the hopes of averting destitution.

Magic Johnson laid out the message that Robinson lived. "Now I've got to teach these brothers that you don't have to sell out to do good. I tell those guys all the time, you don't realize how much power you've got. Use it in your community. You can make money and keep it real back home and lift all of us up."[38]

Robinson, Magic, and Keyshawn have all been confronted with the same issue: "What are you doing for your community?" White athletes are rarely asked a similar question. Not Arnold Palmer, Jack Nicklaus, or Babe Ruth. None of the modern-day athletes, either. For them, the obligatory United Way commercial may be enough. African American athletes are expected to go so much further. Greg Norman does not have to "give back" to Australia. Michael Chang was not expected to invest in Chinatown or Asian American Communities.[39] A mere monetary contribution to a charity or an appearance in one of their commercials is not enough for poor African American communities and loyalists.

Wealth motivating escape from the African American community is not an affliction solely of the professional athlete. Flight has been the fate of other sectors of the African American community since integration allowed those who could afford it to depart for "better" neighborhoods.

While both Johnsons provide good comparisons for understanding the legacy of Sugar Ray Robinson, there is one way in which the comparison comes up short. Robinson's pioneering efforts in self-management and entrepreneurial activity were not simply unheard of, they were dangerous. Robinson was not well liked by much of white America because of his seeming arrogance, which was simply understanding his worth and having the business acumen and gumption to attempt to earn his market worth. Robinson sat at the bargaining table where previously only whites were invited to discuss how they could profit from the ethnic gladiators. His presence was a threat to the order of business and the continued exploitation of the African American athlete. Even more telling, Robinson negotiated some of the first, if not the first, pay-per-view boxing deals and began his own foundation, the Sugar Ray Foundation. He was a pioneer in many respects that have yet to be paralleled by athletes, white or African American, even with the multimedia machine and ever increasing globalization of sports and American popular culture.

Notes

1. Rinaldi, Tom. 1999. "Keyshawn Gets a Taste of Ownership, 'Gridiron to Griddle: Keyshawn's business is food for thought,'" in CNN/SI—NFL Football—Thursday, July 8, 1999 at http://sportsillustrated.cnn.com/.
2. Clarification is necessary because the number and depth of Keyshawn Johnson's business enterprises changed between the beginning of this research and completing this paper.
3. Robinson, Ray (with Dave Anderson). 1969. *Sugar Ray*. New York: DaCapo Press.
4. The authors understand that the notion of "black communities" is a social construction. The fact that black athletes are expected to take care of their communities is indicative of the extent of institutional and social racism in the U.S. In *Race and Racism: A Comparative Perspective* (New York: Wiley, 1967), Pierre Van den Berghe refers to the United States as a *herrenvolk* democracy: "democratic for the master race but tyrannical for the subordinate groups due to structure of racial" (18). In this context blacks are held by the larger society to a different standard than are whites, due to the relative position of the groups.
5. Details of the Bing Group were found on the company's website, http://www.binggroup.com/.
6. Holmes, Larry (with Phil Berger). 1998. *Larry Holmes: Against the Odds*. New York: St. Martin's Press.
7. Holmes, 1998.
8. Platt, Larry. 2000. "Magic Johnson Builds an Empire," The New York *Times*, December 10, 2000, Section 6: 119.
9. *Time*, June 25, 1951 vol. LVII, pp. 58–65.

10. Mailer, Norman. 1957. "The White Negro." *Dissent* (Spring 1957). *Newsweek*, 50, Sept. 9, 1957: 98.
11. Stroud, Rick. 2000. "Keyshawn Johnson," in the St. Petersburg *Times* Online, Sept. 1, 2000, Sports Section, found at http://www.stpetersburgtimes.com/.
12. *Newsweek*, 50, Sept. 9, 1957: 98.
13. *Newsweek*, 1957.
14. *Newsweek*, 1957.
15. Platt, 2000.
16. Platt, 2000.
17. Stadiem, William. 1999. "Reign Supreme," in *Los Angeles* Magazine, Nov. 1999, Review/Restaurant Reviews.
18. Rinaldi, 1999.
19. Rinaldi, 1999.
20. Hutchinson, Dave. 1999. "Jets: Just Let Him Tell It: Keyshawn Has It All," in Newark *Star-Ledger*, Sept. 12, 1999, Sports Section.
21. Rinaldi, 1999.
22. Hughes, Samuel. 2001. "Commercial Development Creates Jobs," in the Community News section on the website for West Angeles Church at http://www.westa.org/.
23. Platt, 2000.
24. Platt, 2000.
25. From interview with Keyshawn Johnson in Los Angeles, September 15, 2001.
26. Robinson, 1969: 156.
27. Robinson, 1969: 156.
28. Robinson, 1969: 155.
29. Robinson, 1969: 155.
30. Rinaldi, 1999.
31. Holmes, 1998.
32. Interview, Los Angeles, September 15, 2001.
33. Robinson, Ray. "Why I'm the Bad Boy of Boxing," in *Ebony*, Nov. 1950, vol. 6, no. 1.
34. *Newsweek*, 1957.
35. Robinson, 1950.
36. Robinson, 1950.
37. Shropshire, Kenneth L., and Timothy Davis. 2003. *The Business of Sports Agents.* Philadelphia: University of Pennsylvania Press.
38. Platt, 2000.
39. Moreover, blacks are expected to fight for social justice whether it has to deal with blacks or others. The recent controversy over Augusta National's (the site of professional golf's Masters Tournament) continuing racism and sexism in their membership admission highlights this. Tiger Woods has been disproportionately burdened with the task of sending a message while other golfers are left alone.

FOSTERING COMMUNITY CONSCIOUSNESS

The Role of Women's Basketball at Black Colleges and Universities, 1900–1950

RITA LIBERTI

In the spring of 1930, when Lucille Townsend graduated from high school in the small town of Hamlet, North Carolina, she thought she was finished with both basketball and school. Unsure of what the future held, Townsend looked forward to spending a few weeks with her aunt in High Point, North Carolina. She welcomed the opportunity to spend some time away from home, in part because she was able to earn a few dollars cleaning up at her aunt's beauty shop. Moreover, getting the chance to leave Hamlet for the far larger town of High Point was exciting.

One morning, as the summer was drawing to a close, Townsend's aunt told her to put on her best clothes for a trip to Greensboro. Townsend gave little thought to her aunt's request, as they often traveled to the nearby town to socialize and shop. A short time later, however, they pulled up to the Bennett College campus. Confused by the turn of events and the trunk that her uncle pulled from the back of the vehicle, Townsend asked where her aunt was going. Lucille's aunt replied, "I ain't going nowhere. You're going to school."

Although Townsend had done well in high school, she was not eager to go to college, especially single-sex Bennett. "I walked in front of the little chapel and Lord, I could have screamed," she remembered. "All I saw was girls, girls, girls." Lucille objected loudly, and even threatened a hunger strike, but to no avail. Prior to leaving the campus, her aunt gave her several envelopes that she soon realized contained varying amounts of money to pay for tuition and expenses. She graduated four years later.[1]

Although Lucille Townsend did not realize it on that day in 1930, her family's carefully planned conspiracy provided her with a host of opportunities she would not have had otherwise, including the chance to keep playing the basketball she loved. Bennett was famous for producing intelligent, capable graduates who lived up to the highest standards of womanhood. It also fielded one of the nation's best women's college basketball teams.[2] At most white colleges, the idea of varsity basketball clashed with the visions of ladylike gentility that they wished their students to embody, and competition was thus limited to intramurals. The faculty at many African American colleges held to a more expansive conceptualization of womanhood, one that could encompass fiercely competitive sports as well as homemaking skills and tea parties.[3]

Lucille Townsend's path to becoming a star on the court started as innocently as the ride to campus with her aunt and uncle in 1930. While participating in a game of field hockey during physical education class, she "saw a lot of girls were gathered and there was a man standing with them." Later that day basketball coach Dean Staley called Townsend to his office and asked her why she was not playing basketball. Townsend told Staley that her mother did not want her getting into anything "rough" because of a childhood surgery to remove her appendix. Dismissing that answer, Staley "got out a pair of shoes and a uniform; he said get dressed, you're going to play tonight. You're going to jump center, you're taller than anything I got out there."[4]

That moment marked a turning point for Townsend. Over the next few years she helped build a basketball dynasty at Bennett College, whose teams were renowned throughout the region during most of the 1930s. Her abilities on the court drew acclaim and recognition from the black press across the South, helping her land a teaching and coaching position in Pinehurst, North Carolina, immediately after college.[5] She continued teaching and coaching for the next four decades, retiring from the profession in the 1970s.

As these stories show, Lucille Townsend's path in life was shaped by the efforts of those around her, notably her extended family and the faculty and staff at Bennett. The commitment among the network of individuals who desired to see Lucille enroll in college and engage in a wide range of school activities underscores a broad legacy of commitment among African Americans to encourage and sustain educational opportunities for young people. The community's preoccupation with education was grounded in the belief that individual academic achievement not only served one person's life, but also resulted in the eventual collective good for all African Americans. Black college personnel sought to complement and continue the work of family by imparting intellectual skills, creating a range of opportunities to build and hone character, and teaching community responsibility. It was hoped that such a process would create leaders for blacks, while disrupting widespread perceptions of African Americans as morally and intellectually inferior.[6]

Examining the place of basketball at colleges such as Bennett illuminates the many goals the school set for female students, as well as detailing an understanding of community that nurtured young women and imbued them with a sense of responsibility to that community. All students entering black colleges and universities learned a variety of lessons about character, community, and social responsibility, but student athletes like Lucille Townsend often learned these lessons through sport. These women entered a college setting that honed academic skills but also stressed the development of leadership, discipline, perseverance, and self-confidence. Such qualities were prerequisites for black women's success as they entered a world reluctant to embrace them. Within the walls of collegiate institutions, presidents, faculty, staff, and coaches set about to shape African American women to enrich, enhance, and elevate the larger communities in which they would live.[7]

Although sport was only one of the means by which school personnel molded female students, it was an important element of the overall educational mission at many black colleges throughout much of the first half of the twentieth century. Drawing upon oral histories and archival material, this paper seeks to examine the place of women's basketball as it informs broader notions concerning self-improvement, character education, and community consciousness. Literature from black colleges makes clear the central position of athletics in relation to character development among students. Schools stressed high standards of moral conduct, and the emphasis on discipline, teamwork, and fair play found in well-conducted sport fit seamlessly into curriculum offerings and extracurricular activities.

Speaking to a crowd of nearly two hundred and fifty people at Christmas Day athletic activities at the Agricultural and Mechanical (A&M) College of Alabama in 1912, the school's president reminded those in attendance that the games were more than mere opportunities to enhance physical skill and socialize. Rather, they were "helpful assets in shaping and molding character." He added that the contests spurred young people to "learn quickly, and above all to govern the temper."[8] Similarly, Mary Mitchell, the Director of Physical Education for Women at Prairie View State Normal and Industrial College in the 1920s, concluded, "a physical expression of consciousness of the race will go far towards the development, not only of physical manhood/womanhood, but also of mind and character."[9]

As with so many aspects of black college life, sport and physical activity were understood both as means toward individual improvement and as serving the collective good of all African Americans. Amelia Roberts, Tuskegee Institute's Girls Physical Education Director and basketball coach, argued with clarity and forcefulness about the uniqueness of physical activity in achieving broader aims. "Leadership, teamwork, and loyalty are developed from games, especially group and competitive games," Roberts argued. "No other branch of the school curriculum is so effective in doing this."[10] Fannie M. Scott, the Director of Physical Education at nearby Talledega College, added that attributes conceived and honed in athletics "can be carried over into all phases of life."[11]

Sports-minded school officials moved well beyond rhetoric by establishing and sustaining opportunities for women's involvement in campus athletics. Parents and educational officials worked toward developing young women of sound character who embodied the qualities of tenacity and self-control that would help them engage the inevitable obstacles placed in their paths by racism and sexism. The basketball court served as one of many laboratories on college campuses where African American women worked to sharpen decision-making and leadership skills amid

conflict and tension. Such practical experience strengthened the likelihood that young women would handle similar situations beyond the
basketball arena with equanimity.

Sports' place in this overall educational strategy was abundantly clear
to the players with whom I have spoken. They understood that the skills
they were developing on the basketball court encompassed much more
than ball-handling and shot selection. "The thing that I remember most,"
explained high school and Shaw University star forward Catherlene
Shaw, "is that we were a disciplined team." She added that coach Lenoir
Cook "taught us to be serious about life as well as the game, because the
game is a preparation *for* life." However, the intensity with which players
competed to win was never permitted to overshadow more valued qualities of sportsmanship and team play, according to Shaw. "No one was
allowed to monopolize the game to try to make all the shots." Players
immediately found themselves "in trouble" with Coach Cook when they
lost sight of their role as a member of the team.[12] The specific ethos
espoused by the Shaw team, contoured and driven by Coach Cook,
demanded excellence from players, both on and off the basketball court.
Coach Cook, along with educators, sought to move students beyond
mediocrity, inspiring in them a sense of determination and steadfastness.
The results, they believed, would be individuals of exceptional character,
who were thus well prepared to speak and act for themselves and other
African Americans. In this regard, both the process and the product were
highly valued.[13]

The focus on the virtues of achievement, excellence, and persistence
ran throughout college life. Francis Jones, both a Bennett student and
the daughter of Bennett President David Jones, recalled that all students
were "expected to be excellent."[14] Yet demands that young women seek
excellence were continually framed within a nurturing and supportive
environment, spurring them to work even harder at a particular task.
Mary Woodruff arrived on the Alabama A&M College campus as a seventh grader in 1924 and soon began playing basketball, competing until
she left the campus in 1932 with a junior college certificate. Her fondest
and most vivid memories were the conversations she and other students
had with campus president Drake. "I liked the way he presented himself

and the things that he talked with us about. He would always talk to you about what you *could* do."[15] Similarly, Francis Jones remembered that her father wanted "everything at [Bennett] to be top quality. He wanted his students to feel about themselves that they were tops! That they were deserving of the best."[16]

Student athletes like Woodruff, Shaw, and others desired to perform their best, in part, because of the attitude and commitment of coaches, teachers, and administrators who were eager to see them excel and be confident in their ability to do so. Catherlene Shaw said of Coach Cook, "We loved him so much, we knew he was excited and wanted to win that game, and we wanted to win [it] for him."[17] Players, intent upon meeting and exceeding expectations established by themselves and their mentors and coaches, often brought a sense of determination onto the basketball court.

Bennett athlete Amaleta Moore recalled an encounter with Shaw University's star forward Frazier Creecy in a 1937 game between the two basketball powerhouses. In an attempt to slow the scoring successes of Creecy, Bennett coach Bill Trent told Moore "to go out there and stop her." Moore, knowing Creecy's moves toward the basket inevitably meant dribbling so hard and fast that the defender was forced to move out of the way, decided to risk injury and stand firm. "I stood there," Moore recalled, "and she dribbled straight at me and I stayed right there." Moore's defiant stance sent Creecy flying across the court, earning her a foul and leaving Coach Trent somewhat bemused, although far from disapproving. "I didn't mean to stop her that way," he calmly observed.[18]

Literally, Moore's actions can be characterized as unshakeable; if read symbolically, her steadfastness illuminates an enterprising attitude and deliberate determination about problem solving that was highly valued. As well as teaching discipline and determination, coaches sought to use experiences on the court to acknowledge and reinforce athletes' agency.

Such efforts could be seen not only in the games themselves but in team travel, which required young women to venture beyond the protective confines of their campuses. Travel away from campus brought with it double-edged feelings for students. On one hand students were excited by the trips and clearly understood the luxury of having the opportunity to travel to colleges dozens or even hundreds of miles away from their own. However, like their coaches, students were keenly aware that travel for African Americans across regions of the South was at best inconvenient and at worst dangerous.[19]

Gladys Martin, a 1942 graduate of Fayetteville State Teachers' College in North Carolina, recalled the last night of a lengthy southern tour that took the team to play in South Carolina, Louisiana, and Alabama. After several hours of driving, with few places where African Americans could stop to refuel, use the rest room, buy food, or simply rest, coach E. T. Martin was exhausted. Just a few miles outside of Fayetteville, the coach fell asleep at the wheel and the "next thing we knew we were sitting in a cow pasture."[20] Fortunately no one was injured and the team was able to continue on its way into Fayetteville.

John McLendon Jr., who coached the men's team and helped with the women's program at Durham's North Carolina College, explained that travel to an away contest demanded two sets of preparation: game strategy and securing safe passage for his team amid threatening, and hostile, racist environments. In McLendon's view, the latter occupied his energy and thoughts as much as the former. "Some trips in some directions were like playing your way through a minefield," he recounted. "You always had that in the back of your mind." An unforeseen confrontation with whites was the most dreaded prospect, as it created a situation in which a coach's respect and dignity were threatened in front of his players. "You are teaching young men and women to be upstanding citizens and to be free to do what they want to do in a society and here you are forced [into] a very bad situation." The key, according to McLendon, was less to shield players from the racist policies and practices than to provide them with the tools and strategies to confront and dismantle racism.[21]

The athletes helped to make sense of these potentially severe exchanges and situations by mocking segregation with levity. McLendon recalls that when a school vehicle or bus was pulled over by the police, athletes joked, "Here comes Charlie, I wonder what he wants now."[22] Female athletes sometimes went further. When the Bennett College team drove to games in the late 1930s, Amaleta Moore recalled, "We would be riding along the highway and you'd meet some white fellas thumbing and we'd hang our heads out the window and say, Jim Crow car!"[23]

Coaches' efforts to encourage a strong sense of self worth, respectability, and self-confidence in the young people they mentored on the court extended the educational missions of institutions and the work of parents and families. In spite of the negativity and racism that surrounded and shaped the lives of African Americans—or possibly because of it—families, communities, and educational institutions strove to constantly remind young people of their potential, value, and abilities. Thus intercollegiate sport and other physical activity programs on college campuses blended well with the narratives of empowerment that were highly preferred to those that stressed victimhood. In this way young women forged a stronger sense of themselves through their involvement in intercollegiate basketball. Basketball not only served as a tool to sculpt desirable character traits among athletes but helped crystallize the integral position of community in relation to individual advancement. Young people entered college campuses where curriculum, extracurricular activities, and student government opportunities were continually framed within a context of serving the larger community.[24]

The relationship was far from one-directional, however, as the community's role in advancing individual development was equally apparent. Racism necessitated that the relationship between the two be a symbiotic one. Individuals were far less likely to excel without collective assistance, and group advancement required the leadership of talented individuals. As a result, strategies employed by the black community to prepare young women for their roles as teachers, homemakers, and community leaders purposefully muted the division between notions of individual achievement and group improvement. Where elements of one objective ended and the other began was ambiguous.

The system of support employed by African Americans during the late nineteenth and early twentieth centuries was conceived around a particular conceptualization of community. Community, according to the historian Stephanie Shaw, was a "diverse group of people . . . who possessed a common understanding of history, mutual interests in the present, and shared visions of the future for the group and all its members."[25] The richness of this community, and the network of support it established, lay in its dynamic and multivocal nature. Community was not organized and sustained out of homogeneity; rather, its cohesiveness was enriched "as much out of difference as out of similarity."[26]

Parents, school officials, and others had different entry points into the dialogue that centered on education; they may even have had differing notions of about how the schooling process should proceed. But their ultimate vision rested with the belief that education advanced individual achievement and promoted collective progress.

Differing opinions resulting in tensions and incongruities surrounding the process, as opposed to the ultimate goal of educating young people, is apparent in a series of letters from parents written to President David Jones of Bennett College in the 1940s. While parents and the larger community generally supported the educational strategies employed by school leadership, acknowledging that their daughters were "there to be governed by the ones in charge," occasional disagreements erupted that illustrate the heterogeneity of thought around the commonly held value placed on education.[27] Jones sent a letter to parents whose daughters had arrived late to campus after a holiday break, drawing businesslike and even curt responses from parents. "In as much as we are not fortunate enough to be able to control the time of illness or train schedules, I consider any comment upon the matter unnecessary," replied Madalene C. Stone.[28] Despite these differences of opinion, parents and administrative staff remained focused on educating young people within the community.

Ruth Glover's experiences highlight ways the African American community's "tangible system of operations" worked to further young people's education, and illuminate the role basketball could play in that process.[29] By high school, Glover's abilities on the court had caught the attention of coach and teacher Zenobia Bost, a 1931 Bennett alumna. With nine other children, Ruth Glover's parents, despite their best efforts, could not provide for all of their daughter's needs. Bost helped Glover to improve her basketball skills, encouraged Glover to attend Bennett, and helped her with gifts of clothing and small amounts of money when needed. Bost's efforts helped the young student enter the college, earn an education, and continue to play the game she loved.[30] When examined in isolation, Bost's efforts to support Glover are regarded solely as a mentoring relationship; however, when contextualized within the Jim Crow South, they become an example of black communities "throwing up highways" to support the growth and achievement of promising individuals.[31]

While basketball helped create an avenue for some to enter college, the sport assisted others in remaining on campus once they got there. Such was the case with Annie Cooke. In the summer of 1939, soon after Cooke completed her first year at Shaw University in Raleigh, North Carolina, her parents informed her that they could not afford to send her back to the private Baptist school. Instead they told her that she would attend Fayetteville State Teachers' College, a public and more affordable institution. Cooke was devastated at the thought of leaving Shaw and immediately called on one of her most trusted mentors—Shaw University women's basketball coach Lenoir Cook. Coach Cook told Annie not to worry and arrived at her home in Wilson, North Carolina, later that same day to convince her parents that Shaw, not Fayetteville, was where Annie should continue her education. Coach Cook reminded Annie's parents that Shaw's biggest rival on the basketball court was Fayetteville and he was not about to lose his starting point guard to them. The next day Cook secured a job for Annie on the Shaw campus, enabling her to finish her athletic and academic career at the Raleigh school.[32] In 1993, over a half a century after Coach Cook persuaded Annie Cooke's parents to permit her to remain at Shaw University, Annie Cooke was inducted into the school's athletic hall of fame. The honor recognized not only Cooke's outstanding leadership and skills on Shaw's top-ranked basketball teams but also five decades of civic, professional, and religious contributions to her community. In her acceptance remarks Cooke recognized a handful of individuals, including Coach Cook, whom she described as her "foundation."[33]

Like so many other women who participated in intercollegiate basketball programs while enrolled at black institutions, Annie Cooke could not see her accomplishments solely as individual achievements. Rather, she understood her actions and the accolades bestowed upon her as part of a collective endeavor. Thus, the academic and athletic achievements earned by young female students were as much testament to the collective will of the African American community as they were markers of

individual diligence. Given widespread interest in helping young people
to excel, it is not surprising that communities and campuses took enormous pride in the achievements of female athletes during the period.
The black press routinely featured female athletes as "excellent example[s] of young womanhood."[34]

Players both understood and relished their celebrity and role-model
status. Catherlene Shaw spoke with pride about the community's
response to her achievements in athletics. Shaw recalled that, soon after
leading her high school squad to a national championship at Tuskegee
Institute in 1937, she "began receiving fan mail" from across the state of
North Carolina.[35] Female athletes often felt as valued as their male
counterparts. Shaw graduate Annie Bowers recalled of the school, "It was
nice to be there because people wanted to see *us* play, rather than watching the men; we liked that."[36] In 1938, a report on end-of-year athletic
festivities at Shaw that appeared in Durham's black newspaper, the
Carolina Times, underscored the status afforded female athletes at the
school and their valued position within the larger community. A "rising
salute and tumultuous [sic] applause virtually shook Greenleaf Memorial
Hall as the members of the girls' team filed across the platform to receive
the gold basketballs, made the letter 'S' in relief and inscribed in their
names, which were given in testimony of the University's recognition of
the unusual proficiency as a team and excellent conduct and decorum
on and off the court as individuals."[37]

The role played by basketball in helping young African American
women aspire to and stay in schools such as Shaw and Bennett represents only a fraction of the varied strategies and elements employed by
the broader community to make education possible. The community's
will to see academic opportunity and success become a reality for young
people was grounded in both altruistic ideals and the practical realities of
being African American and female in the early to mid-twentieth century. With female employment prospects limited to domestic service and
other less than advantageous options, it was especially imperative that
black women attend college and excel. The historian Stephanie Shaw
underscored the urgency and magnitude of this enterprise, arguing that
"these women were educated to the best abilities of their families and

communities, not in spite of their being black women but *because* they were black and female and would otherwise have few economic alternatives to a lifetime of 'work-oxen and hoes,' 'brooms and cook-pots.' "[38]

While the hardships families endured in order to create educational opportunities for their daughters were tremendous, the very dearth of alternatives helped provide the impetus to instigate change. The focused intensity with which young people approached the activities in their lives, including basketball, illuminates their desire to transform both themselves and the world around them. The road to attaining an education demanded an unwavering commitment many were willing to give, despite its many challenges. Gladys Martin recalls how the difficult days in her young life created the drive to move beyond it.

> *Our parents just insisted that we must get an education. In the fall when it was harvest time we would rush to get home so we could pick the peas, or help put in the tobacco, or pick up the potatoes before it got dark. Then we'd go inside and do our homework and turn around and do it all again the next day. It was hard, but I guess we learned some fundamental lessons from it, that you have to be persistent and you have to have somewhere where you're going—why you're doing. We were pretty well focused and that focus was to get our education, so we didn't have to earn our living on the farm.*[39]

Such ambitions were difficult to realize for African Americans who lived in the South. Martin recalls walking past at least one white school on the two- or three-mile journey to the only accredited black high school in Madison County, North Carolina. She and her five siblings walked together for "protection," and were troubled less by the distance they had to traverse than by the insults shouted from white children passing by in school buses. Tellingly, Gladys' sister and teammate, Eudoxia, often read aloud from Victor Hugo's *Les Miserables* to pass the time as they walked to and from school and basketball practice.[40] Gladys Martin and her siblings learned lessons about moral fortitude in the face of relentless injustice, just as *Les Miserables'* main character Jean Valjean encounters in the text. Serving on so many levels as a metaphor for their lives, Hugo's narrative "intricate[ly] intertwin[es] individual development and collective endeavor" while it "challenges the reader to *realize*—both to apprehend and to create—the wonders of the utopian world to come."[41] The schooling process gave the Martins the tools to deal with the realities of social injustice that they faced daily and the skills to work toward achieving Hugo's utopian vision.

Student athletes at Bennett College in the 1930s describe the "duty work" they performed on campus as part of this larger strategy in helping to build a sense of community among themselves, with the hope of ultimately eradicating racism and oppression.[42] For an earlier generation of black college students, duty work may have included actually helping to build the structures on campus. In the 1930s, students polished brass, laundered and ironed table linens, and dusted woodwork, among other tasks. Student work gave financially struggling black colleges a cost-effective way to get needed work done; but equally important, according to Bennett students, was that the work symbolized that no one, regardless of financial standing or social status, was above doing physical work. Mary Martin, a 1931 graduate, detailed the "Bennett Ideal" in the school's catalog, stating, "wealth is no honor and poverty no shame; where honorable labor, even labor of the hands, is glorified by high purpose and strenuous desire for a clearer and larger view."[43] One of the intended outcomes was that individual effort served to unite them as "Bennett sisters"—a community laboring to reach a desired goal. In much the same way, Ruth Glover and her teammates from the 1930s describe the "spirit" that resonated on the campus and among basketball team members.[44] This collective presence was constantly rearticulated and promoted within classrooms and across campus activities.

Students took their moral lessons quite seriously, but these highly spirited young women occasionally bent, if not broke, stated codes of conduct. Although better known for her athletic skills on the track at Tuskegee Institute, Alice Coachman found success on the school's basketball team as well. At the conclusion of an away game versus Tennessee State, Coachman recounts the events that almost led to her dismissal from the team and Tuskegee:

> At the end of the game some of the players asked the coach's permission to
> go across the campus to buy hamburgers. When the coach said no [we]

found a window open in the matron's room. The entire first team climbed out of the window. We got the hamburgers; we met some fellows from a nearby school and went dancing at two clubs. We ended up at the home of one fellow whose parents had gone away for the weekend. Most of the girls danced and drank.[45]

Despite having broken a number of campus rules, after much deliberation school officials permitted the young women, including Coachman, to remain at Tuskegee and complete their degrees. Tuskegee personnel may have extended a degree of leniency rarely afforded those who broke codes of behavior because they believed in the greater good that basketball and other sports promoted.

Transgressions like this aside, students' cognition of the multitude of skills and strategies they were taught, both on and off the basketball court, about character and community is evident in the way they led their adult lives after college. The women with whom I have spoken took a wide variety of lessons and put them into action through teaching, coaching, parenting, and community and church work over the course of the rest of the twentieth century. The students' "duty," according to Catherlene Shaw, was "to make a contribution to humanity. To be concerned about other people and that somebody paved the way for us and we must do likewise."[46] Articulation of a collective consciousness and the desire to act as a result of it was nurtured throughout the collegiate careers of black women in the first half of the twentieth century. Many women moved into their professional lives with the same zeal with which they undertook college, to improve theirs and others' surroundings. Basketball served as one of many ways in which the women who were athletes in college gave something back to the communities in which they lived and worked. Teaching in chronically underfunded black schools in the South during segregation tested the perseverance of educational staff and required them to draw on a wide array of creative problem solving-skills developed in college and honed over the rest of their lives.[47]

Helen Shipman left Winston Salem Teachers' College in the early 1940s and entered the teaching and coaching profession, where her skills in the classroom and on the basketball court reflected only a portion of the attributes she embodied. For example, just prior to a championship basketball game, a parent informed Shipman that his daughter could not play because there were crops in the field that needed to be harvested. Not willing to enter the game without one of her starting players, Shipman asked the parent's permission and the rest of the team "went out there and picked [cotton and peas]" all day and then "went to the tournament [that night] and won the game!"[48]

Occasionally, lending support to sustain an athletic program rested not with coaching a girls' basketball squad, but with assisting a boys' program. Dorothy Hammond recalled that her service as coach of the boys' football team was needed in 1942 because so many male instructors at the school were called to military duty during the war. Concerns that might have been raised about a woman's ability to coach a boys' football team or the appropriateness of such an arrangement were apparently not an issue. Hammond fondly recalled her short tenure as coach and the warm responses she received for her efforts, despite "not knowing much about the game."[49] Her attitude and willingness to take on an unfamiliar task far outweighed the particular expertise she brought to the situation. The expectations and responsibilities of African American female college graduates from the first half of the twentieth century were many and varied. Graduates relied on the skills they learned in classrooms, laboratories, and gymnasiums to navigate their own way—and to lead others as well.

Lucille Townsend's priorities when she graduated from Bennett College campus in the spring of 1934 differed greatly from those of four years earlier. Boys, and the lack of them on Bennett's campus, occupied Townsend's energies when she first entered the school. However, she left Bennett with an agenda that positioned education and community uplift prominently. This change in Townsend's outlook—the result of an array of curricular and other campus activities, including competitive basketball—served an integral role in fostering self-improvement and community consciousness among African American female athletes during the period. For these women basketball was a game *and* a tool of a larger educational strategy. Players were aware of the game's importance in their lives as African American women and the lives of those around them. "I think you learn a lot other than how to play [a] basketball game. You have to learn to be respectful of other people and of other peoples' weaknesses and appreciate their strengths; that's life," concluded Fayetteville State's Gladys Martin. "[Basketball] takes some courage, some hard work, some stamina, some endurance. It takes some forgiveness and it takes some questioning. It helped me in my living."[50]

Notes

I wish to extend my thanks to Pamela Grundy for her assistance in reading earlier drafts of this paper.

1. Lucille Townsend, interview with author (Richmond, VA), August 6, 1995.

2. Bennett won several North Carolina state basketball titles in the 1930s. See for example: "Livingstone College Defeats Shaw University and Fayetteville State Normal," *Baltimore Afro-American* (March 26, 1932), 14; "They Set the Pace for the Old North State," *Baltimore Afro-American* (April 16, 1932), 15; "Bennett Girls Win; Top Field," *Chicago Defender* (March 10, 1934), 16; Bennett is Victor, Now Heads List," *Chicago Defender* (March 16, 1935), 16; "Meet the Nation's Best Female Cage Team," *Chicago Defender* (March 27, 1937), 14.

3. Martha H. Verbrugge, "The Institutional Politics of Women's Sports in American Colleges, 1920–1940" (paper presented at the North American Society for Sport History, Auburn, AL, May 1996); Cindy Himes-Gissendanner, "African American Women and Competitive Sport, 1920–1960," in Susan Birrell and Cheryl Cole, eds., *Women, Sport, and Culture* (Champaign: Human Kinetics, 1994), 81–92; Susan Cahn, *Coming on Strong: Gender and Sexuality in Twentieth-Century Women's Sport* (New York: Free Press, 1994), 68–70, 117–118; Rita Liberti, " 'We Were Ladies, We Just Played Basketball Like Boys': African American Womanhood and Competitive Basketball at Bennett College, 1928–1942," *Journal of Sport History* 26 (1999), 567–584; Pamela Grundy, *Learning to Win: Sports, Education, and Social Change in Twentieth-Century North Carolina* (Chapel Hill: University of North Carolina Press, 2001), 128–157.

4. Townsend interview with author.

5. Notable among the featured articles and photographs in the black press of Lucille Townsend is the photo of Townsend and teammates Clara Humphrey and Victoria Jackson standing in their Bennett College varsity sweaters. "Bennett Three Aces Graduate," *Baltimore Afro-American* (June 23, 1934), 19.

6. Much has been written on education, community, and African Americans. See, for example, James D. Anderson, *The Education of Blacks in the South* (Chapel Hill: University of North Carolina Press, 1988), 4–32; Adam Fairlough, *Teaching Equality: Black Schools in the Age of Jim Crow* (Athens: University of Georgia Press, 2001), 1–19; Jas M. Sullivan and Ashraf M. Esmail, "From Racial Uplift to Personal Economic Security: Declining Idealism in Black Education," *Southern Studies* 9 (Summer/Fall 1998), 147–176; Vanessa Siddle Walker, *Their Highest Potential: An African American School Community in the Segregated South* (Chapel Hill: University of North Carolina Press,

1996), 13–39. On white perceptions of African American female inferiority and education's place, see Deborah Gray White, *Too Heavy a Load: Black Women in Defense of Themselves, 1894–1994* (New York: W.W. Norton, 1999), 21–55; Stephanie Shaw, *What a Woman Ought to Be and to Do: Black Professional Women Workers During the Jim Crow Era* (Chicago: University of Chicago Press, 1996), 77–79; Amy Thompson McCandless, *The Past in the Present: Women's Higher Education in the Twentieth-Century American South* (Tuscaloosa: University of Alabama Press, 1999), 121–158; Victoria W. Wolcott, " 'Bible, Bath, and Broom': Nannie Helen Burrough's Training School and African-American Racial Uplift," *Journal of Women's History* 9 (Spring 1997), 388–411; Glenda Elizabeth Gilmore, *Gender and Jim Crow: Women and the Politics of White Supremacy in North Carolina, 1896–1920* (Chapel Hill: University of North Carolina Press, 1996), 32–50; Evelyn Brooks Higginbotham, *Righteous Discontent: The Women's Movement in the Black Baptist Church, 1880–1920* (Cambridge: Harvard University Press, 1993), 188–204.

7. Shaw, *What a Woman Ought to Be and to Do*, 68–103. On the relationship between sport, self-improvement, and community uplift for African American men, see Patrick B. Miller, "To 'Bring the Race along Rapidly': Sport, Student Culture, and Educational Mission at Historically Black Colleges during the Interwar Years," *History of Education Quarterly* 35 (Summer 1995), 111–133. I argue that attributes colleges wished to build upon in students, among others thrift, respectability, and character, were first introduced to young people by their parents and families. Colleges in many instances were complementing skills parents worked to instill in their children well before college. On this point, see Wolcott, " 'Bible, Bath, and Broom,' " 89–110.

8. "Athletic Notes," *The Normal Index* (December 1912), 13.

9. Mary Mitchell, "Physical Education," *Prairie View A&M Catalogue 1925–1926*, 36.

10. Amelia C. Roberts, "Women in Athletics," *Chicago Defender* (March 12, 1927), 9.

11. Fannie M. Scott, "Women Have Ability As Athletes Says Miss Scott," *Chicago Defender* (February 19, 1927), 9.

12. Catherlene Shaw Thompson, interview with author (Fayetteville, NC), June 6, 1996.

13. Various athletes spoke of their coaches in ways similar to how athletes at Shaw University spoke of Coach Cook. Players had very vivid and generally fond memories of coaches. According to the athletes I interviewed, coaches were extremely serious about athletic and academic training of their players. However, they combined this strictness with a sense of compassion and understanding that gained respect of athletes and endeared players to their coaches.

14. Frances Jones Bonner, phone interview with author, February 1, 1998.

15. Mary Zuma Woodruff Cain, phone interview with author, September 3, 2000.

16. Frances Jones Bonner, interview.

17. Catherlene Shaw Thompson, interview.

18. Amaleta Moore, interview with author (West Cape May, NJ), July 30, 1995.

19. For a telling primary source account of travel across the South during the Jim Crow era, see Henry Hooten in William H. Chafe et al., *Remembering Jim Crow: African Americans Tell About Life in the Segregated South* (New York: New Press, 2001), 293–296.

20. Gladys Martin McNatt, interview with author (Madison, NC), November 7, 1997.

21. John B. McLendon, Jr., phone interview with author, July 29, 1996. Similar stories recounted by McLendon can be found in Grundy, *Learning to Win*, 158–159; Grundy, " 'A Position of Respect': A Basketball Coach Who Resisted Segregation," *Southern Voices* (Summer 2001): 84–91.

22. John B. McLendon, Jr., interview.

23. Amaleta Moore, interview.

24. Monroe H. Little, "The Extra-Curricular Activities of Black College Students 1868–1940," *Journal of Negro History* 65 (Spring 1980), 135–148.

25. Shaw, *What a Woman Ought to Be and to Do*, 42. My understanding of community is informed by Shaw's work, as well as by Allison Dorsey " 'To Build Our Lives Together': African American Community Formation in the Redeemed South, Atlanta 1875–1906," (Ph.D. dissertation, University of California, Irvine, 1995), 3–4, 78; Elsa Barkley Brown "Uncle Ned's Children: Negotiating Community and Freedom in Postemancipation Richmond, Virginia," (Ph.D. dissertation, Kent State University, 1994), 1–16.

26. Brown, "Uncle Ned's Children," 6.

27. J. E. Kersey, (December 17, 1946) in Box 7, Folder "Correspondence—Letters to and from parents 1946–1947." David D. Jones Papers, Amistad Research Center, Tulane University, New Orleans, LA.

28. Madalene C. Stone, (1948) in Box 7, Folder "Correspondence—Letters to and from parents 1947–1948." David D. Jones Papers, Amistad Research Center, Tulane University, New Orleans, LA. It was clear from parents' responses to Jones' letter that their daughters risked expulsion because of their late arrivals back to campus after break. I found no evidence to suggest the outcome of the matter for students.

29. Shaw, *What a Woman Ought to Be and to Do*, 42.

30. Ruth Glover Mullen, interview with author (West Cape May, NJ), July 30, 1995.

31. Shaw, *What a Woman Ought to Be and to Do*, 1.

32. Annie Cooke Dickens, interview with author (Wilson, NC), January 9, 1996. Several other players with whom I have spoken noted that as a result of their basketball skills, they too received employment on campus (contemporary version of work-study positions). Campus jobs were scheduled around games and practices to alleviate any conflicts.

33. Annie Cooke Dickens, quoted in "She was blessed with 'foundation' for Hall of Fame," by Tom Ham, *Wilson Daily Times* (December 14, 1993), 1, 5B. For further details on Cooke's induction to the Shaw Hall of Fame, see "Annie Cooke Dickens— Basketball Class of 1942," *Shaw University Founder's Day/Homecoming 1993—The Sixteenth Annual Athletic Hall of Fame Banquet Program.*

34. "Athlete," *Norfolk Journal and Guide* (April 17, 1937), 9. The "excellent example of young womanhood" referred to Frazier Creecy of Shaw University. Numerous other examples of female athletes featured in the black press include a tribute to Ruth Glover Mullen of Bennett College, "Fast Forward," *Norfolk Journal and Guide* (March 14, 1936), 14; Maude Gatty of Shaw University, "Plans Teaching," *Norfolk Journal and Guide* (February 24, 1940), 18; and Vandalia Wood of Fayetteville State, "Farewell, Cagers," *Norfolk Journal and Guide* (April 13, 1940), 12. On the role of the black press

and community consciousness, see Michael Fultz, " 'The Morning Cometh': African-American Periodicals, Education, and the Black Middle Class, 1900–1930," *Journal of Negro Education* 80 (1995), 97–112.

35. Catherlene Shaw Thompson, interview. For a feature article and photograph in the black press about Shaw, see "Members of Championship Sextet," *Philadelphia Tribune* (January 13, 1938), 12.

36. Annie Bowers, interview with author (Charlotte, NC), July 18, 1996.

37. "48 Athletes Awarded at Shaw University," *Carolina Times* (June 11, 1938), 2.

38. Shaw, *What a Woman Ought to Be and to Do*, 1.

39. Gladys Martin McNatt, interview.

40. Similar stories about the experience of walking to school for young African American children can be found in: Chafe et al. (eds.), *Remembering Jim Crow*, 13–14, 77, 119, 142, 155.

41. Kathryn M. Grossman, *Les Miserables: Conversion, Revolution, Redemption* (New York: Twayne, 1996), 11, 125.

42. Grundy, *Learning to Win*, 133–134; Shaw, *What a Woman Ought to Be and to Do*, 90–93.

43. Mary E. Martin, "Bennett's Ideal," *Bennett College for Women—Catalogue 1929–1930*, in Box: "Miscellaneous Box." Bennett College archives, Greensboro, NC.

44. Ruth Glover Muller, interview; Amaleta Moore, interview; Clarice Gamble Herbert, interview with author (Philadelphia, PA), July 31, 1995; Edythe Robinson Tweedy, interview with author (Rocky Mount, NC), August 10, 1995.

45. Alice Coachman, quoted in *Jumping Over the Moon: A Biography of Alice Coachman Davis* by Nellie Gordon Roulhac (Philadelphia: Roulhac, 1993), 66.

46. Catherlene Shaw Thompson, interview.

47. On the disparity of financial support to African American schools as compared to white schools, see Walker, *Their Highest Potential*, 1–4, 21–25; Anderson, *The Education of Blacks in the South*, 148–185; Gil Kujovich, "Public Black Colleges: The Long History of Unequal Funding," *Journal of Blacks in Higher Education* (Winter 1993/1994), 73–82.

48. Helen Shipman Brown, interview with author (Clarkton, NC), May 31, 1996.

49. Dorothy Hammond Ellis, interview with author (Wilson, NC), November 6, 1997.

50. Gladys Martin McNatt, interview.

MAJOR LEAGUE BASEBALL'S SEPARATE-AND-UNEQUAL DOCTRINE

The African American and Latino Experience in Spring Training, 1946–1961

MICHAEL E. LOMAX

From 1946 to 1961, both African American and Latino players in Major League Baseball (MLB) endured a "separate-and-unequal" experience during spring training in Florida. Barred from white owned hotels and motels, separate accommodations were provided for players of color, primarily in black communities. Finding restaurants that would serve them on road trips during the "grapefruit" season posed problems for black and Latino players that their white teammates never experienced. They were also separated from their white counterparts in participating in leisurely activities like golf or going to the beach. By 1961, however, following the lead of Dr. Ralph Wimbish, President of the NAACP's St. Petersburg branch, African American and Latino players spoke out against the racial indignities they endured, bringing national attention to their plight for the first time.[1]

This paper analyzes the forces that shaped the African American and Latino experience in spring training from 1946 to 1961. The paper will also explore the forces that led to what became known as the "spring training ritual," and explain why these players became outspoken regarding their treatment when they had previously held their peace. Four questions will serve to guide the narrative: What were the forces that shaped the African American and Latino experience in spring training prior to 1961? What were the owners' responses to this experience? What, if any, policy emerged regarding the treatment of players of color during spring training? What were the forces that led to the efforts to desegregate spring training conditions in 1961?

African Americans took the lead in improving the plight of players of color during spring training. Their relatively small numbers on major-league rosters resulted in black players accommodating the spring training ritual, leading to a sense of insecurity and alienation. Due to the major league establishment's ambivalence toward their predicament, African American players were left with few options. By 1961, black players had pledged their support to Dr. Wimbish's efforts to end segregation in housing. At the same time, *Pittsburgh Courier* sportswriter Wendell Smith mounted a media campaign in the black press to intensify pressure on the owners. Several black ballplayers filed a formal protest with the Major League Baseball Players Association (MLBPA) to improve conditions in spring training. Voicing their opposition to the spring training ritual, pledging their support to Ralph Wimbish's attempts to end it, and filing a protest with the MLBPA represented a radical departure from their previous accommodation.

Although they would not enter the major leagues in significant numbers until the mid-1950s, Latino players were also subjected to the spring training ritual. However, several factors made their experience unique. Nothing in their experience prepared them to deal with the way race was politically, economically, and socially constructed in America. As a result they had to overcome several cultural differences. Language was the primary barrier that led to many Latino players being exploited by the major-league establishment; they also had to adjust to playing in a foreign country. Nevertheless, in the early 1960s several Latino players not only challenged the status quo but also grew more outspoken. They especially defied the stereotypes that often led to racial indignities, which included the spring training ritual.

This radical departure, however, yielded only a few minor concessions. Neither the NAACP nor civil rights activists aggressively protested the conditions black and Latino players experienced. The diversity of Florida's population, particularly where major-league clubs trained, helped to marginalize direct-action protests. More important, black and Latino players did not seek to impose integration on the respective cities in which MLB clubs trained. Rather, they desired the choice to stay in the same hotels and eat in the same restaurants as their white teammates. Their performance on the field, and their behavior off it, afforded them these privileges.

Major-league baseball's first encounter with the South's laws, customs, and traditions of racial segregation during spring training occurred in 1946, when the Brooklyn Dodgers' farm club, the Montreal Royals, traveled to Florida. Dodgers president Branch Rickey and members of the Committee on Baseball in New York City made arrangements with city officials in Daytona Beach, Florida to train there. Recognizing the potential economic boom to the local economy, city officials agreed to ease segregation laws prohibiting blacks and whites from using its ballpark at the same time. Simultaneously, Rickey arranged for African American sportswriters Wendell Smith, Sam Lacy, and Billy Rowe to meet Jackie Robinson and his wife Rachel upon their arrival in Florida. These sportswriters had connections in the black community that Rickey did not have and would make the necessary arrangements for the Robinsons to insure a smooth transition into their new environment. With the assistance of a local NAACP official, Mary McLeod Bethune, the journalists located a family who offered their house to the Robinsons. In addition, Rickey signed Negro League pitcher John Wright to join Robinson on the Montreal roster.[2]

The initial plan to house the Robinsons called for providing accommodations in Daytona Beach and Sanford, Florida. In Daytona Beach they stayed at the house of Joe Harris, a pharmacist and influential black leader. The Dodgers and Royals were scheduled to begin spring training on March 1, so the Robinsons moved forty miles south to Sanford, the site of the Dodgers' baseball school or "Rickey University," as sportswriters had labeled it. There the Robinsons stayed at the home of Mr. and Mrs. David Brock, a prominent black couple, while the white players stayed at the lakefront Mayfair Hotel, which excluded blacks. Rickey's plan for the Royals to train in Sanford, however, was thwarted when a delegation from the town told the Dodgers president they would not allow blacks and whites on the same field. As a result, Robinson and Wright returned to Daytona Beach.[3]

Rickey's plan to house the Robinsons was based on what could best be described as a separate-and-unequal doctrine. He accommodated southern law, custom, and tradition by finding the best living arrangements in the black community. Rickey had personally visited the Brock home and declared: "If we can't put them in the hotels, then they should stay some place that represents something. This is the type of home." Rickey's focus on developing a plan to house the Robinsons was understandable because this was one venue he had control over. What he could not plan for was Robinson's reaction to these segregated living arrangements, nor what would occur when the Royals began playing exhibition games.[4]

Robinson's initial response to this imposed segregation was annoyance, due primarily to the harrowing experience he and his wife, Rachel, had endured just getting to spring training. Upon their return.to Daytona Beach from Sanford, the Robinsons found themselves back in their small room at the Harrises. Separate accommodations were found for Wright, while the rest of the players lodged in the Riviera Hotel on the oceanfront. Although the Riviera was in an unpleasant state after its wartime use, Robinson wanted to stay with the rest of the players. Arnold Rampersad states that Robinson later wrote that he and Rachel disliked this distinction "almost as much as we resented being chased out of Sanford, but we knew that there could be no protest." They would have to "bear indignities and humiliations without complaint." Robinson added: "[Mr. Rickey] had said that I would have to be 'a man big enough to bear the cross of martyrdom.'" In other words, not only would Robinson have to tolerate this segregated living arrangement, he would also have to accommodate to what Aldon Morris described as a system of domination that protected the privileges of white society and generated tremendous human suffering for blacks.[5]

The city of Daytona Beach honored its commitment to ease segregation laws to allow for interracial contests to take place. Yet when the Royals returned there, they found themselves practicing in the city's black district while the Dodgers trained in the white district: Daytona Beach officials had eased segregated practices but were not about to completely eliminate them. In any event, on March 17 Jackie Robinson became the first African American in the twentieth century to play alongside whites on the same field, in an exhibition game between the Royals and the Dodgers. He faced the game with some trepidation because of the uncertainty how the public would receive him and, most important, how he would perform against major leaguers like Pee Wee Reese, Pete Reiser, or Dixie Walker. A crowd of four thousand fans greeted Robinson with a resolute volley of cheers—and a scattering of boos—when his name was called.

Robinson and Wright's experience outside of Daytona Beach, however, told a different story. On March 21, George Robinson, executive secretary of the Playground and Recreation Commission in Jacksonville, forbade Robinson and Wright to play in an exhibition game at Durkee Field against the Jersey City Giants. He explained: "It is part of the rules and regulations of the Recreational Department that Negroes and whites cannot compete against each other on a city-owned playground." Rickey's initial response was not to make waves. He stated that the Dodgers "have no intention of attempting to counter any government's laws and regulations. If we are notified that Robinson cannot play at Jacksonville, of course he cannot play." The Giants requested that the Royals leave Robinson and Wright at Daytona Beach. Instead, Rickey requested that he be notified of the ruling on the "official stationary of the city of Jacksonville." In this way he attempted to place the responsibility of canceling the game on the city officials' shoulders. The Jacksonville Parks Commission voted unanimously to cancel the game.[6]

Two exhibition games in Deland and Sanford illustrated the types of barriers local officials erected to prohibit interracial contests. On March 25, the Royals were scheduled to play in Deland, Florida. Upon their arrival, they learned that the game had been canceled due to a malfunction in the lighting system. The contest was scheduled for the afternoon. Responding to the cancellation, Robinson stated: "What this had to do with the fact that the game was to be played in the daytime, no one bothered to explain." On April 7, the Royals were scheduled to play the St. Paul Saints at Sanford, where local townspeople had previously expelled Robinson and Wright. Rickey ignored a request by city officials to leave the two black players at the Dodger camp. Robinson did start in the game, and in his first at-bat beat out an infield single and promptly stole second base. When the next batter singled, he scored the game's first run on a close play at the plate. As Robinson was about to step out onto the field for the third inning, the local chief of police ordered Montreal manager Clay Hopper to remove his second baseman or risk prosecution. Hopper replaced him.[7]

Several other cancellations occurred. These disruptions were both costly and bad for team morale. Without question, Robinson and Wright recognized that this chaotic spring training season was a direct result of their presence, undoubtedly causing insurmountable pressure on both of them. The pressure was further exacerbated by the fact that they still had to make the ball club. Even when they made the club, both players still had to deal with the issue of being segregated from the other players, a distinction that frustrated Robinson from the outset. Despite these obstacles, Robinson and Wright persevered, keeping to themselves and speaking when spoken to.

Branch Rickey stuck with the overall experiment. His willingness to cancel exhibition games sent a subtle message that he was committed to Robinson despite the barriers erected by officials in these Florida cities. According to Wendell Smith, he answered the offended cities with defiance: "Without Robinson and Wright, there'll be no games!" These exhibition games occurred in the context of an era when southern whites had an established, comprehensive system of domination over blacks. The "tripartite system of domination" kept blacks under control economically, politically, and socially in cities and rural areas of the South. This system of domination was sanctioned by legislation and enforced by southern governments. Moreover, exhibition games from baseball clubs from the North would in no way change "their southern way of life."[8]

In 1947, to avoid southern segregation and ensure a smooth elevation for Robinson to the major leagues, Branch Rickey moved the Dodger base from Florida to Cuba, scheduling additional games in Panama. He kept Robinson on the Montreal roster and scheduled a series of games between the Royals and the Dodgers to showcase his talents. Three additional black players were assigned to the Montreal club: Roy Campanella, Don Newcombe, and Roy Partlow.

When Robinson reported to training camp in Cuba, he was stunned to learn that the black players would be segregated not only from the Dodgers but also from the other Royals. The Dodgers stayed at the luxurious Hotel Nacional overlooking the Caribbean, while the Royals quartered at the National Military Academy, a new boarding school for the Cuban elite. Robinson and the other black players were housed in a shabby downtown hotel. Sam Lacy described the accommodations as a third-class hotel "with ample ceiling leakage and toilet facilities which left no doubt as to their purpose for being there." At first, Robinson blasted the Cuban government for insisting on these Jim Crow arrangements. However, it was Rickey's idea. The ever-cautious Dodgers president wanted to avoid any disruptive racial incident that might occur. Such occurrences might involve American tourists, many of whom insisted on segregation in local hotels and nightclubs.[9]

Predictably, Robinson was furious at having this segregated living arrangement once again imposed on him. While white players enjoyed steaks flown in from the mainland, black players received a meal allowance to spend at Havana's restaurants and cafés. Living and dining away from the white players posed other problems. Campanella spoke a limited amount of Spanish, but when he was unavailable the rest of the players felt helpless. Adjusting to Cuban cuisine cause the most serious problem. Robinson experienced a severe reaction to the Cuban diet, which resulted in significant weight loss. To add to his frustration, Robinson was expected to learn a new position—first base.

The imposed segregation these black players confronted exemplified the experiences black and Latino players endured during spring training in the 1950s and 1960s. Living away from the rest of the players facilitated a sense of alienation among them. Additional arrangements had to be made by either the ball club or the players to make it to and from the ballpark. What if there was an emergency? How would the parent club get in contact with the players? After all, the players did not always remain in the hotel.

In 1948, Branch Rickey made three decisions that resulted in placing a proverbial crimp in Jim Crow's armor. First, for the second straight year Rickey moved the Dodger camp overseas, this time to Ciudad Trujillo, capital of the Dominican Republic. The Montreal Royals accompanied the Dodgers to provide the competition there. Each club had two blacks on their rosters. The Dodgers brought Robinson and Dan Bankhead, a former Negro League pitcher, while Don Newcombe and Roy Campanella came with the Royals. For the first time black players stayed in the same hotel as whites, lodging at the Hotel Jaragus.

According to the *New Jersey Afro-American*, staying at the Hotel Jaragus should have erased any doubt in Robinson's mind that he was a "big league" player. Robinson described his experience in the Dominican Republic on the pages of the *Pittsburgh Courier*. He indicated that the island was "one of the most beautiful places I've ever been," and that the Dodgers stayed in a "great big hotel," ate the best food, and could swim in a pool on the front lawn after practice if they chose to do so. Robinson pointed out that the majority of the inhabitants were "colored," and although they spoke Spanish, they had things in common with "colored people in America." According to Robinson, "They show it every time Dan Bankhead or I walk on the field by cheering and clapping as enthusiastically as if we were one of their native players."[10]

Establishing Vero Beach, Florida, as the Dodgers' permanent training facility represented the second decision Rickey made to deal with Jim Crow. He acquired an old naval facility that was exempt from Jim Crow law, and in 1949 Vero Beach became the Dodgers' spring training home. The barracks served as the players' quarters, and they could also bring their families to spring training. In addition, Rickey's four AAA and AA franchises—St. Paul, Montreal, Mobile, and Fort Worth—trained at Dodgertown. The Dodgers and Royals arrived there on March 31, 1948, and played a three-game series.[11]

Finally, Rickey divided the Dodgers into two squads to barnstorm the South before the start of the regular season. Robinson and Roy Campanella, who was called up by the Dodgers prior to leaving Ciudad Trujillo, accompanied the "A" squad that barnstormed through Texas, Oklahoma, North Carolina, and Maryland. The A squad played to packed ballparks throughout the South. In Dallas, a reported crowd of 11,370 fans watched the Dodgers play the local Texas League club in their rebuilt Rebels Stadium. Supposedly, 8,328 black fans witnessed

Robinson and Campanella lead a ten-hit attack en route to a 4–0 victory. In Fort Worth, 15,507 spectators saw Robinson make several spectacular plays in the field as the Dodgers defeated the local club, 4–3.[12]

In 1949, Rickey expanded his spring training tour to include the states of the old Confederacy. The Dodgers played the Boston Braves, the Philadelphia Athletics, and the Washington Senators in Florida, and barnstormed Texas, Oklahoma, Georgia, North Carolina, Virginia, Maryland, and Washington, D.C. As the *New York Herald Tribune* pointed out, Robinson and Campanella were playing in southern ballparks outside of Texas and North Carolina for the first time. Rickey saw this as progress from his Triple A Royals having had three games canceled in Florida three years earlier.[13]

The announcement of these plans summoned an outburst from Dr. Samuel Green, Grand Dragon of the Ku Klux Klan. Green questioned the legality of allowing blacks and whites playing on the same field, and planned to investigate thoroughly the state laws regarding segregation. Rickey regretted that anyone should object to the Dodgers playing a game with their regular team and indicated it was not the club's intention to break the law. When asked by *New York Times* sportswriter John Drebinger if the Dodgers would still go through with their exhibition games in Georgia if Robinson and Campanella could not play, Rickey replied: "Is that a hypothetical question?" Informed that it was, Rickey responded with an emphatic "No!" Nobody anywhere could tell the Dodgers president what players he could or could not use. Rickey, however, was quick to point out that he was not on a crusade to have other people change their laws. He stated: "We'll always observe the laws wherever we go. But if we are not allowed to use the players we want to play, or are informed that by using certain players we are violating a law, why the Dodgers simply won't play there and that is all there is to that."[14]

Robinson and Campanella's reaction to the conflict in Georgia were similar. Robinson declared on his radio show that he would play wherever the Dodgers told him to play. He added: "I don't know how far the Klan objection can go, but I hope very much that the fans in Atlanta, or all over America for that matter, will not allow this objection to cause a cancellation of the game." Campanella pointed out that while the Klan's objection could be a "serious thing," he was not too gravely concerned. "If we are sent to some town where the Ku Klux Klan may resent our presence," Campanella continued, "it will be only because we are pursuing our means of livelihood and not because we have any particular social aspirations."[15]

Concurrently, the *Atlanta Constitution* conducted an informal survey to assess fan reaction to Robinson and Campanella's presence in the Dodgers lineup. Out of 10 people surveyed in sidewalk interviews, one objected to their presence. His reason for objecting was that the "KKK [would] raise a stink and give the South a bad name." A typical response was that "Robinson and Campanella are paid entertainers, just like musicians or dancers." If there was a "race problem," it would be among the players themselves and not the fans.[16]

Reaction among Southern sportswriters was similar to the *Constitution*'s informal survey. *Asheville Citizen* sportswriter L. P. (Red) Miller pointed out that Robinson played to packed stands in Asheville the previous year and another sellout was expected. Wilton Garrison of the *Charlotte Observer* stated that professional football had broken the color line and he saw no reason why black players in baseball would not be received in the same way. *Atlanta Constitution* sportswriter John Bradberry indicated that some would raise indignation regarding the negative impact an interracial contest would have on the southern way of life. Others, however, would recognize the situation for just what it was—an exhibition game between a major- and a minor-league baseball club. Ed Danforth of the *Atlanta Journal* declared that, "Men of good will have no earthly objection to the Dodgers' playing their full team."[17]

Political officials found no laws prohibiting Robinson and Campanella from playing in Georgia. The Fulton County Attorney said the county had no jurisdiction over such matters. City Attorney Jack Savage stated he knew of no city ordinance against interracial contests. Attorney General Eugene Cook made the most definitive statement. "We have no law dealing with segregation except in the school system, transportation, marriage and such," Cook said. "There is no prohibition in Georgia against Negroes playing baseball with white people."[18]

As the exhibition games in Georgia drew near, Robinson felt a mixture of fear and loathing. He admitted he hated the thought of "putting foot on Georgia soil." When he stepped off the plane in Macon, two white girls approached him and asked for his autograph. From that time on, Robinson declared, "things weren't going to be so bad after all." Sixty-four hundred fans, the majority of them white, crammed into Macon's four-thousand-seat ballpark. Wendell Smith observed that Robinson "was the center of every eye, every minute he was on the field." In one game in Atlanta, 25,312 fans jammed through the turnstiles and, according to the *Pittsburgh Courier*, set an all-time record for the minor-league club.[19]

The spring training tours of 1948 and 1949 represented what Jules Tygiel has referred to as a softening of Jim Crow rule. Robinson's presence in the lineup resulted in sellout crowds, and minor-league operators in several southern cities began to take notice. This postwar phenomenon placed pressure on those cities where officials sought to maintain their southern way of life. Southern laws, customs, and traditions conflicted with the minor-league magnates' efforts to maximize their profits generated by the Robinson craze. Therefore, by 1949 efforts were made to ease somewhat the sting of these restrictions. At least in the Dodgers' case, the fact that no reported incidents of racially motivated conflicts occurred when the team came to town made this transition easier.[20]

The spring training tours coincided with what historian Manning Marable described as blacks making "decisive cracks in the citadel of white supremacy." In 1945, President Harry Truman appointed Irvin C. Mollison, a black attorney, an associate judge of the U.S. Customs Court. Black sociologist Charles S. Johnson was appointed to the National Commission advising the U.S. State Department on participation in the United Nations, Education, Scientific, and Cultural Organizations (UNESCO). Ralph J. Bunche, a former socialist and co-organizer of the militant National Negro Congress in the 1930s, was appointed to the Anglo-American Caribbean Commission of the State Department. African Americans in the upper South—Virginia, North Carolina, and Tennessee—were elected in small numbers on city councils and school board posts.[21]

Yet at the same time, Branch Rickey's response to Jim Crow segregation was grounded in a separate-and-unequal doctrine. Rickey provided accommodations for blacks and whites to be housed under one roof in Vero Beach, Florida. He became more militant when southern officials in some towns voiced objections to interracial contests. The economic imperative provided the Dodgers president with some leverage for his militancy. However, Rickey became more cautious when it came to dealing with segregation outside of Vero Beach. Black players were still housed separately from whites on road trips. They still had to eat at separate restaurants. This cautiousness on Rickey's part was based on his assertion that he was not on a crusade to change southern laws, customs, and traditions.

Although the 1948 and 1949 spring training tours, along with African Americans making inroads into government positions, represented some semblance of progress, the tripartite system of domination remained firmly entrenched. As Vincent Harding accurately pointed out, African American veterans still found the United States to be a battleground, with confrontations occurring more frequently in the South than anywhere else. In Georgia, for example, black men returning from the war were still murdered on lonely country roads when they tried to register to vote. White policemen in South Carolina gouged out black soldiers' eyes while they still wore their uniforms. A veteran's defense of his mother in Tennessee against a white man sparked a black–white confrontation, leading to the incarceration of several black men. Despite these confrontations, returning servicemen, in conjunction with other courageous African Americans, continued their determined movement against the tripartite system.[22]

Larry Doby's experience in spring training illustrates the postwar confrontations African Americans faced more in the South than elsewhere. In 1947, Doby broke the color line in the American League, appearing in twenty-nine games and batting an anemic .156. The following year, he was instrumental in leading the Indians to the American League pennant and a World Series victory over the Boston Braves. *Cleveland Press* sportswriter Franklin Lewis described Doby as a "six hour ball player per day" on the field and "an 18-hour Jim Crow personality the rest of the time." At Lubbock, Texas, for example, gate attendants refused to admit him because he was not wearing his uniform. Doby went from gate to gate, trying to explain his predicament, before Indians traveling secretary Spud Goldstein arrived and confirmed that he was a member of the team. In Texarkana, a city straddling the Texas–Arkansas border, Doby put on his uniform in a black family's home and attempted to catch a ride to the ballpark. When Doby found out that both Jim Crow taxis were out of service, he started to walk the streets in his baseball uniform. Upon his arrival to the ballpark, Doby was, once again, banned from entry. He stood outside the ballpark, humiliated, until Cleveland manager Lou Boudreau rescued his angry young outfielder from a hostile white crowd that had gathered. In the game, Doby left his position in centerfield when a salvo of bottles and other objects came down around him in the fourth or fifth inning. Boudreau replaced Doby to protect him from the Texarkana fans.[23]

Doby's trials and tribulations continued as the regular season approached. At Buffalo Stadium in Houston, Doby endured a barrage of racist insults as he came to bat against New York Giants pitcher Larry Jansen. He responded by belting a long home run that, according to sportswriters, must have traveled five hundred feet. As Doby circled the bases, the enormity of his home run registered, and he received an ovation from most of his teammates. Even the fans applauded him as he approached home plate. Their cheers, so soon after their jeers, did not appease him. Doby stated: "In fact, I resented their cheers."[24]

Jackie Robinson and Larry Doby's plights during spring training illustrated the kinds of challenges black players faced that whites never endured. The fact that they performed at such high levels under these circumstances attested to their exceptional athletic ability and character. Team sports are based on a philosophy that stresses the need for team unity and discourages activism against mounting injustices. Players are regimented into a lifestyle that requires them to play together on the diamond and to travel, eat, and sleep together. However, African American players had a regimented lifestyle imposed upon them that was dramatically opposed to the team unity concept. While they were expected to, and did, play together as a team on the field, they were segregated from the club off of it. Moreover, black players were expected to accommodate this imposed segregation and voice no opposition to it. Black players responded in kind and focused on, as Campanella previously stated, "pursuing our means of livelihood."[25]

How would Major League Baseball officials respond to the challenges spring training engendered in the 1950s and 1960s? Branch Rickey was the first to deal with southern law, custom, and tradition and more or less established a blueprint for other officials to follow. Yet this plan was based upon a separate-and-unequal notion. While he was able to house all his players under one roof, at great expense to the Dodgers organization, his ball club was still subjected to Jim Crow at restaurants, hotels, and on road trips. Would other major-league owners follow Rickey's blueprint or would they attempt to maintain the status quo?

GOING ALONG WITH THE PROGRAM

In the 1950s, African American players continued to accommodate the imposed segregation during spring training. In many ways, they emulated the Robinson model of bearing the indignities to open doors for future players of color to enter the major leagues. The number of Latino players on major-league rosters increased throughout that decade. While Latinos also endured this imposed segregation during spring training, their experience was significantly different. Moreover, the response by black and Latino players to this segregation was by no means a monolithic one.

Major-league owners and officials never developed a policy to deal with the obstacles players of color confronted during spring training. The major factor contributing to a lack of a formal policy was the owners' overall commitment to integrating their rosters. In August 1946 major-league owners voted unanimously to approve a "revised" version of New York Yankees general manager Larry MacPhail's "Report for Submission to National and American Leagues on 27 August 1946." While the report covered several topics, like the player raids of the Mexican League, the player pension fund, and problems related to scheduling and ticket prices, MacPhail also analyzed the "Race Question." He argued that baseball should maintain its segregated status and pointed out that few if any Negro League players were ready for the major leagues. Integration by only a few players would "jeopardize" the viability of the Negro Leagues themselves, and result in a loss of revenue from allowing Negro League teams to play in the major-league parks. MacPhail's argument suggested that black participation in major-league games might attract such large numbers of blacks that they would discourage white fans from attending games.[26]

Although the race issue was not included in the final report the owners approved, undoubtedly many were aware of the content of MacPhail's original draft. More importantly, many of these owners were against bringing Jackie Robinson up from the minors. However, as Jules Tygiel and William Marshall point out, there is no evidence to support claims later made by Branch Rickey and Commissioner Alfred B. (Happy) Chandler that the owners voted 15–1 to prevent Robinson from playing in the major leagues. National League counsel Louis Carroll testified before the Subcommittee on the Study of Monopoly Power that the owners voted on a much modified version of MacPhail's original draft. He added that most of the original copies were destroyed the day after the owners met on August 27, 1946.[27]

While it is somewhat problematic to suggest that the owners accepted MacPhail's controversial analysis, their subsequent actions illustrated their lack of commitment to integrate their player force. Integration throughout the late 1940s and 1950s was conducted at a snail's pace. Only six of sixteen major-league clubs had blacks on their rosters by 1953. By the late 1950s, the last three major-league clubs—the Philadelphia Phillies, the Detroit Tigers, and the Boston Red Sox—integrated their all-white casts.

If the owners were slow to commit to integrating their player force, dealing with the plight of black players during spring training was the furthest thing from their minds. No doubt they delegated this responsibility to their general managers and traveling secretaries. To the owners' way of thinking, the greater number of ballplayers should not be inconvenienced for the sake of a few. By the 1950s, the protocol for the African American and Latino experience during spring training had been established. With the exception of Dodgertown, general managers and traveling secretaries made arrangements to house minority players in the homes of black families, boarding houses, or all-black hotels.

Club officials or the players themselves arranged transportation to and from the ballpark. The players were also given meal money to find restaurants that would serve them.

Often referred to as the spring training ritual, the response to this imposed segregation ranged from accommodating it to outright frustration and alienation. In 1954, Milwaukee Braves outfielder Henry Aaron experienced his first spring training with the club in Bradenton, Florida. Aaron, Jim Pendleton, Charlie White, and George Crowe were housed in Mr. and Mrs. K. W. Gibson's home, while the white players stayed "across the tracks" in the Manatee River Hotel. Aaron declared that he was accustomed to this treatment because he grew up in the South. This is not to say, however, that Aaron was either happy about his predicament. As we shall see later, Aaron became one of the most outspoken black players regarding the spring training ritual.[28]

St. Louis Cardinals outfielder Curt Flood, born in Oakland, California, was utterly stunned by his first experience with the spring training ritual. In 1956 the Cincinnati Reds signed Flood to a one-year contract at $4,000 with no signing bonus. The following spring, Flood trained with the Reds in Tampa, Florida, before being assigned to a minor-league club. Upon his arrival at the Reds' hotel in Tampa, Flood was instructed to follow a bellhop who led him through the lobby to a side door. The bellhop instructed a black cab driver to take Flood to "Ma Felder's" boarding house. "Until it happens you literally cannot believe it," Flood explained. "After it happens you need time to absorb it." At Ma Felder's, Flood met Frank Robinson, George Crowe, Chuck Harmon, Joe Black, and Brooks Lawrence. While many of the older players did not mind living in the boarding houses, the initial experience of Jim Crow left a lasting impression that gnawed at Flood's gut.[29]

Among the indignities that angered Flood (and undoubtedly other black and Latino players) was a ritual they were subjected to known as the "routine on the bus." On road trips, it was customary for a team to stop in a town to eat after a game. Black players would either remain on the bus while their white teammates went into the restaurant or go to the back door to be served. If they were lucky, an all-black restaurant would be within walking distance from the bus. To save them from the humiliation of waiting at the back door of a restaurant, some white players brought food to them on the bus. Flood's frustration was evident when he explained that it was "absolutely maddening to sit all sweaty and funky in the rotten bus instead of walking like a human being into a restaurant."[30]

Toward the end of his career, Jackie Robinson voiced his frustration with enduring the spring training ritual. Outside of Dodgertown, Vero Beach was a lonely place for black players. His biographer Arnold Rampersad states that blacks and whites down South at times tried his patience. "This is one real bad town," Robinson wrote about a particular stopover in a segregated hotel. "There is absolutely nothing to do here." He added: "I have been to the movies once and am going again this afternoon. It's like the worst we saw in Daytona Beach." Even though he could stay with his white teammates at Dodgertown, Robinson still expressed this sense of alienation many players of color experienced during spring training.[31]

Black players whose clubs trained in Arizona were also subjected to the spring training ritual. In 1950, New York Giants outfielder Monte Irvin reported to his first spring training in Phoenix. While Irvin could stay in the same hotel with the rest of the club, certain restrictions were placed on him. He could not hang around the lobby and on entering the hotel had to go straight to his room. He also couldn't eat in the dining room, so he ordered room service. When Irvin asked Giants traveling secretary Eddie Brannick why he was not allowed in the dining room, Brannick told him: "Well, for some reason, that's the law out here, and until they get the law changed, we'll just have to suffer with it." Since Irvin was trying to make the team, he "accepted it and went along with the program."[32]

With the spring training ritual established, Latino players entered the major leagues in substantial numbers. As historian Rob Ruck has noted, when Jackie Robinson broke the color barrier in 1947 it sent "shock waves throughout Caribbean baseball." Black and mulatto ballplayers from the Dominican Republic, Cuba, Puerto Rico, Venezuela, and Mexico could now consider major-league careers. During 1947, only Cuban-born catcher Fermin Guerra and Mexican pitcher Jesse Flores, both with the Philadelphia Athletics, were in the major leagues. Between 1950 and 1955, however, forty-two Latinos played in the majors. Historian Sam Regalado points out that given the fact that only fifty-four Latinos made the big leagues in more than fifty years prior to 1950, this was a considerable increase.[33]

While Latino players were subjected to the same protocol as American blacks—segregated housing, the routine on the bus, and finding restaurants that would serve them—other factors made their experience significantly different. From the outset, many Americans thought poorly of Latinos. Research published by the Office of Public Opinion Research in 1940, for example, indicated that 49 percent of Americans viewed Latinos as "quick tempered"; 44 percent described them as "lazy"; and 34 percent classified them as ignorant. In terms of positive traits, only 15 percent of those who responded believed Latinos to be intelligent, and a paltry 5 percent felt Latinos were efficient as a people. Sportswriters characterized Latino players like Puerto Rico's Vic Power and Cuba's Minnie Minoso as "rebellious in the clubhouse" and selfish—not team players—on the diamond. The press dismissed their flamboyant play on the field as mere "showboating" or "hot dogging."[34]

In 1951, Orestes "Minnie" Minoso became the first Latino to play for the Chicago White Sox. Minoso acknowledged that racial discrimination and the language barrier made things more difficult, but not impossible. Cultural pride and charm were weapons he used to respond to these obstacles. In his autobiography, Minoso states that he felt like he was defending his uniform each time he put it on. He added: "I respected my uniform, and I wore it as if I was representing each Latino country." One year Cleveland general manager Hank Greenberg threatened to fine Minoso for arriving late to spring training. In an effort to reprimand his star outfielder, Greenberg asked Minoso what the latter would do if the roles were reversed. The Cuban astutely replied: "I say 'Minnie fine fellow. He always in good shape. He all the time hustle. He worked hard during winter. I no mind if he come late.'" Greenberg never issued the fine.[35]

Felipe Alou's experience in spring training typified the frustration bought on by the language barrier. On April 7, 1956, Alou began his American baseball career in the Giants' spring training facilities in

Melbourne, Florida. He arrived with only ten dollars in his pocket, speaking only Spanish. Dinner that evening foretold the increasing sense of isolation he felt as the days passed. His menu included "no rice, no beans." Alou recalled: "They kept feeding me steaks, a food that I found to be very rich and one which I had eaten only on rare occasions in the past. And I faithfully drank my cold, cold milk. Back home we always boiled it and drank it warm." This new diet resulted in Alou losing a considerable amount of weight in just one week. Adjusting to his new environment took much longer.[36]

The racial environment was another obstacle most Latinos were not prepared for. "I didn't even know about the stuff when I get here," claimed a puzzled Roberto Clemente. "I don't believe in color; I believe in people." In his first spring training in 1955, Clemente was disturbed by a Fort Myers journalist, who characterized him as a "Puerto Rican hot dog." What disturbed Clemente the most was that this particular sportswriter knew nothing about him. However, he knew Clemente was Puerto Rican. "As soon as I got to camp," Clemente explained, "they tell me I'm a Puerto Rican hot dog." The label irritated the Pirates outfielder, who felt he was being derogatorily stereotyped. When Clemente approached the other Latino players in camp, Roman Meijas and Felix Montemayor, he was told to keep his mouth shut or risk being returned to the minor leagues. Clemente replied: "I don't care one way or the other. If I am good enough to play, I have to be good enough to be treated like the rest of the players." He added: "So I don't want to be put in the bathroom because I came from Puerto Rico." Clemente expressed his cultural pride through his athletic ability, which to his way of thinking, should have afforded him the same treatment as the rest of the players.[37]

To most Latinos Jim Crow society was irrational, particularly in the way it was practiced. Puerto Rican-born pitcher Ruben Gomez stayed in segregated facilities at the Giants' Florida-based spring training camp. He discovered that some restaurants were selective in their bias. For example, one evening after he and his black teammate confronted a "whites only" restaurant, Gomez "went in, but the other guy didn't want to. The owner came over and said 'how are you?' and started to talk to me, and they served me. The other guy saw this through the restaurant window.

He came in [but] they wouldn't serve him." Gomez recognized "how crazy the whole question of race is in America—if you speak Spanish you're somehow not as black."[38]

Puerto Rican infielder Felix Mantilla also confronted this racial inconsistency. During his first spring training in the Milwaukee Braves organization in 1956, a club official took a group of rookie players to attend the movies in a nearby town. Unfortunately, they were unknowingly left at a Jim Crow theater. "We had to sit on the sidewalk from seven until the bus game back at ten," he recalled. The Braves did little to orient black Latinos about American racial customs. "We used to play a lot of exhibition games down South and nobody used to tell us where we had to go and things like that," Mantilla explained. "We were on our own. I remember times when the white players used to go to the good hotels and we had to find some flea bag somewhere to stay."[39]

One club, the New York (and later the San Francisco) Giants, recognized the problems of adjustment. The Giants assigned Alessandro "Alex" Pompez to help their Latino players make the transition into American culture. Pompez's experience with Latino blacks dated back to his days as the owner of the Negro League New York Cubans. He developed a friendship with Giants owner Horace Stoneham when the Cubans used the Polo Grounds. When the Cubans collapsed, Stoneham hired Pompez to work for the Giants. He was given the unenviable task of orienting Latino players to American culture during spring training. A specific task was to educate Latinos regarding America's racial mores. Pompez explained, "When they first come here they don't like it [racism]. Some boys cry and want to go home." He added: "But after they stay and make big money they accept things as they are. My main thing is to help them. They can't change the laws." Therefore, accommodating these racial mores was the first lesson in adapting to American culture.[40]

Treatment on and off the field remained uncertain during spring training. This was an era when major-league clubs barnstormed their way to their respective cities before the start of the regular season. They played several exhibition games throughout the Deep South, Texas, California, and Arizona. The Pittsburgh Pirates were scheduled to play an exhibition game with the Baltimore Orioles in Birmingham, Alabama.

Because of a sports segregation ordinance adopted by the city in 1954, the Pirates' players of color—Roberto Clemente, Roman Meijas, and Curt Roberts—could not dress for the game. For Clemente, this marked the first time he had been told he could not play because of the color of his skin.[41]

In 1956 several black and Latino players on the Milwaukee Braves found out how problematic it was to be segregated from the rest of the club. Henry Aaron, George Crowe, Bill Bruton, and Humberto Robinson were scheduled to catch the team plane in Mobile, Alabama, en route to Houston. Before they caught the plane, they had to travel from the ballpark to the "colored side of town" through a maze of traffic to gather their belongings. Simultaneously, their white teammates, many of whom would be sent to the minor leagues after the season began, had a police escort for their chartered bus to a downtown hotel. Once they had checked out, they reboarded the bus and were escorted to the airport. When Aaron, Bruton, Crowe, and Robinson arrived at the airport, they discovered that they were left behind with instructions to catch the next flight. Angered by being stranded in Mobile, they refused to board the flight and returned to the house where they had been quartered. According to Sam Lacy, being left behind in Mobile almost resulted in a "tan rebellion." The following morning, however, Braves traveling secretary Duffy Lewis made a flight reservation to enable them to rejoin the club in Houston. Instead of an open revolt, the players acquiesced, boarded the flight, and rejoined the club.[42]

In 1958, Henry Aaron and Felix Mantilla were run off the road by a young white driver on their way to Bradenton. When Aaron reached Tampa, a big Buick pulled up behind him and began tapping his rear bumper. Aaron thought the kid wanted to pass him, so he pulled over to one side and allowed the latter to pass. The driver proceeded to pass Aaron and then slowed down to fifteen miles per hour. The Braves outfielder attempted to pass the kid again, but he swerved into Aaron's car, causing them to land in a ditch.[43]

When Aaron and Mantilla arrived at camp, they talked to the other players about the incident. They were told not to mention the episode to the press. According to Aaron, one player supposedly said: "The NAACP will get a hold of it and there you go." Aaron replied: "I almost lost my life and you want to me keep it a secret?" When he reported the affair to the local press, it didn't appear in the newspaper. It was a puzzling response to a player who was a major contributor to the Braves' success in the late 1950s.[44]

Aaron and Mantilla's near-death experience occurred during a period when the South had become what Aldon Morris referred to as "an extremely dangerous place for blacks." In 1955 alone, several hideous murders took place. The most notable crime was the killing of a fourteen-year-old black boy named Emmett Till who was visiting Mississippi from the North. Till was murdered for allegedly whistling at a white woman. A coordinated attack against the NAACP throughout the South became highly organized and effective from 1954 to 1958. An emotional wave of massive resistance to public school desegregation permeated the South in response to the *Brown* decision. Several states—Alabama, Georgia, and Louisiana in particular—attempted to push through legislation banning interracial sporting contests.[45]

By 1961, African American and Latino players endured the spring training ritual within the context of a racially hostile environment. They could not rely on the major-league establishment to rectify their plight. With the owners' lack of commitment to integrate and their numbers relatively small, they were left with few options but to put up with it. As Sam Lacy accurately has pointed out, black and Latino players were "inwardly seething but outwardly silent over the discrimination [they were] subjected [to during their] six-week sojourn in Dixie." As the 1961 grapefruit-league season approached, these players of color would no longer remain silent regarding their plight.[46]

WITH ALL DELIBERATE SPEED

In 1961 two members of the NAACP chapter in St. Petersburg, Florida, Dr. Ralph Wimbish and Dr. Robert Swain, publicly denounced the spring training ritual and urged the major-league owners to remedy the situation. Several African American and Latino players pledged their support to Wimbish and Swain's efforts. Their support was predictable, since the owners had expressed little or no concern for their plight for fifteen years. Simultaneously, Wendell Smith mounted a "media campaign for racial equality in major league training camps" on the pages of the *Pittsburgh Courier*. For the first time, national attention was focused on the conditions black and Latino players experienced during spring training. Moreover, African Americans took the lead in exerting pressure on the major-league establishment to correct the situation.

The response by the major league establishment to this external pressure was essentially to stonewall the issue until the media storm subsided. Several of their comments in the press resulted in black and Latino players voicing their opposition to the spring training ritual. Although Chicago White Sox owner Bill Veeck and New York Yankees co-owner Dan Topping made attempts to house their players of color "under one roof," their efforts were minimal at best. Some concessions were made to improve the conditions of these players during spring training, but they would be based on a separate-and-unequal notion.

Efforts to remedy the spring training ritual occurred simultaneously with what historians August Meier and John Bracey referred to as a "revolution in expectations" among American blacks. A new sense of urgency to dismantle barriers to racial equality emerged, resulting in an outpouring of nonviolent direct action that, by the early 1960s, came to characterize this most recent phase of the civil rights movement. Tens of thousands of people—black and white—were mobilized for the first time, leading to the rise of new organizations, like the SCLC and SNCC. Several local organizations mounted a frontal assault against all existing racial barriers to political, economic, and social equality.[47]

It was within this context that Ralph Wimbish publicly denounced the spring training ritual. A medical doctor and a prominent member of St. Petersburg's black community, Wimbish was the president of the local chapter of the NAACP. He had spearheaded a successful drive to desegregate several variety stores and department-store lunch counters. Wimbish owned rental property and for years reaped the financial rewards that came with housing black players in St. Petersburg for the New York Yankees and the St. Louis Cardinals. In an era that historian

John Hope Franklin referred to as "the most profound revolutionary change in the status of black Americans . . . since Emancipation," Wimbish came to terms with the paradox of the practice. He concluded that if he continued lodging black players, he would be contributing to the condition of forced segregation, conflicting with the very cause he fought for—racial equality. Wimbish added: ". . . it [was] not logical to battle for integration of lunch counters with one hand and to further the cause of segregation by arranging separate housing with the other."[48]

At a January 31, 1961, press conference Wimbish told reporters he would no longer act as the Yankees' unofficial housing representative. He had located accommodations for black players for years and even put up Elston Howard in his own home. To demonstrate his commitment, Wimbish announced that he would not offer the Yankees catcher accommodations that season and urged other black landlords to follow suit. He also called on Yankees and Cardinals officials to push for an end to segregated practices at their respective headquarters, the Vinoy Park and Soreno hotels.[49]

Wimbish asserted that he had heard complaints from Yankees and Cardinals players about "the lack of suitable housing in the Negro section." While the housing was described as "satisfactory," Cardinals players Bill White, George Crowe, and Curt Flood complained about the lack of privacy and various other inconveniences. Wimbish also pointed out that the biggest "bone of contention [was] over the poor eating facilities." Prior to desegregating the lunch counters, eating facilities for black and Latino players were virtually nonexistent. The Cardinals' black players lived in one house, but had to eat in another.[50]

The following day, the New York Times reported that Yankees co-owner Dan Topping took what appeared to be the initial step toward ending segregation at the American League champions' spring training camp. Topping stated that he would like very much to have the whole team—particularly the club's minority players Howard, Hector Lopez, and Jesse Gonder—"under one roof." He added that it was time for the Yankees and Cardinals to take the first steps to end segregation. Topping advised Soreno Hotel officials that he was prepared to abandon their St. Petersburg training base, unless the club's minority players were granted the same privileges as their white teammates. The Yankees president requested that F. C. Robinson, chairman of the local baseball committee, "follow through" on his request. Despite Topping's reported aspiration to end segregation, a spokesman added that the hotel remained firm on their policy of excluding blacks. The spokesman added that the Soreno would be happy to continue to house the Yankees "on the same basis," meaning that black and Latino players would have to seek separate accommodations.[51]

On February 3, Topping announced that the Yankees would move to Fort Lauderdale for the 1963 grapefruit-league season. Confirmation of the move came supposedly by accident during a press conference dealing with another matter. Topping went to great lengths to indicate that this decision was in no way related to the segregation problems that hampered the Yankees' spring training housing arrangement. According to Yankees publicity director Bob Fishel, Fort Lauderdale interests attempted to lure Topping to their city by making concessions to deal with integration. Fishel, however, did not elaborate whether the city's hotels offered integrated facilities. He did say an "integrated area" was part of the Fort Lauderdale bid for the Yankees. The city of Fort Lauderdale approved a half-million-dollar general-obligation bond issue to build a modern eight-thousand-seat stadium that would include an air-conditioned clubhouse and offices at an abandoned airport called Prospect Field.[52]

Simultaneously, White Sox owner Bill Veeck made efforts to house all of his players under one roof in Sarasota, Florida. Veeck told Wendell Smith that he did not like his minority players segregated from the rest of the team and he intended to do something about it. In addition, he stated that the situation was unfair and the sooner the owners corrected it the better. Veeck was only partially successful in rectifying the segregation imposed on black and Latino players in Sarasota. He arranged for his minority players to lodge in a "first class" motel, while the rest of the team stayed at the New Terrace Hotel. In Miami Veeck did manage to house his entire club at the Biscayne Terrance Hotel for a series of exhibition games. Hotel manager Randy Kippel gave considerable thought whether to lodge the White Sox there and concluded that it was just "a matter of time before these things are bound to happen in Miami."[53]

Whereas Bill Veeck and Dan Topping attempted to redress the segregation situation, the majority of major-league clubs essentially chose to stonewall the issue. St. Louis Cardinals general manager Bing Devine responded to Wimbish's challenge to remedy the spring training ritual with caution. While it was desirable to have all the players stay together, Devine pointed out that the Cardinals did not "make the rules and regulations for the various localities." Prior to the start of spring training, Devine called Curt Flood into his office to discuss the living arrangements in Florida. According to Devine, Flood was straightforward in voicing his displeasure with the spring training ritual. When told there was nothing the Cardinals could do about the situation, Flood retorted, "train someplace else." When told moving would be costly, Flood replied that baseball "had a hundred years and money you haven't even counted." What bothered Flood the most was that white rookies got better treatment in Florida than black veterans. According to the *Pittsburgh Courier*, Flood declared: "The rookie who is trying to win my job can bring his wife to camp and live in the most lavish surroundings. Me, I'm forced to leave my wife at home because we can't find a decent place to stay. It just doesn't make sense."[54]

Comments made by Milwaukee Braves vice-president George "Birdie" Tebbetts resulted in several black and Latino players voicing their opposition to the segregated living arrangements. Tebbetts asserted that racial segregation had never presented a problem for the Braves in spring training in Bradenton, Florida. When asked if the Braves planned to follow the lead of the Yankees in attempting to house black and white players at the same hotels, Tebbetts replied that such a problem did not exist among the Braves' black players. He added, however, that if any of their black players requested hotel accommodations, the organization would attempt to accommodate them.[55]

Braves outfielders Henry Aaron and Wes Covington were two of the most vocal players expressing their dissatisfaction with the living arrangements. Aaron stated that blacks "resented having to live away from the rest of the club." Their feelings were never made known because no one asked them. Pointing out Tebbetts' claim to have "carefully selected" the black players' accommodations, Aaron responded: "Carefully selected?

From what? There's not but one place down here for us to stay in." Covington indicated that the situation didn't affect him directly, because he owned a home in Bradenton; however, he was quick to point out how problematic it was when a black player brought his family to spring training. He added: "They [hotel and boarding house owners] see you coming and they want to make a fortune off you." Black players got less than whites for the same money. Aaron and Covington asserted that there was no decent housing in Bradenton and most restaurants and entertainment outlets denied them service.[56]

Throughout Florida black and Latino players spoke out against the indignities of Jim Crow segregation. Elston Howard desired to bring his family to spring training like the rest of the players, but he could not make any plans until he arrived in St. Petersburg to see what kind of housing was available. "The other players can rent from an agent in advance," Howard explained, "but I can't. It is not pleasant." Chicago White Sox outfielder Al Smith was uncertain about the new arrangements Veeck made for black and Latino players in Sarasota. He accurately pointed out that the "motel they speak about getting for us may be alright but it is still segregated." Detroit Tigers outfielder Bill Bruton pondered who or what gave anyone "the idea that we [black players] shouldn't have wanted the same accommodations as were afforded the rest of the guys." He perceptively added: "I realize the ball clubs are small compared to states, but they take a lot of money into cities and they're important enough to be listened to." Bruton continued: "After all, take the Braves out of Bradenton and what have you got?" Cincinnati Reds outfielder Frank Robinson pointed out that the spring training ritual had hurt all the minority players. "It could be nothing but their indifference that kept the owners from understanding how we felt," Robinson declared. "You don't have to be told that you're digging a pin in a man's face." Pittsburgh Pirates outfielder Roberto Clemente indicated that he was "against segregation in any form." and that he didn't "like it in Fort Myers and never will so long as we are treated on a segregated basis."[57]

Additional pressure was exerted on the major-league establishment to end the spring training ritual. Wendell Smith mounted a media campaign in the *Pittsburgh Courier* aimed to secure equal treatment during spring training for all "Negro players in the major leagues." Several former and current executives like Branch Rickey, Bill Veeck, and Chicago Cubs general manager John Holland supported Smith's campaign. Former players Roy Campanella and Larry Doby also endorsed Smith's aim to end the spring training ritual. Florida State NAACP President A. Leon Lowry asked all major-league clubs to break down segregation barriers against their black players. Lowry's purpose was to bring national attention to the plight of black and Latino players during spring training, and called for all teams to follow the Yankees' lead to end racial bias.[58]

Efforts to end the spring training ritual coincided with the wave of direct action protest against all forms of segregation that swept across the South. In St. Petersburg, for example, black students in cooperation with the NAACP launched a boycott and picketing movement against segregated lunch counters, beginning with a McDonald's restaurant. The NAACP provided the financial support and organizational experience, while the students supplied the manpower and youthful energy. By January 1961, seventeen establishments had ended their discriminatory policies. Professional sports were also caught in the web of direct action protests. In 1960, *Houston Informer* sportswriter Lloyd Wells—in conjunction with the Progressive Youth Association, a local civil-rights group— urged black fans to boycott the Houston Oilers' home games. The protest was in response to Oilers owner Bud Adams' segregated seating policy in Jeppensen Stadium.[59]

Although the NAACP advocated an end to the spring training ritual, there is no evidence to indicate that attempts were made to initiate a coordinated boycott or protest. Essentially, the assault against spring training conditions was a two-man show. A. Leon Lowry aspired to bring national attention to the plight of black and Latino players during spring training. Undoubtedly, efforts to attract the national spotlight could also tacitly shed light on the problems Florida's black community confronted; Major League Baseball served as an excellent lure to bring national attention to the Sunshine State, since thirteen of the eighteen teams trained there. Why was there no coordinated boycott or protest against the spring training ritual?

Two factors contributed to the lack of a coordinated effort. Reluctance to relinquish the revenue private homeowners generated by housing black and Latino players constituted the first factor. As Jack Davis pointed out, the lack of support from black and white landlords was somewhat disappointing to the advocates of change. It was problematic to ask these landlords and hotel owners to give up these economic residuals. Moreover, this loss of revenue would end up in the coffers of rich white hotel chains. Therefore, it was understandable when most landlords at Florida spring training sites declined to join Wimbish and Swain's stand against imposed segregation in housing.[60]

The other factor was the small size of Florida's African American population. The relatively low percentage of blacks in an increasingly diverse population helped marginalize inflammatory rhetoric and direct-action protests. As V. O. Key Jr. states, the smaller the percentage of blacks in a state's population, the less chance there was for intense racial animosities. With many immigrants from the Northeast and Midwest settling in the urbanized, southern region of the state, Florida's diverse population tended to moderate racial confrontations. In addition, Florida's heavy economic reliance on tourism also provided a steadying influence that served to inhibit those reactionary demonstrations that would have tarnished the state's "vacation land" image. This could possibly explain why no local civil-rights groups outside the NAACP protested against the spring training ritual.[61]

The NAACP's conservative protest, combined with Wendell Smith's media campaign, did yield some minor concessions; the Milwaukee Braves, for example, desegregated Bradenton Field. According to General Manager John McHale, the Braves "insisted to the city officials of Bradenton, and they have acquiesced, that under our interpretation of the local ordinances, we are free to run the ballpark as we see fit." Under the Braves' new policy, tickets could be made available to all fans for exhibition games. It also included the removal of discriminatory signs on men's and women's washrooms, and at the gates and ticket windows. Birdie Tebbetts and manager Chuck Dressen suggested that this policy change was a sign of "good faith," since they could do nothing immediately about the hotel situation.[62]

This policy change did not satisfy the Braves' black and Latino players. On March 8, 1961, the Sporting News reported that an official and formal protest was filed with Frank Scott, general director of the Major

League Baseball Players Association. According to sportswriter Dan Daniel, the strongest protest came from the Milwaukee club. The fundamental underpinning of the protest centered on black and Latino players receiving the same human decency as whites. In the minds of these players, enduring the spring training ritual constituted second-class citizenship. These players were treated well in the private homes where they frequently resided; the complaints were against the principle that forced this discrimination upon some of the game's highest-paid players.[63]

Pressure also came against the major-league establishment regarding an incident involving the St. Petersburg Chamber of Commerce. The Chamber of Commerce sponsored an annual "Salute to Baseball" breakfast in honor of the Yankees and Cardinals. Bill White and the other black players discovered they had been excluded from the invitation list. Cardinals public relations director Jim Tooney stated that White had misinterpreted the exclusion of the black players from the list. He defensively added that white players like Stan Musial, Lindy McDaniel, and Joe Cunningham were not invited because they lived outside the hotel. "Since the Negro players do not live in the hotel," Tooney explained, "they were not invited." But the aforementioned white players were not excluded from living there. On the other hand, Yankees PR man Bob Fishel invited all their players. When Elston Howard asked if it included him, Fishel answered in the affirmative.[64]

As a form of damage control, Tooney took full responsibility for White's mistaken impression. Concurrently, the St. Petersburg Chamber of Commerce issued a "personal invitation" to the "Negro players" to attend the breakfast. No doubt this included Latino players Julian Javier (Cardinals) and Hector Lopez (Yankees). These gestures did not satisfy White, who decided to use the incident to publicly condemn the discriminatory practices at spring training locations in Florida. The black players called for team officials to pressure their respective headquarters, the Vinoy Park and Soreno hotels, to end their segregated practices. According to Bob Gibson, White mentioned the invitation list to Joe Reichler, an Associated Press sportswriter out of St. Louis. Reichler wrote a story that was published in a black newspaper in St. Louis calling for a boycott of Anheuser-Busch, the brewery that owned the Cardinals.[65]

This unwanted publicity resulted in Cardinals owner August A. Busch, Jr., taking up the cause. Busch threatened to move the Cardinals if conditions didn't change. Local and team officials in St. Petersburg began working behind the scenes to arrange integrated accommodations at hotels other than the Soreno and Vinoy Park. In 1962, the Colonial Inn housed the newly arriving New York Mets, while the Cardinals bought their own hotel in St. Petersburg.[66]

Voicing their opposition to the spring training ritual, supporting Ralph Wimbish's efforts to end it, and filing a formal protest with the MLBPA represented a radical departure by African American and Latino players from their previous accommodation of discrimination. Staying in the same hotels and eating in the same restaurants as the white players appear to be minor concessions by today's standards; however, as historian Vincent Harding asserted, every move black people made out of the place whites assigned them politically, economically, and socially, symbolized a "revolutionary move." Black and Latino players put up with the spring training ritual for fifteen years. Unlike the student activists in the sit-in movement, they were limited in their opportunities to challenge the status quo. This was the reserve-clause era, where players were the property of their respective clubs until traded, sold, or released. African American, Latino, and white players alike were beholden to the power of the owners. Why did black and Latino players nevertheless suddenly depart from their accommodating ways in 1961?[67]

Essentially, three factors contributed to this radical change. First was the increase in number of African American and Latino players on major-league rosters. By 1961, approximately 92 (51 African American and 41 Latino) players of color appeared on the eighteen clubs that made up the major leagues. Their growing numbers freed them from the insecurity of the early years of integration and encouraged them to speak out against inequitable conditions. As Larry Doby declared, it was "impossible for us [in the early stages of integration] to openly oppose the system. But this is the right time—exactly the right time—to fight it. Segregation is crumbling everywhere, so why not in baseball?"[68]

What can best be described as the post–Jackie Robinson generation represented the second factor. The majority of these outspoken black and Latino players entered the major leagues in 1954 or later. They exemplified this new sense of urgency to dismantle barriers to racial equality. Aaron states that blacks represented the best players in the National League and earned the right to stay in their teams' hotels during spring training. Although it was not a coordinated effort, this generation of black players refused to accept the status quo. Cincinnati Reds outfielder Vada Pinson declared black players no longer wanted to be regarded as "inferior," particularly when their performances on the field said otherwise. The post–Jackie Robinson generation expected to mature in a different America, in a different sports world. Their youth had been marked by sweeping changes in the economy, in demography, and in American racial attitudes. Their opposition to the spring training ritual reflected the changing racial landscape.[69]

Finally, black and Latino players' stand for principle was grounded in the ideological foundation that governed team sports—unity, morale, and most important of all, teamwork. Many of the outspoken players like Aaron, Elston Howard, Bill White, Frank Robinson, and Roberto Clemente, contributed significantly to their clubs' success during the regular season. If these players performed as a team in the pursuit of pennants and World Series championships, it was hypocritical not to afford them the same privileges—eating, sleeping, and traveling with the team—off it. African American and Latino players' stand against their plight during spring training illustrated Malcolm X's distinction between desegregation and integration that civil-rights leaders like James Farmer, A. Philip Randolph, and Thurgood Marshall could never grasp. "It is not a case of [dark mankind] wanting integration or separation, it is a case of wanting freedom, justice, and equality. It is not integration that Negroes want in America, it is human dignity."[70]

African American and Latino players efforts to end segregation during spring training illustrated the need to exert external pressure to change the status quo, despite the fact that they led to only a few minor concessions. It should be noted, however, that no effort was made to impose integration on the respective cities in which MLB clubs trained. Rather, the players simply desired the choice to stay in the same hotels, engage in leisurely pursuits when they were not playing exhibition games, and eat in the same restaurants white players took for granted.

Their performances on the field and their behavior off it earned them these privileges.

Notes

1. To date, Jack Davis has provided the most definitive scholarly inquiry on spring training. See "Baseball's Reluctant Challenge: Desegregating Major League Spring Training Sites, 1961–1964," *Journal of Sport History* 19 (Summer 1992): 144–62. Jackie Robinson's first training experience has received the most scholarly attention. See Jules Tygiel, *Baseball's Great Experiment: Jackie Robinson and His Legacy* (New York: Oxford University Press, 1983); David Falkner, *Great Time Coming: The Life of Jackie Robinson From Baseball to Birmingham* (New York: Simon & Schuster, 1995); Arnold Rampersad, *Jackie Robinson: A Biography* (New York: Alfred A. Knopf, 1997). Popular sources that provide information on the spring training ritual include Jackie Robinson, *Baseball Has Done It* (Philadelphia: J. P. Lippincott Co., 1964); Idem., *I Never Had It Made: An Autobiography* (Hopewell, NJ: Ecco Press, 1995); Frank Robinson and Al Silverman, *My Life Is Baseball* (Garden City, NY: Doubleday, 1968); Curt Flood, *The Way It Is* (New York: Trident Press, 1970); Henry Aaron, *Aaron*, rev. ed. (New York: Thomas Y. Carroll, 1974); idem., *I Had A Hammer: The Hank Aaron Story* (New York: HarperCollins, 1991); Bob Gibson, *Stranger To The Game* (New York: Penguin, 1994).

2. Tygiel, *Baseball's*, 99–105; Falkner, *Great Time*, 126–28; Rampersad, *Jackie*, 237–46.

3. Rampersad, *Jackie*, 245–46.

4. Ibid., 247.

5. Ibid., 251. Aldon Morris, *The Origins Of The Civil Rights Movement: Black Communities Organizing for Change* (New York: Free Press, 1984), 1–4.

6. George Robinson's comments in *New York Times*, March 22, 23, 1946; *New York Herald Tribune*, March 23, 1946. Rickey's comments in Tygiel, *Baseball's*, 108.

7. Robinson quote in Rampersad, *Jackie*, 259.

8. *Pittsburgh Courier*, April 13, 1946. Morris, *Origins*, 4.

9. Lacy's comments in *New Jersey Afro-American*, March 13, 1948. Tygiel, *Baseball's*, 164–65; Rampersad, *Jackie*, 284–85.

10. *New Jersey Afro-American*, March 13, 1948. For Jackie Robinson's articles, see, for example, *Pittsburgh Courier*, March 13, 1948.

11. *Sporting News*, 136 (March 2, 1949); 136 (March 9, 1949); 136 (March 23, 1949); *New York Herald Tribune*, February 2, 1961.

12. *New Jersey Afro-American*, January 17, March 27, April 10, 1948.

13. *New York Herald Tribune*, January 14, 1949; *Atlanta Journal*, January 14, 1949; *Pittsburgh Courier*, March 27, 1949.

14. *New York Times*, January 15, 1949; *New York Herald Tribune*, January 15, 1949; *Atlanta Constitution*, January 15, 1949; *Atlanta Journal*, January 15, 1949. Although the Grand Dragon of the Ku Klux Klan raised objections to interracial contests, the Miami baseball commission in Florida announced that the Dodgers would play exhibition games with Robinson and Campanella in the lineup. Dr. Ralph B. Ferguson, the chairman of the commission, stated that they had received authorization from the city commission to allow the two black players to play against the Boston Red Sox.

Ferguson added that if the Dodgers were playing a team from Miami the circumstances might have been different, but the conditions were acceptable since the Dodgers were playing another major-league team. The Miami baseball commission's decision was in response to a broader effort by the state of Florida to lure all sixteen major-league teams to train there. Led by Florida Governor Fuller Warren, efforts were made to attract major league clubs to increase tourism and generate revenues to address the state's poor tax situation. Miami was targeted specifically due to the New York Giants' move to Phoenix, Arizona. See *Atlanta Constitution*, January 15, 1949; *Sporting News* 136 (January 19, 1949); 136 (March 9, 1949).

15. *New Jersey Afro-American*, January 22, 1949.

16. *Atlanta Constitution*, January 18, 1949; *New York Times*, January 18, 1949; *New York Herald Tribune*, January 18, 1949.

17. *New York Times*, January 16, 1949. Bradberry's comments in *Atlanta Constitution*, January 16, 1949; Danforth's comments in *Atlanta Journal*, January 16, 1949.

18. *New York Times*, January 18, 1949; *New Jersey Afro-American*, January 29, 1949.

19. *Pittsburgh Courier*, April 16, 1949; *New Jersey Afro-American*, April 16, 1949; *Sporting News* 136 (April 20, 1949).

20. Tygiel, *Baseball's*, 267–68.

21. Manning Marable, *Race, Reform and Rebellion: The Second Reconstruction in Black America, 1945–1982* (Jackson: University Press of Mississippi, 1984), 15–16.

22. Vincent Harding, *The Other American Revolution* (Los Angeles: Center for Afro-American Studies UCLA, 1980), 138.

23. Franklin Lewis quote in Joseph Thomas Moore, *Pride Against Prejudice: The Biography Of Larry Doby* (New York: Prager, 1988), 72. *Sporting News* 136 (April 20, 1949). Doby was also excluded from hotels in Tucson, Arizona, and Los Angeles, California. See *New Jersey Afro-American*, March 5, 12, 1949; *Pittsburgh Courier*, March 12, 1949. See also Moore, *Pride*, 68–71.

24. *New Jersey Afro-American*, April 16, 1949.

25. For an account on the ideology of teamwork in baseball, see David Q. Voigt, *American Baseball*, Vol. 1 (Norman: University of Oklahoma Press, 1966), 37–57.

26. *U.S. Congress, House of Representatives, Study of Monopoly Power: Organized Baseball* (Washington, DC: Government Printing Office, 1951), 474–88.

27. Tygiel, *Baseball's*, 82–86; William Marshall, *Baseball's Pivotal Era 1945–1951* (Lexington: University Press of Kentucky, 1999), 134–35. Carroll testimony in *U.S. Congress*, 496.

28. Aaron, *Aaron*, 38–39.

29. Flood, *The Way It Is*, 34–35.

30. Ibid., 43.

31. Rampersad, *Jackie*, 514–15.

32. Monte Irvin, *Monte Irvin: Nice Guys Finish First* (New York: Carroll & Graff, 1996), 125–26.

33. Rob Ruck, *The Tropic of Baseball: Baseball in the Dominican Republic* (Westport, CT: Meckler, 1991), 99; Samuel O. Regalado, *Viva Baseball! Latin Major Leaguers and Their Special Hunger* (Urbana: University of Illinois Press, 1998), 50.

34. Office of Public Opinion survey in Regalado, *Viva Baseball*, 67. For an account dealing with Latin players being stereotyped, see Peter C. Bjarkman, *Baseball with a Latin Beat: A History of the Latin American Game* (Jefferson, NC: McFarland, 1994), 89–90.

35. Bjarkman, *Baseball*, 207–17; Minnie Minoso, *Just Call Me Minnie: My Six Decades in Baseball* (Champaign: Sagamore, 1994), 131–32; William Barry Furlong, "The White Sox Katzenjammer Kid," *Saturday Evening Post* 227 (July 10, 1954): 78.

36. Felipe Alou with Herm Weiskopf, *Felipe Alou: My Life and Baseball* (Waco, TX: Word Books, 1967), 26.

37. Phil Musick, *Who Was Roberto? A Biography of Roberto Clemente* (Garden City, NY: Doubleday, 1974), 111; Bruce Markusen, *Roberto Clemente: The Great One* (Champaign: Sports Publishing, 1998), 38–39.

38. Kal Wagenheim, *Clemente!* (New York: Praeger, 1973), 88.

39. Regalado, *Viva Baseball*, 78.

40. Donn Rogosin, *Invisible Men: Life in Baseball's Negro Leagues* (New York: Atheneum, 1985), 111–18; Robert Boyle, "The Private World Of The Negro Ballplayer," *Sports Illustrated* 12 (March 21, 1960): 18.

41. Markusen, *Roberto*, 39.

42. Aaron, *Aaron*, 39–40; *Milwaukee Journal*, February 3, 1961; *New Jersey Afro-American*, February 11, 1961.

43. Robinson, *Baseball Has Done It*, 127–28.

44. Ibid.

45. Morris, *Origins*, 12–16. For an account on the proposed banning of interracial contests, see Charles H. Martin, "Racial Change and 'Big-Time' College Football in Georgia: The Age of Segregation, 1892–1957," *Georgia Historical Quarterly* 80 (Fall 1996): 532–62; John Sayle Watterson, *College Football: History, Spectacle, Controversy* (Baltimore: Johns Hopkins University Press, 2000), 308–31.

46. *New Jersey Afro-American*, February 11, 1961.

47. August Meier and John Bracey, Jr., "The NAACP as a Reform Movement, 1909–1965," *Journal of Southern History* LIX (February 1993): 26–27.

48. John Hope Franklin, *From Slavery to Freedom: A History of Negro Americans*, 5th ed. (New York: Alfred A. Knopf, 1980), 463. Davis, "Baseball's Reluctant Challenge," 148. Wimbish quote in *St. Petersburg Times*, February 1, 1961. See also *St. Louis Globe Democrat*, February 1, 1961; *New York Times*, February 1, 1961.

49. Ibid.

50. *St. Petersburg Times*, February 1, 1961.

51. *New York Times*, February 2, 3, 4, 1961; *St. Louis Post-Dispatch*, February 2, 1961; *New York Post*, February 3, 1961.

52. *St. Petersburg Times*, February 4, 1961.

53. *Pittsburgh Courier*, February 4, 1961; *Sarasota Herald Tribune*, February 2, 3, 1961; *Chicago Sun-Times*, February 2, 3, 1961; Kippel's comment in *Bradenton Herald*, February 3, 1961.

54. Flood, *The Way It Is*, 78–79. *Pittsburgh Courier*, February 11, March 18, 1961.

55. *Milwaukee Journal*, February 2, 4, 1961. See also Chicago *Defender*, February 11, 1961.

56. Aaron and Covington's comments in *Milwaukee Journal*, February 3, 1961; *New Jersey Afro-American*, February 11, 1961; see also Chicago *Defender*, February 11, 1961.

57. *Miami Herald*, February 2, 1961; *New York Times*, February 3, 1961; *New Jersey Afro-American*, February 11, March 11, 1961; *Pittsburgh Courier*, March 4, 1961.

58. For Smith's media campaign, see, for example, *Pittsburgh Courier*, February 4, 11, 18, 25, March 4, 25, 1961. For A. Leon Lowry bringing national attention to the spring training ritual, see *Bradenton Herald*, February 3, 1961.

59. Davis, "Baseball's Reluctant Challenge," 150–51. For the protest in Houston, see Charles K. Ross, *Outside the Lines: African Americans and the Integration of the National Football League* (New York: New York University Press, 1999), 144–45; F. Kenneth Jensen, "The Houston Sit-In Movement of 1960–61," in Howard Beeth and Cary D. Wintz, eds., *Black Dixie: Afro-Texan History and Culture in Houston* (College Station: Texas A&M University Press, 1992), 216.

60. Davis, "Baseball's Reluctant Challenge," 160.

61. V. O. Key, Jr., *Southern Politics in State and Nation* (New York: Alfred A. Knopf, 1949), 86–87; David R. Colburn and Richard K. Scher, "Race Relations and Florida Gubernatorial Politics since the Brown Decision," *Florida Historical Quarterly* 55 (October 1976): 154; David R. Colburn, "Florida Politics in the Twentieth Century," in Michael Gannon, ed., *The New History of Florida* (Gainesville: University of Florida Press, 1996), 358–60; Norman V. Bartley, *The New South 1945–1980* (Baton Rouge: Louisiana University Press, 1995), 142–43; Patricia Dillon, "Civil Rights and School Desegregation in Sanford," *Florida Historical Quarterly* 76 (Winter 1998): 318–19.

62. McHale's comment in *Milwaukee Journal*, March 6, 1961. *Bradenton Herald*, March 6, 1961; *New Jersey Afro-American*, March 11, 1961.

63. *Sporting News*, 151 (March 8, 1961).

64. *Miami Herald*, March 9, 1961; *New York Post*, March 9, 1961; *New York Times*, March 9, 1961; *Pittsburgh Courier*, March 18, 1961.

65. *St. Petersburg Times*, March 9, 1961. *Pittsburgh Courier*, March 18, 1961; Gibson, *Stranger*, 57–58; Aaron, *I Had A Hammer*, 212.

66. Ibid. For an account on the Mets moving into the Colonial Inn, see *Pittsburgh Courier*, March 10, 1962.

67. Harding, *The Other*, 162–63.

68. These numbers were an estimate of black and Latin players that appeared on major league rosters in 1961. See David S. Neft and Richard M. Cohen, *The Sports Encyclopedia: Baseball*, 16th ed. (New York: St. Martin's Griffin, 1996). Doby's comments in *Pittsburgh Courier*, February 4, 1961.

69. Aaron, *I Had A Hammer*, 210. Pinson's comment in *New Jersey Afro-American*, February 11, 1961.

70. Malcolm X's comments in Marable, *Race*, 62.

THE AMERICAN IMPERIAL CRUSADE
Race, Religion, and Sport in the Pacific

GERALD R. GEMS

Events following September 11, 2001, have caused Americans to question the role of the United States in the world and its foreign policies. They have caused us to wonder how non-Americans perceive that role. Our national policies have a long history, and many historians have recognized the influence of race and religion in their formation. Such factors have been closely intertwined for more than a century, producing a variety of results, ranging from resistance, adaptation, acculturation, and even retaliation.[1]

By the late nineteenth century the United States had consolidated its own national boundaries in a series of racial wars that sealed the fate of Native Americans, forcibly seized territory in the Mexican War, and ostensibly "freed" African Americans in a racial conflict known as the Civil War.

Race permeated such encounters. Native Americans were characterized as barbaric heathens or savages; even the so-called "civilized" tribes who adopted white ways, such as the Creeks or Cherokees, faced painful expulsion from their lands. Mexicans, labeled a "mongrel" race, fell victim to the Anglos' westward thrust. Blacks were stigmatized by rudimentary Darwinian science as lower beings on the evolutionary scale. As early as 1882 the Chinese Exclusion Act severely limited Asian immigration and determined that Caucasians would prevail within the continental United States.[2]

Religious views proved equally important. The Puritans' early utopian experiment in the "city upon a hill" had lasting influence on American thought and culture well beyond New England. They were followed by successive and divergent sects who established their own communities in a westward march, each ensuring that the United States would be dominated by white, Anglo-Saxon Protestantism. By the mid-nineteenth century such strong nativist sentiments were epitomized by the Know-Nothing political party with its xenophobic tendencies. Anti-Catholicism and anti-Semitism persisted on a widespread scale throughout the twentieth century. By the 1890s Frederick Jackson Turner unabashedly claimed an American exceptionalism, while Theodore Roosevelt preached an American duty to assume the white man's burden and moral leadership of the world.[3]

William F. "Buffalo Bill" Cody displayed white Americans' racial conquests in his wildly popular Wild West show throughout the urban areas of the United States for those who had not experienced the process firsthand. By 1887 Cody had transplanted his vision of Anglo triumph to European audiences, with Indians assuming the status of exotic "others" caught in the progress of modernization.[4] Cody's exhibition proved a celebrated sideshow in the larger cultural spectacle of the Columbian Exposition, or 1893 World's Fair, held in Chicago.

The stunning "White City," constructed for the fair under the direction of famed architect Daniel Burnham, symbolized the achievement of modern American civilization. Classical architecture symbolized the order, discipline, harmony, grandeur, and idealism of the organizers' social vision. The Social Darwinian perspective of the planners displayed three distinct models of development—the savage, the semi-civilized, and the civilized, with white Europeans and Americans assuming the latter role. Racial categorization clearly defined social status. Native American exhibits and Buffalo Bill's Wild West show relegated the Indians to inferiority; African Americans, despite their protests, were denied any representation on planning committees or exhibition space, save for the inclusion of Hampton Institute in the Education Department's display on the value of education to non-white groups. African tribal displays suggested a universal black experience, and in keeping with the organizers' moral and educational mission, the *Columbian Exposition Album* "hoped the Dahomans would take back the influence of civilization to West Africa."[5]

Racialization persisted in the St. Louis Fair of 1904, where American organizers displayed the headhunting Igorot tribe of the recently

colonized Philippines despite vehement objections of middle-class Filipinos. The educated Filipinos asserted that "the Igorottes [sic] were no
more representative of the Philippines than the most savage Indians
are representative of Americans."[6]

Some Filipinos clamored for independence, while others requested
statehood, only to be rebuffed by Secretary of State Elihu Root, who
replied that "statehood for Filipinos would add another serious problem
to the one we have already. The Negroes are a cancer in our body politic,
a source of constant difficulty, and we wish to avoid developing another
such problem."[7] The American-owned *Manila Cablenews* further charged
that "All of us who have lived in the Far East know that in practice these
yellow and brown peoples must be guided and often driven in a forward
direction so that they do not obstruct the progress of the world nor
infringe on the rights of other nations."[8] The Filipino retort to such
charges emphasized racial, class, national, and cultural differences in
stating that "The charge is that 'the Filipinos will not work.' The sen-
tence is not complete; it should read: 'The Filipinos will not work for foreigners.' That is to say, they will not work for the vampire and the wolf
whose sole intent is to amass wealth by the labor of others."[9]

Such acrimony and recrimination suffused racial politics throughout
the period, and administrators, entrepreneurs, teachers, missionaries,
and military personnel all invoked the seemingly apolitical gospel of
sport to allay the animosity and bridge cultural chasms. Alexander
Cartwright, secretary of the New York Knickerbockers club, codified
baseball rules as early as 1845 and transported them to Hawaii soon after.
American expatriates brought the game to China as early as 1863;
American teachers introduced it to the Japanese throughout the next
decade.[10] Albert Spalding, president of the Chicago White Stockings,
leader of the National League, and a sporting goods entrepreneur, organized a world tour of ballplayers in 1888–1889 to promote the values of
sport.[11] Progressive reformers believed that sport possessed the power to
change perceptions, attitudes, and behaviors. It thus became a subtler
tool in commercial, colonial, and hegemonic cultural efforts.[12]

After the British forced commercial trade with China in the Opium
War of 1839–1842, the United States quickly secured its own entrée to

such markets in the Treaty of Wanghia in 1844. Baseball and rowing clubs formed in Shanghai as early as 1863, and the YMCA organized a branch in that city in the 1870s. Protestant missionaries poured into China throughout the remainder of the nineteenth century, numbering more than one thousand by the 1890s. They preached both Christianity and sport as a means to save and modernize the ancient civilization. Under the guidance of the Protestants, Chinese colleges began fielding baseball teams by 1895. A year later the YMCA introduced basketball in Tiansin. At the same time, foreign governments carved up pieces of the Chinese territory as commercial settlements. Great Britain, France, Germany, Russia, and Japan all claimed portions of China before the United States declared an Open Door policy by 1900 to safeguard its own interests in the vast Asian market. Such impositions fostered a nativist backlash that same year, as Chinese Boxers retaliated by killing foreigners and Christian countrymen until overwhelmed by western military might.[13]

Undeterred by the so-called Boxer Rebellion, the U.S. emissaries renewed their commercial, religious, and athletic efforts. Missionaries and educators particularly promoted baseball, America's national game. St. John's University defeated the Shanghai YMCA in 1905 as Chinese Protestants slowly adopted western recreational practices. Educated and upper-class Chinese had traditionally considered active forms of leisure to be decidedly inferior to scholarly endeavors.[14]

Race, perhaps, figured more prominently than religion in the adoption of western sport forms. After the Japanese victory in the Russo-Japanese War of 1905, Japan assumed a preeminent role in Asian affairs. U.S. immigration laws excluded the Chinese, so as many as 30,000 Chinese students traveled to Japan for their education, where many learned the Japanese passion for baseball. By 1907 Chinese schools engaged in intercollegiate contests. The following year the YMCA initiated basketball leagues; these would expand to include women's play by the 1930s. The YMCA organized track and field meets as early as 1902 in Shanghai and Tientsin, and Max Exner, a physical educator, arrived from the United States in 1908 to institute gymnastics and teacher training. Within two years, ten thousand spectators witnessed the national athletic games at Nanking, held in conjunction with the National

Industrial Exposition as organizers adopted the western ideology that mixed sport and commerce.[15]

Resentment festered among many Chinese over the foreign invasion and the alien religious practices that were transforming their traditional way of life. Sun Yat-sen, a nationalist revolutionary who had been educated in Hawaii, found a practical political use for baseball. He reputedly founded a baseball club to unite his followers, who quickly transferred their throwing skills to grenade tossing.[16] By 1913 the Chinese had found in sport another means to assert their nationalistic pride in the first Far Eastern Olympics when they agreed to compete against the Japanese and the Filipinos in Manila. While such an association, organized and administered by the American YMCA, drew the Chinese further into the Anglo sphere of sport, it also provided the Chinese, who lacked the military might to repulse foreign subjugation, an opportunity to reclaim their national pride.

W. Cameron Forbes, the American governor-general of the Philippines, welcomed the participants with a speech that stated, "I hope that all your contests will be carried on in the spirit of fair play, which in after years may govern your conduct in business and other vocations of grownups."[17] Forbes thus reiterated the Anglo perception of infantile Asians, incapable of fair play or commercial enterprise without Anglo guidance. Nevertheless, China sent at least forty competitors, led by Americans from the YMCA. They participated in the volleyball and basketball contests despite little success, but took succor in finishing first and second in the decathlon.[18]

The Chinese learned quickly, however. When they hosted the 1915 Games, local athletes won the pentathlon, swimming, soccer, and volleyball competitions. They placed second to the Filipinos in baseball. The Chinese schools, under the leadership of Willard Nash, an American missionary, had formed an intercollegiate athletic association that featured six baseball teams the year before.[19]

Despite persistent opposition to Christianity in the 1920s, sport continued to grow. The YMCA, based in urban areas, had little influence in the largely rural country. Yet the Chinese formed a national soccer association in 1924, and Anglo sports such as cricket, tennis, golf, and polo continued along with the American-induced baseball, basketball, volleyball, and track and field. Shanghai's citizens even attended equestrian events at the local race course.[20]

Political events slowed sporting pursuits thereafter, as Japan invaded Manchuria in 1931, precipitating the struggles that would engulf Europe a decade later. Both the Japanese and the Chinese Communists embraced baseball, however, and it emerged as the premier sporting enterprise in Taiwan in the postwar years, before Chinese ping-pong players, gymnasts, swimmers, and runners became dominant. Following the Japanese model and adopting the Confucian tenets of work ethic and discipline, the Taiwanese Little Leaguers first defeated their Japanese counterparts in 1968. The Japanese team had been world champs. Japan had instilled baseball during its many years of repressive occupation before World War II, and the Taiwanese employed it to exact a measure of athletic revenge. The Taiwanese took on an even bigger foe in the U.S.A. the following year and won the Little League championship outright. They garnered seventeen championships within twenty-seven years to restore Chinese pride and dignity, eventually forcing the American administrators to temporarily ban non-American teams in 1975 and restrict their participation after continued Asian dominance in the 1990s. By that time mainland Chinese athletes had restored their stature in international competition against their Asian and Anglo rivals.[21] Sport, in fact, served the Chinese as an important political force. Introduced by the colonial powers with the intent of modernizing and converting the traditional culture to white, Anglo, Protestant norms, the foreigners failed to subdue the nationalistic impulses of the Chinese people. They adapted sport to their own multiple visions of society and used it to construct their own futures with "ping pong diplomacy," Little League championships, and Olympic victories that reinforced, rather than diminished, loyalties to race and the established culture.

JAPAN

American sporting influences had an equally long history in Japan. Commodore Matthew Perry sailed to Japan in 1853 and soon secured the Treaty of Friendship that opened the country to American commercial enterprise. The ensuing Meiji era (1852–1912) witnessed rapid modernization, industrialization, and the adoption of many Western models in clothing, arts, and government. The samurai faced formal abolition by 1876; but the warriors' *bushido* tenets of discipline, loyalty, courage, honor, and self-sacrifice found ready application in sports. Tokyo students played baseball by the 1870s, a game introduced by American teachers; but the western values that the mentors intended to transfer gave way to nationalistic, patriotic, and imperialistic aspirations.[22]

Once again, race proved a prominent factor in cultural transformation and the role of sport. The Anglos deigned to teach the game to the Japanese, but they would not play with them. Nor could the Asians even observe games as spectators at the prestigious Yokohama Athletic Club, which barred natives from the grounds. American immigration policy had begun excluding the Japanese from the United States as early as 1882. Such overt racism stung the Japanese, and students at the elite Ichiko school bristled at Anglo condescension. Their repeated challenges for a baseball game with the Yokohama A. C. met with derision from 1891–1896, until an American English teacher at Ichiko managed to arrange the contest. Buoyed by a recent victory in the Sino-Japanese War of 1895, the collegians vowed to "fight to the bitter end" in a written statement, and the team captain claimed that "the name of the country was at stake."[23]

A train of supporters followed the Ichiko team to the Yokohama grounds, where home team fans taunted their perceived inferiors. Ichiko responded with bonsai chants as the team overwhelmed the stunned Anglos, 29–4. They celebrated with sake toasts as they sang the Japanese national anthem. The student body president proclaimed that "This great victory is more than a victory for our school, it is a victory for the Japanese people."[24] Players basked in the glory of their heroic status, as the surprised Americans clamored for a rematch. They recruited the top players from U.S. Navy ships anchored in Yokohama harbor, but despite their reinforcements they were embarrassed once again by a score of 32–9. This time the Japanese returned the years of indignity by spitting on the Americans' sacred ground in ritual defiance of their past exclusion as their fans shouted obscenities. English language newspapers offered excuses as yet another U.S. Navy team arrived to retrieve American honor. Despite the presence of a naval band and a U.S. government representative, the Japanese schoolboys humbled yet another symbol of Social Darwinism might, 22–6, before ten thousand onlookers. Outside the sold-out field, Japanese workers who had suffered shame and dishonor in the employment of white bosses cheered the warriors who had redeemed their pride and self-esteem.[25]

The Ichiko baseball team's annual report left no doubt that the contest was more than a baseball game with underlying political and cultural ramifications. It stated that

> *"The Americans are proud of baseball as their national game just as we have been proud of judo and kendo. Now, however, in a place far removed from their native land, they have fought against a 'little people' whom they ridicule as childish, only to find themselves swept away like falling leaves. No words can describe their disgraceful conduct. The aggressive character of our national spirit is a well-established fact, demonstrated first in the Sino-Japanese War and now by our great victories in baseball."*[26]

The Americans finally won yet another rematch on the Fourth of July. The victory proved a narrow one, 14–12, as the westerners succeeded by garnering an all-star team from the U.S. Navy, including a former professional player. The international series continued over the next eight years, Ichiko winning eight of nine confrontations. Such superiority fueled nationalistic sentiments and proved to the Japanese people that they could not only compete but succeed in the modern world. As the western powers colonized the world Japan developed imperialistic visions of its own.[27]

By 1897 white settlers in Hawaii feared a Japanese takeover and called for annexation by the United States. The Hawaiian government responded by restricting Japanese immigrants to the islands, which brought a protest from Japan. The *Honolulu Star* claimed that "It is the white race against the yellow. . . . Nothing but annexation can save the islands."[28] The U.S. government formally granted territorial status in 1898, and Japanese attentions were soon diverted closer to home when Russian forces moved into Korea. Japan emerged victorious in the Russo-Japanese War of 1904–1905 and annexed Korea in 1910. By that time the so-called Gentleman's Agreement had excluded Japanese workers from entering the United States. Nevertheless, the competing cultures continued testing each other in the athletic arena.[29]

Baseball expanded rapidly throughout the Japanese school system after 1900, where it reinforced the *bushido* spirit of the samurai. Relieving a pitcher and bunting were perceived as cowardly acts, and defeat brought shame. Baseball players assumed the status of warriors who fought for the honor of their school. International contests acquired even greater dimensions as primary tests of racial comparison and symbolic military might. In 1905 the Waseda University team made an extended tour of the United States, but managed to win only seven of twenty-six games. Keio University fared better at home, defeating a team from the U.S. Atlantic Fleet in 1908 and then finishing second in a Hawaiian tournament. The A. J. Reach Sporting Goods firm sent a troop of barnstorming professionals to Japan after the 1908 season, and the universities of Washington, Wisconsin, and Chicago arrived between 1908 and 1910. Such excursions were characterized as "invasions." Wisconsin lost three of its four games against Keio in Tokyo, and American publicists admitted that the Japanese were "inbred with bushida [sic] spirit" and "play with an indomitable fighting spirit which is lacking in most American college teams."[30]

The University of Chicago stipulated particular conditions and took extensive precautions to insure a better performance in 1910. Coach Amos Alonzo Stagg informed his hosts that his players were in "strict training" and unable to accept Japanese "hospitality." He feared that the Washington and Wisconsin athletes had compromised both their morality and ability by frolicking with geisha girls. The Chicagoans were instructed to "keep away from such places in Japan . . . which are commonly visited from impure motives or morbid curiosity" and "without exception add to the warfare each and every man has to fight for his own self control . . . do not go where you would not be willing to take your mother and sister and sweetheart."[31] An accompanying faculty member assured compliance.

Stagg also refused to play Japan's best teams on successive days and he received extensive scouting reports for Americans already there, some of whom coached Japanese teams. One such report stated that

> . . . *they are proud and usually count themselves superior to all foreigners . . . they root like mad, arouse themselves, and fight like the soldiers they really are. . . . The little fellows are sometimes tricky . . . they are tempted sorely by the rough American tactics sometimes used against them. They bear such things in silence usually, but feel it deep inside. . . . Don't call the little brown players "Japs" for they are sensitive . . . never show anger under any provocation . . . a few "banzais" (cheers) for the opposing team will add spirit . . . and create good feeling.*[32]

Further correspondence referred to both sides as "warriors" in the invasion and meeting one's "Waterloo."[33] Stagg's charges prepared by practicing with Chicago pro teams, while Waseda University played in the Oahu Baseball League in Hawaii during the summer. Stagg's diligence paid off as enormous crowds witnessed ten straight victories by the Chicagoans, who declared themselves "champions of the Orient."[34]

Japanese athletes continued to challenge such notions in the ensuing years. They made their first appearance in the Olympics in 1912 as Japan also increased the size of its navy. Both militarily and athletically Japan exerted its growing dominance in Asia.

The YMCA organized a Far Eastern Olympics in Manila, part of its vision for a pan-Asian alliance in 1912. The Japanese borrowed the YMCA model in organizing thirty thousand youth clubs throughout the land, which served nationalistic and imperial purposes but without the YMCA's inherent Christianity. By 1917 Japanese athletes dominated the Far Eastern Games, held in Tokyo before twenty thousand fans per day.[35]

Sport became an ongoing means for the Japanese to test their growing power and to fuse a nationalistic pride. Baseball exchanges continued between Japan and the United States. Tobita Suishu, the famed authoritarian coach of the Waseda University team, spent years infusing *konjo*, the Japanese fighting spirit, in his charges. When the previously undefeated University of Chicago team returned to Japan for a third time in 1925, it won only two of eight games, four of them with Waseda. In six contests the Chicagoans failed to score.[36]

In 1930 Chicago went 5–9–1 on its Japanese tour and managed to win only two games against the Japanese college teams. In the Far East Games that same year Japan dominated the Philippines, China, and India. The nearest competitor in the track and field events lagged nearly 100 points behind, as Japan demonstrated its athletic mastery of Asia.[37]

In 1931 Japanese swimmers defeated the United States in a dual meet, as the government mandated compulsory martial arts training in the schools. Japan seized Manchuria that same year and began extending its economic influence throughout eastern Asia. Sport enhanced Japanese pride, power, and confidence as athletes garnered international prestige. Track stars and swimmers began winning medals in the 1928 Olympics, and by 1932 Japanese swimmers overwhelmed their competition by winning eleven of the sixteen possible medals, including five of six golds. Despite such prowess, American journalists continued to refer to them as "little brown men" who were "diminutive but doughty."[38]

Such remarks tarnished Japanese honor and fueled ambitions to prove self worth and national dignity. When America's premier educational institution, Harvard University, traveled to Japan in 1934, its baseball team lost most of its games, with six different opponents inflicting defeats. An American League all-star team fared better, winning all of its games in a barnstorming tour but providing the impetus for the formation of a Japanese professional league and a true World Series to determine baseball superiority.[39]

Sport both promoted and masked political tensions. The Japanese government renounced its treaties with Washington in 1934, while a Japanese baseball team traveled to the United States the following year, winning ninety-three of its 102 games. Real war soon intervened, however, as Japan invaded China in 1937. United States hopes for progressive assimilation through sport were superceded by Japanese nationalism. The adoption of western sport forms served both racial and imperialistic ends, in which the Japanese confronted Anglo perceptions of superiority, western colonialism, and notions of Asian leadership. Sport provided a vehicle for cultural identity and the reemergence of traditional values—in particular the warrior ethic of *bushido* that culminated in a resistive and eventually aggressive force against foreign transgressors.[40]

PHILIPPINES

The United States had its most sustained influence in the Philippines, which remained an American colony for nearly half a century after the Spanish-American War of 1898. The racialization of Filipinos, however, had preceded that tumultuous event. Dean Worcester, a zoology professor at the University of Michigan, began a number of expeditions to the islands in 1887 in search of specimens. He later augmented his income with lectures and publications portraying the islands' inhabitants as half-naked savages, primitive barbarians, and headhunters. Worcester assumed the role of authority in the developing field of anthropology, and President McKinley appointed him to the First Philippines Commission in 1899. His final report recommended U.S. rule, despite the fact that the Filipino rebellion had nearly secured independence from their Spanish overlords when U.S. troops arrived. Worcester then served on the Second Philippines Commission and as Secretary of the Interior in the colonial administration. Despite his resignation under scandalous circumstances in 1913, his racial characterizations of Filipinos held a lasting influence that supported Social Darwinian beliefs in Anglo superiority and the necessity to assume the white man's burden.[41]

Worcester claimed that the Negrito tribe "are probably the lowest type of human beings known and have been described as 'not far above the anthropoid apes.'" He declared the Ilongots "a tribe so primitive that they are unable to count beyond ten" and the "moros . . . unexcelled pirates and slave traders, treacherous and unreliable to the last degree."[42]

Robert Bennett Bean, an anatomist at the University of Michigan, also emphasized racial differences, and such publications rationalized the Filipinos as genetically inferior beings incapable of self-government. The need for American guidance extended to religious matters: Protestant missionaries swarmed to the archipelago to "Christianize" a land that had been largely Catholic for more than three hundred years. Filipinos did not suffer such indignities gladly and American troops faced a vicious and bloody guerrilla war for independence that persisted until 1916.[43]

One way in which the American officials intended to co-opt such revolutionary notions involved education via sport. In a 1914 book, Worcester suggested baseball as a remedy to "strengthen muscles and wits."[44] By that time the process had long been under way; American soldiers began introducing the game as early as 1898. Spalding's *Base Ball Guide* proclaimed the occurrence "an auspicious opening of our national game in the 'expanded' territory of Uncle Sam."[45] The American national game intended to link both players and spectators in common cultural beliefs that emphasized the progressive democratic vision and American self-righteousness. One American expatriate claimed that "baseball was as cleansing and creative as total immersion to a Baptist," while the American-owned *Manila Times* proclaimed it "more than a game, a regenerating influence, or power for good."[46]

Filipino schoolchildren played baseball even before American teachers arrived in 1901. Mary Fee, a migratory instructor, stated that girls, too, engaged in the game by 1903. She felt that "those children got more real Americanism out of that corrupted ballgame than they did from singing 'My Country 'tis of Thee' every morning."[47]

Baseball proved only one of the American impositions as Anglos tried to refashion the colony into their own image. A variety of Protestant missionaries began arriving in March of 1899, and proselytizing and Bible distribution soon followed. The Episcopalian bishop, Charles Brent, and the YMCA assumed undue influence with the American administrators, who banned gambling houses, lotteries, and the Filipinos' beloved cockfighting. Colonial educators introduced English language instruction as a medium to replace the multitude of dialects and tribal languages. The Massachusetts public schools and the vocational programs of the Tuskegee Institute served as models for the education system of the

Philippines; and like Tuskegee, segregation practices between the races found ready acceptance in the colony, as whites secluded themselves in separate social and athletic clubs. Filipino men served as house "boys" for the wives of U.S. bureaucrats, while respectable American businessmen employed Filipino women in their brothels.[48]

The Americans attempted to change not only the language and culture of the Philippines, but its physical geography as well. They restructured streets and housing in the villages to more clearly approximate their own norms, and taught the populace to observe American holidays. Former American soldiers and expatriates soon began exploiting natural resources and cheap Filipino labor; the U.S. government solicited famed architect Daniel Burnham to transform the historic capital of Manila and design a summer capital at Baguio, where cool mountain breezes better suited Anglo constitutions. Burnham sailed to the islands in the fall of 1904 for "the purpose of . . . adopting . . . Manila to the changed conditions brought about by the influx of Americans, who are used to better conditions of living than had prevailed in those islands . . . the two capitals of the Philippines, even in their physical characteristics, will represent the power and dignity of this [U.S.] nation."[49]

Burnham intended to display the seemingly contradictory features of both American democracy and imperialism. Parks, playgrounds, and natural preserves served the people, while government buildings sat elevated along the bay, with the Hall of Justice at the highest point. Diagonal streets radiated from the civic center "because every section of the Capital City should look with deference toward the symbol of the Nation's power."[50]

A grand boulevard, later named for Admiral George Dewey, the hero of the conquering fleet, accentuated the bay, while dredgings provided for the Luneta, and elegant downtown park. The opulent Manila Hotel rested on prime property described by Burnham as the "most prominent spot" in the city and leased to Americans for a period of 99 years.[51]

The public buildings copied Burnham's designs for Washington, D.C., and Manila's streets assumed the names of American heroes and politicians. Forbes Park, its wealthiest suburb, honored W. Cameron Forbes, the governor-general who attempted most assiduously to Americanize his Filipino charges. Such sites and monumental structures relied upon American ideals of aesthetics and social order and both established and objectified white dominance.[52]

Burnham enacted similar plans at Baguio, based on his Washington design and the layout of Simla, the British summer capital in their Indian colony. At Baguio the commercial district lay on a meadow situated below a ridgetop municipal building and government structures placed "on the natural Acropolis formed by Governor's Mountain and its flanking hilltop."[53] Burnham intended the government complex to provide "preeminence over all other buildings of the city."[54]

Burnham also designed Forbes' private residence at Baguio. As mutual friends they had recommended each other to President Theodore Roosevelt for the posts in the islands. Forbes, A Boston patrician and former Harvard football coach, served as a Philippines commissioner before his appointment as vice governor in 1908. He became governor-general the following year, and his firm belief in the values of sport led him to implement an extensive plan for athletic competition that surpassed stateside models in its comprehensiveness.[55]

Forbes used his own money to construct a polo field at Baguio, which also served as a baseball diamond and cricket pitch. He paid for part of the magnificent golf course, where the local Igorot boys caddied for the white colonists. Only selected Filipino politicians might play at the expansive Baguio Country Club that featured facilities for billiards, tennis, swimming, croquet, and equestrian activities. Bishop Brent also founded his private school at Baguio, which enrolled only pure American or European youths. The Banquet Road, which traversed the mountainous approach to Baguio, enabled wealthy patrons to cavort in a lavish resort similar to those of the Adirondacks. The passage required thousands of laborers and years of construction that cost nearly $3 million, more than a tenth of the cost of the entire archipelago.[56]

Forbes's plan extended well beyond Baguio, however. Mandatory physical education and formal interscholastic competition began in 1905. A principal's report stated that "each boy's class has a team . . . [of] baseball, indoor baseball, volley ball and basket ball. Each girls' class has a team in indoor baseball and volleyball."[57] Tennis courts and tracks were added to the schools by 1910 to inculcate discipline, work ethic, and competitiveness, and to instill community pride in local teams, who competed for district and interprovincial laurels. Worcester opined that "gymnastic exercises taught in the public schools are converting puny youths into vigorous athletes."[58] The emphasis on competitive sorts proved so great that by 1916 the Bureau of Education adopted a formal policy that awarded bonus points for provincial qualifiers, who could then apply them to their grade point averages or use them to rectify academic deficiencies. Those who competed in the annual Manila Carnival enjoyed even greater benefits.[59]

Initiated in 1908, the Carnival served as a commercial fair to promote business and featured the national championships in an athletic spectacle. The festival integrated the Filipino love of pageantry and revelry, while spurring town and tribal rivalries in the sports competitions. By 1912 the extensive program crowned national titlists in men's and boys' baseball, basketball, volleyball, track and field, and girls' basketball, with open competition in swimming, tennis, rowing, golf, polo, soccer, football, and bowling. The baseball game between the Philippines and Japan soon evolved into the Far Eastern Olympic Games under the leadership of the YMCA.[60]

Sports and physical education became a primary means of acculturating Filipinos to American values, and Governor-General Forbes served as president of the Philippines Amateur Athletic Federation from 1911–1914. He rewarded the top baseball and basketball teams with full uniforms, while track athletes got trophies, and additional prizes were awarded at the provincial competitions. Forbes's incentives proved alluring; 95 percent of schoolchildren participated in the program by the end of his tenure, and more than fifteen hundred baseball teams vied for the honors. Patnongon, the 1913 provincial volleyball champ, enjoyed a police escort, a parade through decorated streets, and a musical tribute from the town band as a thousand fans cheered their conquering victors.[61]

Filipino educators soon adopted the Americans' competitive spirit. Luis Santiago, a middle school principal, organized his own intramural farm system so teams at lower grades could feed their best players to his varsity. He sent the pitcher and catcher to Fort McKinley to learn from the American military teams. They learned well, for by 1911 his school-boys had beaten their American tutors in three of five contests. When Santiago's San Mateo team made it to the interprovincial championship game, he himself even pitched.[62]

The colonial government worked closely with the YMCA to create a comprehensive sports program that included schools, playgrounds, clubs, and recreational facilities. The director of education bragged, "It is believed that no country in the world, certainly no State in the American Union, has such a carefully worked out plan to make athletics national in scope and to determine who are the athletic champions."[63]

The nepotistic involvement of the YMCA assured that such plans carried a particular white, Anglo-Saxon Protestant tint. The Y enjoyed tax-exempt status, and its director, Elwood Brown, assumed an authoritative role. He informed his superior that "a great many of the evils that grew up in athletics in the States before definite control was established will never find a foothold in the Philippines or in the Far East."[64] Within a year of his arrival in 1910 Brown prepared the schools' recreation manual, while another YMCA staffer served as acting director of public education. Brown trained the playground directors and soon served on the Playground Committee. He founded the Philippine Amateur Athletic Federation in 1911 with Forbes as president and himself as secretary-treasurer. Brown gained control of the Manila Carnival and transformed it into a regional competition by including Japan and China under the auspices of his Far Eastern Athletic Association. The stature of Brown and the YMCA grew rapidly, and by 1915 the colonial government provided institutional support.[65]

International competition was intended to foster in tribal factions a greater sense of Filipino nationalism against foreign rivals, but continued racist practices within the country limited that objective. The YMCA allowed for interracial competition, but assumed white superiority and maintained separate structures for whites, Chinese, and Filipinos. The latter employed their newfound nationalism by testing the precepts of Social Darwinism against their colonial rulers as well as other Asians. When Filipino clerks defeated their American bosses in the 1915 PAAF volleyball tournament, the Anglos changed the rules by declaring the locals' deceptive plays unsportsmanlike.[66]

American officials persisted in their consummate beliefs in the powers of sport. The director of education stated that baseball replaced the cockpit and that "this new spirit of athletic interest . . . is actually revolutionary, and with it came new standards, new ideals of conduct, and what is more important, new ideals of character."[67] The Bureau of Education even claimed that "exercise was necessary to make Filipinos taller and bigger . . . and that the stock of the race can be improved considerably despite many handicaps."[68] The Philippine Constabulary asserted that its recruits had grown in only a decade, "due, no doubt, to athletic training the younger generation has been and is receiving in the primary, intermediate, and high schools of the Islands."[69]

By the 1920s the stronger Filipino bodies took the form of boxers, who challenged notions of racial superiority. Pancho Villa became the world champion as a flyweight, and welterweight Ceferino Garcia later created his famed "bolo punch" to symbolize his Filipino sentiments. The growth of Filipino nationalism occurred at the United States' expense, as Washington continually delayed an emancipation date. The promise of sport rang only half true; Filipinos adopted American sport forms and a greater sense of nationhood but did so discriminately. Wholesale assimilation surrendered to cultural adaptation in a polyglot population inhabiting more than seven thousand islands that still resists religious and cultural cohesion.[70]

Protestants gained few converts, and those faced ostracism or worse. By 1922 the YMCA's executive secretary admitted that "as far as the work that we came out here to do, there seems little likelihood of its immediate accomplishment."[71] Forty years of American rule failed to inculcate English; as late as 1948 only 26 percent of Filipinos could or would speak the colonial language and 40 percent remained illiterate.[72]

Sport fared somewhat better. Baseball virtually vanished, but basketball became the national game; yet neither managed to banish cockfighting. Fencing, a residual sport introduced by the Spanish, reappeared in the 1920s, and women's sports gained greater acceptance with national championships gaining greater scope and visibility during the era. Gambling persisted, as Filipinos wagered on human competitors; and they openly flaunted the YMCA and PAAF dictates on amateurism by fielding teams of ringers by the 1920s.[73]

Ultimately the Filipinos both adopted and adapted the cultural forms of their choosing, rather than those imposed on them. Youth gravitated toward American popular culture with its fashions, music, and movies, as well as sports. Combined with existing native practices this produced a hybrid culture, evolving from the traditional but still unusurped by the colonial.

Notes

1. The various responses to and hegemonic interrelationships of cultural factors are detailed in Quintin Hoare and Geoffrey N. Smith, eds., *Selections from the Prison Notebooks of Antonio Gramsci* (New York: International Pub., 1971); Reginald Horsman, *Race and Manifest Destiny: The Origins of American Racial Anglo-Saxonism* (Cambridge: Harvard University Press, 1981); Matthew Frye Jacobson, *Barbarian Virtues: The United States Encounters Foreign Peoples at Home and Abroad, 1876–1917* (New York: Hill and Wang, 2000); Hazel M. McFerson, *The Racial Dimension of American Overseas Colonial Policy* (Westport, CT: Greenwood Press, 1997); Deborah Wei and Rachael Kamel, eds., *Resistance in Paradise: Rethinking 100 Years of U.S. Involvement in the Caribbean and the Pacific* (Philadelphia: American Friends Service Committee, 1998); and Amy Kaplan and Donald E. Pease, eds., *Cultures of United States Imperialism* (Durham, NC: Duke University Press, 1993), are among the many that address race.

Religion is prominent in the analyses of Jon Thares Davidann, *A World of Crisis and Progress: The American YMCA in Japan, 1890–1930* (Bethlehem, PA: Lehigh University Press, 1998); Clifford Pritney, *Muscular Christianity: Mangood and Sports in Protestant America, 1880–1920* (Cambridge: Harvard University Press, 2001); and Robert J. Higgs, *God in the Stadium: Sports and Religion in America* (Lexington: University Press of Kentucky, 1995).

Among the growing literature on the political role of sport are Joel S. Franks, *Crossing Sidelines, Crossing Cultures: Sport and Asian Pacific American Cultural Citizenship* (Lanham, Md: University Press of America, 2000); Mark Dyreson, *Making the American Team: Sport, Culture, and the Olympic Experience* (Urbana: University of Illinois Press, 1998); Wanda Ellen Wakefield, *Playing to Win: Sports and the American Military, 1898–1945* (Albany: State University of New York Press, 1997); S. W. Pope, *Patriotic Games: Sporting Traditions in the American Imagination, 1876–1926* (New York: Oxford University Press, 1997); as well as seminal works such as J. A. Mangan, *The Games Ethic and Imperialism Aspects of the Diffusion of an Ideal* (New York: Viking Press, 1986); and Allen Guttmann, *Games and Empires: Modern Sports and Cultural Imperialism* (New York: Columbia University Press, 1996).

See David Cannadine, *Ornamentalism: How the British Saw Their Empire* (Oxford: Oxford University Press, 2001) for an emphasis on social class rather than racial or religious factors in imperialism.

2. Gail Bederman, *Manliness and Civilization: A Cultural History of Gender and Race in the United States, 1880–1917* (Chicago: University of Chicago Press, 1995), 178–184; and Horsman, *Race and Manifest Destiny*, 100–248.

3. John A. Garraty, *The American Nation: A History of the United States* (New York: Harper & Row, 1983), 43–45; John M. Blum et al., *The National Experience: A History of the United States* (New York: Harcourt, Brace, Jovanovich, 1981), 22–30, 61–68.

For Puritans' attitudes toward sport, see J. Thomas Jable, "The English Puritans: Suppressors of Sport and Amusement," *Canadian Journal of the History of Sport and Physical Education*, 7 (May 1976), 33–40; Nancy L. Struna, "Puritans and Sport: The Irretrievable Tide of Change," *Journal of Sport History*, 4 (Spring 1977), 1–21.

On the westward push and martial spirit, see Patricia Nelson Limerick, *The Legacy of Conquest: The Unbroken Past of the American West* (New York: W. W. Norton, 1987); Allan G. Bogue, *Frederick Jackson Turner: Strange Roads Going Down* (Norman: University of Oklahoma Press, 1998); H. Paul Jeffers, *Colonel Roosevelt: Theodore Roosevelt Goes to War, 1897–1898* (New York: John Wiley & Sons, 1996); H. W. Brands, *The Reckless Decade: America in the 1890s* (New York: St. Martin's Press, 1995), 287–335.

4. Joy S. Kasson, *Buffalo Bill's Wild West: Celebrity, Memory, and Popular History* (New York: Hill and Wang, 2000) and Richard Slotkin, "Buffalo Bill's 'Wild West' and the Mythologization of the American Empire," in Kaplan and Pease, eds., *Cultures of United States Imperialism*, 164–181.

5. Reid Badger, *The Great American Fair* (Chicago: Nelson Hall, 1979); Robert Rydell, *All the World's a Fair: Visions of Empire at American International Expositions, 1876–1916* (Chicago: University of Chicago Press, 1984); Maurice F. Neufeld, "The Contribution of the World's Columbian Exposition of 1893 to the Idea of a Planned Society in the United States" (Ph.D. dissertation, University of Wisconsin, 1935).

Columbian Exposition Album (Chicago, 1893), 98. Quote cited in Larzer Ziff, *The American 1890s* (New York: Viking Press, 1973 ed.), 4.

6. See the *Greatest of Expositions* (St. Louis: Louisiana Purchase Exposition Co., 1904), 225–239, 272 on Depictions, *St. Louis Post-Dispatch*, June 19, 1904, 4, cited in Paul A. Kramer, "The Pragmatic Empire: U.S. Anthropology and Colonial Politics in the Occupied Philippines, 1898–1916" (Ph.D. dissertation, Princeton University, 1998), 235. For a similar reaction see an editorial entitled "How the Filipinos Feel About the Exhibition of the Igorottes in the United States," in *The Public*, 8 (March 3, 1906) reprinted in *BoondocksNet.com*. http://www.boondocksnet.com/expos/wfe_public060303.html/.

7. Stanley Karnow, *In Our Own Image: America's Empire in the Philippines* (New York: Random House, 1989), 176–177. See Bonifacio S. Salamanca, *The Filipino Reaction to American Rule, 1901–1913* (Hamden, CT: Shoe String Press, 1968) on Filipino political movement.

8. *Manila Cablenews*, August 8, 1907, cited in Peter W. Stanley, *A Nation in the Making: The Philippines and the United States, 1899–1921* (Cambridge: Harvard University Press, 1974), 107.

9. Sixto Lopez and Thomas T. Patterson, "The Filipinos Will Not 'Take Up the White Man's Burden,'" *The Public*, 7 (May 21, 1904), cited in Jim Zwick, ed.,

Anti-Imperialism in the United States, 1898–1935, http://www.boondocksnet.com/kipling/lopez_umb.html/.

10. Joseph A. Reaves, *Taking In a Game: A History of Baseball in Asia* (Lincoln: University of Nebraska Press, 2002); Frank Ardolino, "Missionaries, Cartwright, and Spalding: The Development of Baseball in Nineteenth-Century Hawaii," *Nine: A Journal of Baseball History and Culture*, 10:2 (2002), 27–45.

11. Peter Levine, *A. G. Spalding and the Rise of Baseball: The Promise of American Sport* (New York: Oxford University Press, 1985).

12. See Antonio Gramsci, *Selections from the Prison Notebooks of Antonio Gramsci*, translation by Quintin Hoare and Geoffrey N. Smith (New York: International Publishers, 1971), on the concept of cultural hegemony. See Guttmann, *Games and Empires*; Maarten Van Bottenburg (translation by Beverley Jackson), *Global Games* (Urbana: University of Illinois Press, 2002); Walter La Feber, *Michael Jordan and the New Global Capitalism* (New York: W. W. Norton, 1999); Joseph Maguire, *Global Sport: Identities, Societies, Civilizations* (Cambridge: Polity Press, 1999) on the diffusion of sport; and Mark Dyreson, *Making the American Team: Sport, Culture, and the Olympic Experience* (Urbana: University of Illinois Press, 1998) on American sporting ideology.

13. Blum et al., *The National Experience*, 308–309, 525, 535–538; Reaves, *Taking In a Game*, xv, 29–36, Kenneth S. Latourette, *World Service: A History of the Foreign Work and World Service of the Young Men's Christian Association of the United States and Canada* (New York: Association Press, 1957), 249–250. On the close ties between sport and religion in the YMCA movement, see Clifford Purney, *Muscular Christianity: Manhood and Sports in Protestant America, 1880–1920* (Cambridge, MA: Harvard University Press, 2001). Matthew Frye Jacobson, *Barbarian Virtues: The United States Encounters Foreign Peoples at Home and Abroad, 1876–1917* (New York: Hill and Wang, 2000), 29–38.

14. Reaves, *Taking In a Game*, xvi, 37.

15. Ibid., 37; James Naismith, *Basketball: Its Origins and Development* (New York: Association Press, 1941), 154–155; Latourette, *World Service*, 266.

16. Reaves, *Taking In a Game*, xvii, 38.

17. Elwood S. Brown, *Annual Report, Oct. 1, 1912–Oct. 1, 1913*, Administrative Reports, 1912–1917, Philippines, NP Correspondence Reports Box, YMCA Archives at the University of Minnesota.

18. Ibid.

19. Reaves, *Taking In a Game*, 40–41, 102, Van Vottenburg, *Global Games*, 182, 244, n. 66.

20. Latourette, *World Service*, 252, 283; Franks, *Crossing Sidelines, Crossing Boundaries*, xiv; Reaves, *Taking In a Game*, 41.

21. Reaves, *Taking In a Game*, 42–47, 140–146.

22. Ibid., 14; Guttmann, *Games and Empires*, 76, credits the introduction of baseball in Japan to Horace Wilson at Kaiser Gakko (Tokyo University) in 1873. Reaves dates the occurrence as early as 1867, with Albert Bates, a teacher at Kaitaku University in Tokyo, organizing formal games by 1873.

Guttmann, *Games and Empires*, and Allen Guttmann and Lee Thompson, *Japanese Sports: A History* (Honolulu: University of Hawaii Press, 2001), 71, offer modernization theory in the explanation of the rapid change in Japanese society during the Meiji period. I agree with Davidann, *A World of Crisis and Progress*, 11, 22, who disputes the unidirectional nature of modernization theory and recognizes the dual interchange of influences in the process of cultural exchange.

See Paul Varley, *Japanese Culture* (Honolulu: University of Hawaii Press, 2000 ed.), 235–270, on the nature of change; Mark Dyreson, "Regulating the Body and the Body Politic: American Sport, Bourgeois Culture, and the Language of Progress, 1880–1920," in S. W. Pope, *The New American Sport History: Recent Approaches and Perspectives* (Urbana: University of Illinois Press, 1997), 121–144; and Shinsuke Tanada, "Diffusion into the Orient: The Introduction of Western Sports in Kobe, Japan," *International Journal of The History of Sport*, 5:3 (Dec. 1988), 372–376.

23. Donald Roden, "Baseball and the Quest for National Dignity in Japan," in John E. Dreifort, ed., *Baseball History from Outside the Lines: A Reader* (Lincoln: University of Nebraska Press, 2001), 280–303 (294, quotes).

24. Ibid., 294.

25. Ibid., 294–299.

26. Ibid., 298.

27. Ibid., 296–298. On imperialism, see Deborah Wir and Rachael Kamel, eds., *Resistance in Paradise: Rethinking 100 years of U.S. Involvement in the Caribbean and the Pacific* (Philadelphia: American Friends Service Committee, 1998); Augustin Kramer, *The Samoa Islands: An Outline of a Monograph with Particular Consideration of German Samoa* (Honolulu: University of Hawaii Press, 1994 [1901]); J. A. C. Gray, *AMERIKA SAMOA: A History of American Samoa and its United States Naval Administration* (Annapolis: United States Naval Institute, 1960); Michael J. Field, *Mau: Samoa's Struggle for Freedom* (Auckland, New Zealand: Polynesian Press, 1991 [1984]); Peter C. Stuart, *Isles of Empire: The United States and Its Overseas Possessions* (Lanham, MD: University Presses of America, 1999).

28. Julius W. Pratt, *Expansionists of 1898: The Acquisition of Hawaii and the Spanish Islands* (Gloucester, MA: Peter Smith, 1959), 217–221 (217, quote).

29. Ikuo Abe, Yasuharu Kiyohara and Ken Nakajima, "Fascism, Sport and Society in Japan," *International Journal of the History of Sport*, 9:1 (Apr. 1992), 1–28.

30. Yuko Kusaka, "The Development of Baseball Organizations in Japan," *International Review for the Sociology of Sport*, 22:4 (1987), 266–279; Francis C. Richter, ed., "Collegiate 1909 Invasion Japan," *The Reach Official American League Base Ball Guide for 1910* (Philadelphia: A. J. Reach Co., 1910), 481 (quote). See Dean A. Sullivan, ed., *Middle Innings: A Documentary History of Baseball, 1900–1948* (Lincoln: University of Nebraska Press, 1998), 17, for an account of a 1905 Waseo victory in Los Angeles.

31. Amos Alonzo Stagg to R. Kurosaura, July 29, 1910; and Stagg to Ralph Cleary, Aug. 30, 1910, in Stagg Papers, Box 63, folder 3, University of Chicago, Special Collections.

32. Fred Merrifield to My Dear Lon (Stagg), June 27, 1910, Stagg Papers, Box 63, folder 3.

33. Pat Page, International Baseball Series, Fall 1910, correspondence; Page to Stagg, Oct. 6, 1910; Oct. 14, 1910, Stagg Papers, Box 63, folder 3.

34. T. Takasugi, Pres. of Waseda Base Ball Assoc., to Prof. A. Alonzo Stagg, July 20, 1910; Pat Page to Stagg, Oct. 20, 1910, in Stagg Papers, Box 63, folder 3.

35. Elwood S. Brown, *Annual Report, Oct. 1, 1912–Oct. 1, 1913,* n.p.; *Annual Report, Oct. 1913–Oct. 1, 1914,* n.p.; *Annual Report, Oct. 1, 1914–Oct. 1, 1915,* n.p., and Philippines Box NP, Correspondence Reports, 1911–1968 at the YMCA Archives at the University of Minnesota for the origin of the Games.

36. William W. Kelly, "Blood and Guts in Japanese Professional Baseball," in Sepp Kinhart and Sabine Fuhstuck, eds., *The Culture of Japan As Seen Through Its Leisure* (Albany: State University of New York Press, 1998), 104–105, on Tobita Suishu.

See Obojski, *The Rise of Japanese Baseball Power,* 15–19, on international baseball games; the 1925 baseball scorebook, Box 28, folder 5, Stagg Papers, indicates that five games were tied when rain and darkness caused an end in several extra inning affairs.

37. 1930 scorebook, Box 29, folder 2, Stagg Papers; Obojski, *The Rise of Japanese Baseball Power,* 19–20; Heita Okabe to My Dear Prof. Stagg, June 30, 1930, Box 2, folder 11, Stagg Papers, on the Far East Games.

38. Guttmann and Thompson, *Japanese Sports,* 121–122; Abe et al., "Fascism, Sport, and Society in Japan," and Masaji Kiyokawa, "My Olympic Golden Moment: Swimming into History," *Journal of Olympic History,* 5:3 (Fall 1997), 10–14. David B. Welky, "Viking Girls, Mermaids, and Little Brown Men: U.S. Journalism and the 1932 Olympics," *Journal of Sport History,* 24:1 (Spring 1997), 24–49 (40, quote).

39. Obojski, *The Rise of Japanese Baseball Power,* 21–30, gives 1934 as the organizational date for the pro league, with actual play beginning in 1936. See Robert Whiting, *The Chrysanthemum and the Bat: Baseball Samurai Style* (New York: Dodd, Mead, 1977), 221–246, for further development of pro baseball in Japan and continued challenges to American teams.

40. Reaves, *Taking In a Game,* 76–77; Richard Crepeau, "Pearl Harbor: A Failure of Baseball," *Journal of Popular Culture,* 15:4 (Spring 1982), 67–74; and Ira Chernus, "The Pearl Harbor Myth," *History News Network,* http://www.historynewsnetwork.org/.

41. Dean C. Worcester Papers, Bentley Library, University of Michigan; Dean C. Worcester, "Field Sports among the Wild Men of Luzon," *National Geographic Magazine,* 22:3 (March 1911), 215–267; ibid., "The Non-Christian Peoples of the Philippine Islands," *National Geographic,* 24:11 (Nov. 1913), 1157–1256; Paul A. Kramer, "The Pragmatic Empire: U.S. Anthropology and Colonial Politics in the Occupied Philippines, 1898–1916," Ph.D. dissertation, Princeton University, 1998.

42. Worcester, "The Non-Christian Peoples of the Philippines," 1180, 1182, 1189 (quotes, respectively).

43. Paul Kramer, "Jim Crow Science and the 'Negro Problem' in the Occupied Philippines, 1898–1914," in Judith Jackson Fossett and Jeffrey A. Trucker, eds., *Race Consciousness: African-American Studies for the New Century* (New York: New York University Press, 1997), 237–241 on Bean.

On Filipino resistance, see Bonifacio S. Salamanca, *The Filipino Reaction to American Rule, 1901–1913* (Hamden, CT: Shoe String Press, 1968); John M. Gates, *Schoolbooks and Krags: The United States Army in the Philippines, 1898–1902* (Westport, CT: Greenwood Press, 1973); and Glenn May, *Social Engineering in the Philippines: The Aims,*

Education, and Impact of American Colonial Policy, 1900–1913 (Westport, CT: Greenwood Press, 1980).

44. Dean C. Worcester, *The Philippines: Past and Present*, vol. 2 (New York: Macmillan, 1914), 514, 515.

45. Henry Chadwick, ed., *Spalding's Base Ball Guide and Official League Book for 1900* (New York: American Sports Pub. Co., 1901), 76–77 (quote).

46. Lewis E. Gleeck, Jr., *American Institutions in the Philippines* (Manila: Historical Conservation Society, 1979), 39.

47. Mary H. Fee, *A Woman's Impression of the Philippines* (Chicago: A.C. McClurg, 1910), 283–286, (286, quote). See William B. Freer, *The Philippine Experiences of an American Teacher: A Narrative of Work and Travel in the Philippines* (New York: Charles Scribner's Sons, 1906), 273, 287, for another account of baseball.

48. Alexander C. Zabriskie, *Bishop Brent: Crusader for Christian Unity* (Philadelphia: Westminster Press, 1948); Lewis E. Gleeck, *American Institutions in the Philippines (1898–1941)*, 57–75; Cecilia Bocobo-Olivar, *History of Physical Education in the Philippines* (Quezon City: University of the Philippines Press, 1972), 49, 54–56, 71; Kenton J. Clymer, *Protestant Missionaries in the Philippines, 1898–1916: An Inquiry into the American Colonial Mentality* (Urbana: University of Illinois Press, 1986).

   See Elsie Parsons, "American Snobbishness in the Philippines," *The Independent*, 60:8 (Feb. 1906), 332–333; Luis Dery, "Prostitution in Colonial Manila, "*Philippine Studies* 39:4 (1991), 475–489; Vicente Rafael, "White Women and United States Rule in the Philippines," *American Literature*, 67:4 (Dec. 1995), 639–666; and Virginia Benitez Licuanen, *Filipinos and Americans: A Love–Hate Relationship* (Manila: Baguio Country Club, 1982), 56–60, 62–67, 117–119; Kramer, "Jim Crow Science."

49. *See Ninth Annual Report, 1910* (Manila: Bureau of Printing, 1910), n.p., in Worcester Papers, Box 3, Bentley Library, University of Michigan, on village restructuring. Stanley Karnow, *In Our Image: America's Empire in the Philippines* (New York: Random House, 1989), 16–17, 211, 214–215; Thomas Hines, "The Imperial Façade: Daniel Burnham and American Architecture in the Philippines," *Pacific Historical Review*, 41:1 (1992), 33–53; Charles Moore, ed., *Plan of Chicago* (Chicago: Commercial Club, 1909), 29 (quote).

50. Thomas S. Hines, *Burnham of Chicago: Architect and Planner* (Chicago: University of Chicago Press, 1979 ed. [1974]), 203.

51. Daniel Burnham Papers, Art Institute of Chicago Library, Series I: Vol. 15, 745–746; Official Plan of Manila; Daniel H. Burnham to Cameron Forbes, Aug. 7, 1905, Burnham Papers, Series I: Vol. 15, 499; Daniel H. Burnham to William H. Taft, Apr. 4, 1905, Burnham Papers, Series I: Vol. 15, 165; Daniel H. Burnham to J. G. White, Apr. 10, 1905, Burnham Papers, Series I: Vol. 15, 194–195 (quote).

52. Karnow, *In Our Image*, 16–17.

53. Ibid., 211, 214–215; Burnham to R. Watson Gilder, Sept. 12, 1904, Burnham Papers, Series I: Vol. 15, 5–7; Moore, *Plan of Chicago*, 28–29; Hines, *Burnham of Chicago*, 207–210; Burnham to William H. Taft, Oct. 6, 1905, Burnham Papers, Series I: Vol. 15, 641 (quote).

54. Hines, *Burnham of Chicago*, 209.

55. Burnham Papers, Series I: Vol. 14, 579–580; Vol. 15, 356–357, 499, 596–599, 629–630, 675; Vol. 16, 11; Vol. 17, 238, 707; Vol. 21, 47. Hines, "the Imperial Façade," 37–39.

56. Licuanen, *Filipinos and Americans*, 35, 42–50, 71–72. Licuanen indicates the Benquet project at $2,754,281.05 over five years. Karnow, *In Our Image*, 215, claims a cost of $3 million over 10 years for the 28-mile road. See Worcester Papers, Box 5, for photos of the Baguio Country Club.

57. Frederic S. Marquardt Papers, Bentley Library, University of Michigan.

58. Photo caption for *Philippines: Past and Present*, in Worcester Papers, Box 5, folder 1.

59. Marquardt Papers; Bocobo-Olivar, *History of Physical Education in the Philippines*, 46–48.

60. Gleeck, *American Institutions in the Philippines*, 75, 245–246; Elwood S. Brown, *Annual Report, Oct. 1, 1911–Oct. 1, 1912*, n.p.; and *Annual Report, Oct. 1, 1912–Oct. 1, 1913*, n.p., YMCA Archives, Philippines box, Administrative Reports file, 1912–1917, at the University of Minnesota.

61. Janice A. Beran, "Americans in the Philippines: Imperialism or Progress through Sports," *International Journal of the History of Sport*, 6 (May 1989), 74; and Sabas Tordesillas, "How Our Team Surprised the People of Patnongon," from *The Teachers' Assembly Herald* (Baguio: Dept. of Pub. Instruct.) 6:19 (May 3, 1913), 112–113, in Geronima T. Pecson and Maria Racelis, eds., *Tales of the American Teachers in the Philippines* (Manila: Carmelo and Bauerman, 1959), 192.

62. Luis Santiago, "The Organization of the San Mateo Baseball Team," *The Teachers' Assembly Herald* (Baguio: Dept. of Pub. Instruct.) 5:26 (1912), 142–143, in Pecson and Racelis, eds., *Tales of the American Teachers*, 195–199.

63. Bocobo-Olivar, *History of Physical Education in the Philippines*, 47.

64. Brown, *Annual Report, Oct. 1, 1911–Oct. 1, 1912*, n.p., YMCA Archives. The Philippines Box, Manila folder, also contains the request for tax exemption.

65. Bocobo-Olivar, *History of Physical Education in the Philippines*, 54, 71; Gleeck, *American Institutions in the Philippines*, 74–75; Philippine Correspondence Reports, 1911–1968, Administrative Reports file, n.p., YMCA Archives.

66. YMCA segregation practices are evident in Philippines, International Division 167, local associations, 1906–1973, Manila file, 1906–1907 and Correspondence file, 1906–1908; William H. Taft to James F. Smith, Dec. 31, 1906; E. Finley Johnson to John R. Mott, Apr. 22, 1909; C. H. Brent to Mr. Mott, Apr. 30, 1909; Chingting T. Wang to My Dear Fletcher, Feb. 19, 1915; and H. W. Lowe to George I. Babcock, March 21, 1921, at YMCA Archives.

The volleyball game is detailed in Brown, *Annual Report, Oct. 1, 1914–Oct. 1, 1915*, n.p.; and Clymer, *Protestant Missionaries in the Philippines*, 66, 92.

67. Bocobo-Olivar, *History of Physical Education in the Philippines*, 49.

68. Ibid., 48.

69. Ibid., 50.

70. T. S. Andrews, ed., *Ring Battles of Centuries and sporting Almanac* (Tom Andrews Record Book Co., 1924), 29; Linda Nueva Espana-Maram, "Negotiating Identity: Youth,

Gender, and Popular Culture in Los Angeles' Little Manila, 1920s–1940s," Ph.D. dissertation, UCLA, 1996, 118–126.

71. J. Truitt Maxwell to Elwood S. Brown, Apr. 18, 1922, corresponding file, 1920–1923, YMCA archives, See Salamanca, *Filipino Reaction to American Rule*, 109–110, 117–120, on conversions.

72. Salamanca, *The Filipino Reaction to American Rule*, 87; Gleeck, *American Institutions in the Philippines*, 45, 301–302; Stanley, *A Nation In the Making*, 315, fn. 2.

73. *Annual Report*, Philippine Amateur Athletic Federation, 1926, n.p.; Gleeck, *American Institutions in the Philippines*, 97, 119; Bocobo-Olivar, *History of Physical Education in the Philippines*, 44.

THE AFRICAN AMERICAN
STUDENT-ATHLETE

EARL SMITH

This essay begins with the fact that most of America's major social problems are embedded within African American civil society. Name the social problem and you will find it in the African American community. These include, but are not limited to, the devastation of HIV/AIDS; the continuation of unfit housing; high rates of both unemployment and underemployment; limited access to decent health care; high rates (but hidden from the public) of intimate partner violence; environmental degradation; unbridled racial discrimination (Wells 2003); and over-representation in America's jails and prisons. This brief list could be easily extended.

This chapter is about the Dionysian nature of young African American males and their relationship to the athletic structure of United States society, especially the intercollegiate athletic empire. Since the author is a sociologist, much of the critique will include presentations of data on the institutional nature of American society and how and where African Americans fit into institutions that make up American society. The reader is reminded that sports are, after all, merely a reflection of the society we live in. None other than the legendary sports announcer the late Howard Cosell put it best when he said (1991, 32):

Once upon a time, the legend had it there was a world that remained separate and apart from all others, a privileged sanctuary from real life. It was the wonderful world of sport, where every competition was endowed with an inherent purity, every athlete a shining example of noble young manhood, and every owner was motivated by his love of the game and his concern for the public interest. . . .

The sports establishment—the commissioners, the owners, the leagues, and the National Collegiate Athletic Association—would have us believe the legend. Their unceasing chant is that sport is escapism, pure and simple: that people have enough daily problems to cope with in a complex, divided, and even tormented society; and that the relief provided by sports is essential to the maintenance of an individual mental and emotional equilibrium. There is something to be said for this argument, but this hardly means that the sports establishment should be left untrammeled and that individual injustices should not be exposed. The plain truth is that sport is a reflection of the society, that it is human life in microcosm, that it has within it the maladies of the society, that some athletes drink, that some athletes do take drugs, that there is racism in sport, that the sports establishment is quite capable of defying the public interest, and that in this contemporary civilization sport does invade sociology, economics, law, and politics.

At the 1980 meeting of the American Sociological Association, President William Foote Whyte noted in his presidential address that sociology had a lot of big, grand theories that abstractly addressed the problems of the world, but at the more practical micro-level sociologists were unable to assist in the day-to-day solving of American social problems.

The point that President Whyte raises moves in the direction of utility. That is to say, what good are these grand theories if they do not assist in the solving of day-to-day social problems?

Therefore, although my chapter is about that breed of student we have come to label student-athletes, at the end of this paper on African American student-athletes a proposal will be presented for changing some of the long-standing practices that are among the problems that plague African American males who participate at all levels of intercollegiate sports.

In opening my chapter on African American student-athletes I define these as typically young women and men between the ages of 17 and 23 who attend any number of different institutions of higher learning. That is, they may be students attending a junior college, the private liberal arts colleges and universities, or they may attend large state controlled universities. These women and men bring to the institutions remarkable athletic skills, many of which help redefine the sport and entertainment business through the games they play.

Because so many also come from impoverished backgrounds, it is also remarkable that they have survived to become college students. This age group has been ravaged by the disease and violence that are a big part of life in African American civil society (National Urban League, 2003). These young people about whom I write in this chapter are survivors of the war against both preventable diseases (e.g., HIV) and violence (e.g., interpersonal violence).

Of the 42,156 new U.S. cases of HIV/AIDS reported in 2002, 19,890 were new cases reported among African Americans, nearly half (47 percent) of all new cases. The disease has been devastating in the way it has hit the cohort of young African American males very hard. Among African American males and females, HIV/AIDS is the leading cause of death for those between the ages of 25 and 44. Among U.S. citizens, African Americans have the highest rate of HIV/AIDS.

Like HIV/AIDS, high levels of violence continue to be a major social problem in the United States. Homicide rates remain among the highest in the world. Young African American males lead the statistics of being both perpetrators and victims of U.S. homicide, and African Americans overall have the highest homicide rate of any race or ethnic group. Because it has had a tremendous impact on the health and well-being of African American young people, violence is a public health issue that needs special attention if African American civil society is to flourish. Violent injury and death disproportionately affect young adults in the United States, and among African American males between the ages of 15 and 44 homicide is the leading cause of death. In 94 percent of these murders both the victim and perpetrator are African American.

The overall homicide rate for the United States has dropped since 1996 and is now in the range of 8.4 to 10.5 per 100,000. Yet the firearm homicide rate for African American males, at 103.4 deaths per 100,000, is ten times higher than for white males in the same age group (10.5 deaths per 100,000). In 1997, 92 percent of homicides of young African American men occurred by firearms, compared to 68 percent in the general population.

In 1996, the African American homicide victim rate (29.8 per 100,000 persons) was more than twice that of Hispanics (12.4) and more than six times that of whites (3.5) and Asians (4.6). This figure has been at least five times higher than those of whites for the last half-century, and has sometimes reached more than ten times the white rate. Among males aged 15 to 24 (the group with the highest homicide victimization rates), the differences across racial and ethnic groups are even more pronounced. In 1996, African Americans had by far the highest rate (123.1 per 100,000), followed by Hispanics (48.9), American Indians (26.6), Asians (15.6), and non-Hispanic whites (6.4).

With a population of approximately 13 percent of the total U.S. population, African Americans (mainly young males) have arrests rates that are astounding when one takes into consideration that they are less than 15 percent of the total U.S. population. Additionally, African Americans account for two-thirds of all arrests for robbery and are perpetrators of approximately one half of all homicide deaths.

Surely there are political, cultural, and economic factors that account for these disparate figures. What is important for this chapter, however, is that the numbers are so high to begin with—the point being that these young African American males are losing ground, caught in the web of disease, devastation, and random violence that drive up the morbidity and mortality rates. Their negative behavior contributes to the myriad of social problems and in the end greatly diminishes the future potential of family and overall community stability in African American civil society (National Urban League, 2003).

The unanticipated consequences (Merton, 1936) of these personally controllable actions wreak havoc in African American communities. It is important to note the influence on social behavior caused by a whole generation of African American children not having fathers in their homes on a regular basis, being raised by single mothers, and/or at times raising themselves (and more recently the large-scale trend taking place in these communities of children being raised by aging grandparents, usually a grandmother).

The picture is complicated by the fact that there is no widespread protest over these deteriorating conditions. Not only do "rap" music and violent TV broadcast approval of these dysfunctional forms of social behavior and living arrangements; you can find the same message conveyed in research by social and behavioral scientists.

In 1938 the sociologist Robert K. Merton, then of Harvard University, published a paper that is now a classic in American sociology. In "Social Structure and Anomie," Professor Merton gave five reasons why the social structure of human society tends toward strain or "normlessness" that in the end has a high probability of leading to criminal activity. These are:

(1) Conformity
(2) Innovation
(3) Retreatism
(4) Ritualism
(5) Rebellion

According to Professor Merton, these five behavioral patterns attempt to control the natural tendencies toward achieving success in U.S. society (which are mitigated by blocked chances for success) and thus send the message to individuals who do not have the requisite resources for success that it is okay to resort to non-conforming behavior.

That is, cultural goals and institutional norms are at odds with each other. Merton's analysis may be one way of attempting to analyze and explain the disproportionate numbers of African American young people (mostly male but a growing number of females) caught up in the maelstrom of behavior that leads to ill health and criminal activity. Avoiding more complicated explanations such as those posed by Professor Merton, some scholars embrace easier theories blaming poverty for the above-mentioned social problems.

POVERTY

Poverty in the United States is staggering. If we define poverty in its most basic sense as the lack of the means of providing material needs or comforts, some 32.3 million Americans (11.8 percent of the total population) are poor, according to the Department of Commerce, whose definition is that a family of four is poor if their annual income is below $18,100.

The most recent data available from the Department of Commerce and Census Bureau show that fully 22.1 percent of African American families are recorded as being poor—and this figure rises in households that are headed by women (24.7 percent). The data also show that poverty for whites remains below 10 percent (7.5 percent) and the rates for Asians and Pacific islanders is around 10 percent. The total number of Americans in poverty is high at approximately 31.1 million people.

The figures for African Americans do not change much with each census count; it is no surprise, then, that a good percentage of African American males convert to a life of crime and that many student-athletes come to campus from abject poverty conditions and on average are poorer than all other students on their campuses. African Americans, even those in the middle class, have fewer resources, poorer housing choices (Fox 2000), fewer community services, less wealth (Oliver and Shapiro 1995), almost no political clout, less than equal schools, and higher incidence of all types of crime.

The number of all Americans is over 287 million; some 31.1 million live in poverty, or 11.3 percent. For African Americans the numbers are 36,748,000, 9.1 million and 26.5 percent; for whites, 211,400,000, 21.2 million, and 7.5 percent. In research that examines poverty differences and why these rates persist into the current era, we find that, unlike whites, African Americans believe their class position (their relationship to the means of production) is a better explanation for their impoverishment than individual culpability because of race—that is, lack of effort to do something about their current situation. This belief is in line with what research consistently tells us about the way whites see the African American ethnic group (and others) and their strong links to generation after generation after of impoverishment. In recent research by Hunt (1996, 310) we learn that the way ethnic individuals see their group's relationship to poverty is "conditioned by the facts of class."

This discussion is relevant in that academic institutions, and coaches and other individuals who make the decisions to recruit African American male athletes, are conditioned by the dominant ideology (class rule) and do not go into their relationships with these student-athlete recruits without bias.

In fact, the decision makers seek out underprivileged, underrepresented African Americans to come to campus to play sports. Otherwise, how do we account for the fact that more African American student-athletes compete in the elite divisions of intercollegiate sport than there are regular African American students? Or, as Shulman and Bowen state (2001, 53), "If it weren't for our programs, you wouldn't see a black face on this campus."

The data for such an understanding of this complex issue is inadequate, but recent empirical research by Shulman and Bowen (2001) begins to shed some new light on what these male African American student-athletes mean to the high-profile colleges and universities that are deeply involved in sports competition. They also reflect the domineering priorities and values these institutions hold.

For example, in *The Game of Life: College Sports and Educational Values*, Shulman and Bowen note the following (52–53):

> *In 1951, less than 1 percent of the students enrolled at the schools in this study were reported to be black, and enrollment data at a number of the schools do not show that they had any black students at all.*
>
> *During these years athletics provided a limited avenue of access at a very few places, with schools like Michigan and Oberlin enrolling black students who played high profile sports in higher proportion than they were represented elsewhere on the campus. For the most part, however African Americans who sought a college degree (regardless of their athletic interests) went mainly to the Historically Black Colleges and Universities.*
>
> *By 1976, the world had changed. All schools in our study were now actively seeking to admit talented black students, although even with race being taken into account in admission only 5 percent of all male students were black. . . . A much bigger change was evident in the high profile sports. The overall proportion of football and basketball players coming from the African American community at the scholarship-awarding schools in Division 1A was now four to five times their proportion in the student body. In the 1989 cohort, the percentage of high profile athletes who were black*

was higher yet. . . . At the scholarship-granting schools, African Americans accounted for nearly 40 percent of all students playing football or basketball. For these students, it seems, the "golden ring" held out to African American high school students who were excellent athletes had been seized, and the campus was more diverse as a result. Not everyone, however, saw the picture this way.

That African American student-athletes outnumber all other African American students on campus, even though the opportunity structure is greater now than ever for college acceptance, raises serious questions. Rising SAT scores and rising class status (Pattillo-McCoy, 1999) that account for college acceptances make it ironic that, at the very point in time those opportunities for access to higher education for African American students at some of the best colleges and universities in the country are at their highest, their acceptance is still being determined by their athletic ability?

The question then becomes, who are these male (and female) student-athletes? Many we can identify by name: Bob "Bullet" Hayes, Kareem Abdul Jabbar (formerly known as Lewis Alcindor), O. J. Simpson, John Mackey, Jim Brown, Cheryl Miller, Ralph Boston, Barry Sanders, Lawrence Taylor, Oscar Robertson, Arthur Ashe, Tiger Woods, Michael Jordan, Willie Whyte, Wilma Rudolph, and Bill Russell all demonstrated exceptional athletic talent in college and became household names in the sport and entertainment business.

THE SPORT AND ENTERTAINMENT BUSINESS

Many other African American athletes whose names are not so familiar never made it out of colleges and universities—let alone into the professional sporting ranks. Some have died in obscurity. One case that comes to mind is that of Kevin Ross, a basketball player at Creighton University. Never again should colleges and universities be allowed to err on the side of illegalities, bad decisions, immorality, and unethical behavior as they did in the Kevin Ross case. Ross enrolled at Creighton University as a 6'9" basketball player. He had scored nine out of a possible 36 on his ACT test; at the time, the average score for Creighton students was 23. When his initial application was rejected, a vice president and officials in the athletic department had the decision overturned, and Ross began his collegiate career taking courses such as "Theory of Basketball," "Introduction to Ceramics," and "Theory of Track and Field." Ross was advanced to his sophomore year; but when the sports program at Creighton was finished with Ross he was dropped from school, and later was diagnosed as functionally illiterate. The case gained national attention when Ross began taking elementary school classes in Chicago.

The priorities of intercollegiate athletics need to be addressed. These programs may attempt to walk a path that is straight and narrow, but they must at the same time be both ethical and honest; it was dishonesty that fooled Kevin Ross and his family (Davis, 1992).

There are many unnamed ex-athletes like Kevin Ross in the graveyard of American intercollegiate sports. These young men accept their college student-athlete status as performers in the sport and entertainment arena and, like so many African American entertainers, end up being ripped off by the very people and corporations who at the time of their prowess support them in ways beyond imagination.

This last point becomes clearer when you read the story in *USA Today* about the teenage music market (*USA Today*, Friday, June 7, 2002, Section E). The story is a feature-length article about teenage singers such as Bow Wow (age 15), Lil Romeo (12), Lil J (16), and Mario (15). Lil Romeo is the son of rapper Master P and will soon have his own TV sitcom. Bow Wow is the star of the basketball movie *Like Mike* (2002). This article makes it clear that there is a market for this level of entertainment, reinforcing my point about young African American males and their one-dimensional pursuit in entertainment and/or in sports. The portrait of these four young males shows the appeal of gangster rap and sports to young fans who covet urban fashion images.

Cartels like the National Collegiate Athletic Association (NCAA) and groups like the Professional Organization of Athletic Directors would have us believe that sports played on college campuses are merely an extension of the mission of the higher-education system they serve.

(Many of the institutions in Division 1A no longer play their games on campus but rather in professional style arenas and stadiums.) Yet a small test completed in one of my sociology of sport classes last year looked at mission statements of all 117 Division 1A institutions that field a football program; not one says anything about athletics.

The sports-as-entertainment label gains added credence if one examines the high-paying contracts supplied to current and former coaches like Steve Spurrier, Bobby Knight, and John Thompson. Coaches of "big sports" programs all have million-dollar base contracts with built-in incentives. The sports programs they run are also connected to TV contracts signed by the NCAA worth billions of dollars—the most lucrative by far being the exclusive rights to broadcast the March basketball championships, now in an 11-year, $6 billion contract with CBS.

The old cliché "It is not whether you win or lose; it is how you play the game" is no longer valid in high-profile intercollegiate sports. It does matter very much whether you win or lose; the firing of football coaches each December and January attests to this fact. The late Vince Lombardi (1913–1970), Hall of Fame coach of the Green Bay Packers, had it right a long time ago in 1962 when he quipped, "Winning isn't everything, it's the only thing." Missing from this fixation on winning is the connection to higher education.

This becomes clear as we head toward the thirtieth anniversary of Title IX. Advocates of Title IX say the opportunity to play college sports is a chance for women to attend our colleges and universities. This assertion becomes hollow when we see women student-athletes at the college level adopting trends that no one would be proud of for male student-athletes.

It used to be said that, for all that is wrong with the system of intercollegiate athletics, at least the women athletes graduate. While this may still be true, it is no longer so by any large margin: according to Shulman and Bowen in *The Game of Life*, graduation rates for female student-athletes now lag behind those of their non-sport female counterparts (see also Gavora, 2002). Shulman and Bowen examined SAT scores across a 13-year period and found that female basketball players had a 177-point difference from other students at public institutions and a 240-point difference at private institutions (see also Gavora, 159). Obviously, this problem is not limited to male basketball and football players.

Remarkably, the NCAA recently approved an extension of the regular football season and the bowl game postseason. These season extensions come at the very moment that there is a call for "reform" from some of the college and university presidents who initially welcomed the Knight Commission reports (Riggs, 2002; see also the *Knight Commission Report* of 2001 entitled "A Call to Action: Reconnecting College Sports and Higher Education").

ON THE GRADUATION RATES OF MALE AFRICAN AMERICAN STUDENT-ATHLETES

Alfred E. Neuman, the cartoon character in *MAD* magazine, was fond of asking the question, "What, me worry?" Applying this question to the probability of success for African American male athletes in college and whether or not they will complete their education, the answer to Neuman would be YES!—worry. Many African American families are not as wise as the Kellen Winslows when they are making decisions about where to send their sons to college. Kellen Winslow, Sr., (member, National Football League Hall of Fame) drove a hard bargain before he would sign the letter of intent for his son Kellen Winslow, Jr. Winslow Sr. wanted to assure that his son's choice of a football program had a diverse staff and personal concern that ran deeper than the usual clichés given to recruits (see the interesting story at ESPN.com entitled "A racial divide between father and son" by Wayne Drehs, May 22, 2002). It is important that coaches do more than pay lip service to the education of a student-athlete.

Even high-profile coaches like the former University of Arkansas men's basketball coach Nolan Richardson fail to pay attention to these young men. According to a story in the *Northwest Arkansas Times* dated July 25, 2002, over a 17-year career as head coach Richardson failed to graduate a single African American basketball player—and only four players total.

The reason to worry is that African American student-athletes have the lowest graduation rate (less than 40 percent) of all race, ethnic, and gender classifications of student-athletes attending Division 1A schools. In fact, eight of the participating institutions in the 2001 NCAA basketball tournament failed to graduate a single African American player.

All else being equal, why do African American student-athletes do less well in the college and university classroom than their white counterparts (Sperber, 2000)? No one knows, because scholars have not taken the time to carefully research this long-standing problem. The issue itself is sensitive; scholars who venture into this territory risk being labeled racist. When he was studying the social problem of urban poverty in the late 1980s and early 1990s, Professor William J. Wilson of Harvard found that the sociopolitical problems associated with poverty research in essence held up a whole field of inquiry for nearly 20 years. Scholars were labeled—in a criminological sense—and consequently abandoned the poverty research agenda.

Regardless of the research or lack thereof, we do have work by William Shockley, Arthur Jensen, and Murray and Herrnstein among others, all of whom in one way or another posit that African Americans may be athletically gifted but intellectually inferior. This intellectual inferiority is coupled with issues like poverty: if you are not smart then you deserve to be poor! (Murray and Hernnstein, 1999; Jensen, 1969; Shockley, 1987).

African American students and African American student-athletes lag behind their white counterparts on all measurable indexes that record academic performance. And while some findings are now emerging that show African Americans graduating from high school at rates greater than their white counterparts, the meaning of this new statistic remains unclear. This finding needs to be analyzed carefully; most who study high school issues know that movement through the high school ranks has been shown to be almost mandatory ("social promotion") in many school districts across the country. These indexes are the most accurate we have.

For this chapter, it does matter that the opening up of the educational opportunity structure for African American student-athletes allows them to attend some of the best public and private universities in the country.

The Harvard University anthropologist Professor Katherine Newman captured the consequences of failing to seize these educational opportunities. She recorded the downside of not getting credentials or skills to sustain one in the pursuit of a happy and long life in her ethnographic study of young African American men in Harlem, in which she says (1999, 22):

> There is nothing quite like slaving over a hot, greasy deep fryer for eight hours to teach people that they need to put some effort into making sure they have credentials to qualify for something better in the future.

To date, the major theory explaining this failure to grab the opportunity of advanced education is posited by anthropologist Professor John Ogbu. He explained that while education and skills attainment are important for upward mobility in American society for African American school children and their parents, these remain elusive goals and aspirations. He put it thus: "An important determinant of school performance is what children and their parents or community expect to gain from their education in adult life" (Ogbu, 1978, 264).

From Professor Ogbu's ethnographic research, much of it carried out in Stockton, California, found that African American parents and their children have low expectations and perceive they will get little in return for their efforts at obtaining an advanced education. This finding appealed to many in the sociological and psychological research communities even though Ogbu did little to verify these findings with comparative research (Ogbu 1978).

Harvard University Professor of Government Jennifer Hochschild contends in her book *Facing Up to the American Dream: Race, Class, and the Soul of the Nation* that upwardly mobile African Americans have simply become too complacent and tired of fighting for social justice. This paradox—as Hochschild labels it "of succeeding more and enjoying it less"—leads to resentment, frustration, and bitterness toward the American Dream (Hochschild, 1995, 140–141).

This American Dream, says Professor Hochschild, is made up of four tenets. Tenet one tells us that in America all can vie for the dream. Tenet two asserts that all of us can reasonably anticipate success. Tenet three is exceptionally valid in that success comes only from one's own actions: the effort, the traits of hard work and sacrifice. Finally, the fourth tenet tells us that success is virtue. Failure, then, is individual lack of will and talent (Hochschild, 1995, 15–32). If we then assume that African American student-athletes are in fact pursuing their own version of the American Dream, then how is it that the dream gets reduced to the flip side of Hochschild's tenet four—to failure?

If they do nothing more than give a snapshot of one six-year time period, graduation rates allow us to measure the value institutions place on the academic side of participation and competition. Many coaches are not happy with the annual printing of graduation rates and have rebutted them year after year. One such coach is Rick Majerus of Utah who has been very vocal about his opposition to making public the student-athlete graduation rates.

Yet the disgruntled coaches are going to have to live with this; beginning with the class of 2000, the major sport weekly *Sports Illustrated* annually prints graduation rates of ranked basketball teams.

TALENT, BUT NO VOICE

Many African American student-athletes have a lot of talent in their respective sports but little or no voice in how they are treated once they reach campus. One problem in drawing correlations between talent, performance, and graduation rates is how best to quantify talent. What is talent? Most dictionaries define talent as having "god-given" abilities to accomplish some enviable task. Does having a lot of athletic talent become a substitute for working hard at academics? Although this may seem an easy question, it is not.

Failure to graduate cripples student-athletes later in life. They do not get the call to become coaches or managers. Legal scholar Ken Shropshire has published on this subject and says that leadership in college sports "resembles a black-bottomed pyramid": African American coach rarely rises above the middle levels of management and corporate structure in sports. No amount of effort on his or her part can alleviate the position inherited (Shropshire, 1996).

IS PAYING THE STUDENT-ATHLETE THE ANSWER?

While the "party line" from the gatekeepers of high-profile college sports is that paying the student-athletes will not solve any of the aforementioned problems, this line sounds very similar to one offered by (non-sports-related) corporate America contending that paying workers a decent wage will only spoil them (Ehrenreich, 2001). While it is not being advocated that institutions start paying college athletes, acknowledgment is being made that the current system must be changed. Workers' low wages, high unemployment rates, companies downsizing to increase profits: all these work to concentrate wealth in the hands of those who own and control corporate organizations and athletic departments. A good case study of this practice can be found in ongoing revelations about L. Dennis Kozlowski, former CEO of Tyco International. With a base salary in the range of $1.65 million, stock options at $80 million, and annual perks packages of $1 million, Mr. Kozlowski profited while the company sank (see, especially, "A Prime Example of Anything-Goes Executive Pay" by David Leonhardt, *New York Times*, June 4, 2002). Also see the glowing stories about Hewlett-Packard CEO Carleton S. Fiorina, who announced that HP would lay off some 15,000 employees by November 2003. In so doing HP should realize $72.8 billion to $73.8 billion in revenues for fiscal year 2002 (see "Hewlett Steps Up Pace of Layoff Plan," *Reuters News Service*, June 5, 2002). Or see the interesting story on greed among company executives after the Enron debacle (Edward Iwata, "Payouts Anger Former Enron Workers," *USA Today*, June 18, 2002).

Among these stories about greed and generous pay for chief executives while denying the basic pay and benefits to staff employees should be included universities like Harvard and Yale that do not want to pay their staff employees decent living wages. Many of those who clean the dorms, office buildings, toilets and windows at these great universities earn annual salaries that keep their take-home pay below the U.S. federal government's poverty line. Contrast this with the $6 billion per year currently paid to the NCAA by CBS for rights to televise the men's college basketball championships, a figure unsurpassed by any other sports spectacle except perhaps the Super Bowl.

Paying student-athletes a stipend, instead of a wage, could boost morale (and stop petty crime resulting from the lack of money). Another proposed solution is to increase the amount of the scholarship aid that student-athletes receive for athletic services rendered. This could come in the form of a modest amount of money based on potential and/or performance. This decision would be reviewed by a board whose responsibilities would include verifying that the student-athlete remained in good academic standing. Taking an approach like this would soon make the idea of paying college athletes a non-issue. Following the same rules that pertain to the awarding of scholarships would also avoid issues related to insurance and worker's compensation.

CONCLUSION: FORGING A NEW AFRICAN AMERICAN STUDENT-ATHLETE

Athletics are important for African American males regardless of their level in school. Some scholars feel that athletics is so important within African American civil society that it is embedded within their culture. African American males in elementary, junior high, and high schools tell researchers in survey after survey that it sports are more important to them than anything else. Most of them cannot, however, tell researchers why sport has become "a way of life" for so many of them.

Recent research by University of Miami sociologist Jomills Braddock II shows that African American males in high school who are involved in sports do better than those who are not. In fact, according to Professor Braddock, "the sport experience can be an agent of socialization" very important for these young men (Braddock, 2000). On the other hand, the role of athletics is one of the most controversial topics today in the social and behavioral sciences whether the focus is high school or university sport programs (Cantor and Prentice, 1996).

Why do so many African American student-athletes each year descend upon our college campuses looking for athletic fame? The number of African American males playing basketball and football at the college and professional levels is astounding. In intercollegiate basketball African American players make up 61 percent of all male players; in football the figure is 52 percent.

At the pro level these numbers get larger. In professional football African American players make up 67 percent of all players, in basketball some 78 percent. Where these numbers get weaker is in baseball, a sport that has strong roots in the African American communities of the past. Today, African Americans make up just 13 percent of all professional baseball players. This figure has dropped precipitously from the number as recently as the 1980s.

In a 1982 essay entitled "Common Myths Hide Flaws in the Athletic System," Professor Harry Edwards saw this growth in the numbers of African American athletes and quipped:

> This is why, when you turn on television—and it doesn't make any difference whether you are watching collegiate or professional basketball and football— all too often, with the exception of the quarterback and a few other positions, it doesn't look like Georgia playing Texas, it looks like Ghana playing Nigeria. (Edwards, 1982, 21)

If these players do not take advantage of the larger educational opportunity, what good does it do them to receive the "free" education? As Andrew Zimbalist points out in his book *Unpaid Professionals: Commercialism and Conflict in Big-Time College Sports* (1999, 38):

> Other than the athletic training and visibility that the fortunate few who go on to the pros receive, the greatest tangible compensation an athlete can hope for is the credential of a bachelor's degree. But, as we have seen, only around half of Division 1 football and basketball players ever manage to get this degree, and many who have the degree have learned little or nothing.

Or is it time to consider what the athletes have long known: that there is no other route to the professional leagues? Few athletes used to go directly from high school to pro basketball. This is changing. In the past decade the numbers have increased considerably, to the point where these "boys" are among the top NBA draft picks, frequently selected ahead of college graduates. LeBron James, a 17-year-old high school senior, became the number one draft pick in professional basketball and is now a star player for the NBA's Cleveland Cavaliers.

The odds against an African American student-athlete going on to play professional basketball are 20,000 to one; for professional football the odds are 10,000 to one. Therefore, we must ask: Is this slim chance of becoming a Michael Jordan or an Emmit Smith reason enough to work against the tide? Do the odds of playing these two sports at the professional level get better by going through the intercollegiate sport system? No! So, is what we have here the "lemming phenomenon"?

Another phenomenon that affects these odds—one this author predicted several years ago in a paper in the *Marquette Sports Law Journal*—is the increasing recruitment of foreign athletes. More and more college sports programs are recruiting athletes from places that almost never field athletes in American high-profile sports. For example, how does a basketball player (Yao Ming) from China get top billing when he has not played in front of an American audience? Dirk Nowitzki of the Dallas Mavericks is a somewhat mediocre player while hundreds of African Americans with enormous talent never make it to the NBA. Foreign players deserve the right to play the games they have come to love, but there is a cost to recruiting and playing foreign players in place of young African American males. Take the use of professionals for the Olympic Games: fewer get a chance for Olympic glory that can be turned into jobs or money, and if the current trend continues, fewer opportunities will be available for African Americans to attend a college or university.

In fact, for African American youth the odds are very high these days. In the 2002 NBA draft of the first ten picks, three were foreigners; of the first 20, five foreign. Of the first fifty basketball players selected, eleven were foreign; in all 17 foreign players were picked.

William Rhoden, columnist for the *New York Times*, wrote recently that this need to see basketball as the be-all and end-all for African American youth and their families is changing, and not because they want it to change. As more and more foreign players are recruited to play both intercollegiate and professional basketball the openings for African American youth grow fewer. The trend for recruiting players from Europe, he wrote, should be a wake-up call for young African American players who see the NBA shining brightly in their immediate futures. Another column appearing in the *New York Times*, by Chris Broussard, quoted Hall of Fame coach Chuck Daly:

> *They better pay attention to what's happening, those guys that want to get into drugs and chasing young girls around and not shoot basketballs better think twice if they want to make it to the N.B.A. because somebody wants their jobs.*

Yet the athletes themselves firmly believe that someday they will play professional basketball (or some other professional sport). How many times and how often can these young men be told to listen, to pay attention? As the legal scholar Ken Shropshire points out in his book *In Black and White: Race and Sports in America* (1996, 103), "the trail of racism runs through collegiate athletics," and much of the support needed to assist athletes to the next level of play is pulled from under them long before they exit college.

In conclusion, the last word belongs to Professor Harry Edwards, a longtime critic of the exploitation of African American student-athletes (1984, 12):

> *Black communities, black families, and black student-athletes themselves also have critically vital roles to play in efforts to remedy the disastrous educational consequences of black sports involvement. The undeniable fact is that through its blind belief in sport as an extraordinary route to social and economic salvation, black society has unwittingly become an accessory to, and a major perpetuator of, the rape, or less figuratively put, the disparate exploitation of black student athletes. We have in effect set up our own children for academic victimization and athletic exploitation by our encouragement of, if not insistence upon, the primacy of sports achievement over all else.*

Edwards digs even deeper into the social fabric, in structural terms under late capitalism and in the last stages of the twentieth century, explaining where the problems lie:

The first principle of sport sociology is that sport inevitably recapitulates the character, structure, and dynamics of human and institutional relationships within and between societies and the ideological values and sentiments that rationalize and justify those relationships. No realm of institutional interdependent relationship better illustrates this principle than that which has emerged at the interface of sport and law. Often ostensibly far removed from specific locus and focus of many of the legal actions in question, sport, nonetheless, has been both judged progressively ahead and sent reeling in reaction by forces of law over the last six decades. It was simply inevitable, given sport's status as an integrated institutional component of society, that laws, regulatory edicts, and executive orders, which so profoundly affected American life in general over this period, would have no less profound impact within sport. And nowhere has this impact been more evident than in the sphere of interracial relations. (Edwards, 1997)

Sport in American society has been described as an ordered activity (Wrong, 1961) giving form and shape to participants' functional abilities. That is to say, sport socializes individuals who participate in that ritual in a number of ways, including but not limited to building character, forging teamwork, and teaching participants the values of cooperation and civility. This is deemed especially true for young men who are student-athletes attending some of the most prestigious institutions of higher learning in America. At this point in time, a critique of this view of sports seems necessary. It may be that sport does no more, and possibly does less, for individuals and families than originally thought; yet there is no denying that sport is an important American institution as we move into the twenty-first century. The noted Washington University writer Gerald Early captures the essence of sport when he says the following in his essay "Two Ways to Think about Sports":

We have come to think in two mistaken ways about sport: that sports are such tawdry spectacles that they are worthy only of disposable commentary and that sports themselves are disposable because they are trivial human activities. The first thought misses the very vital point that day-to-day events in high-performance sports competitions are, indeed, news, to be gathered and presented in a highly professional way, in the same way that other aspects of popular culture such as film, music, and theater are. The writing itself may be disposable, a reflection of our disposable popular culture, but there is, ironically, an act of preservation in making something newsworthy that means, in effect, we have made something a part of our history, a reference point, a defining instance, something that must be returned to by future generations if they are to understand us and themselves. With the exception of our politics, nothing comes as close to being recorded almost completely as an epic narrative in our news as our sports. The second thought confuses the content of sports performance with its meaning. The goal of any particular game or even of any particular sports season is trivial, but the fact that it is being played and being supported by a huge corporate and technological apparatus is not. Teams and individuals may be beaten, but the kingdom of sports is unstoppable. (Early, 1998)

How Professor Early captures the essence of sport is a fitting way to sum up its meaning for African Americans. African Americans are still the poorest of American citizens, their youth the biggest sufferer of HIV/ AIDS, the ethnic group with the least amount of social capital or wealth (but the most debt)—and we wonder why so many "eggs" are thrown into the sport/entertainment basket by these young athletes? Speculation would have it that these young men have few other options (LaVeist, 2002).

Long before the sports prowess of Jackie Robinson and Joe Louis were on show for all Americans to see, the quickest route to social and economic prosperity had been marked as the route to the boxing gym, the football or basketball stadium, or the baseball field. Today, the belief about upward mobility in African American civil society remains the same.

African American males are encouraged and taught from an early age to hone their athletic skills by long sessions of practice. Popular commercials (such as those for Nike) that run during the month of March will show an African American youngster playing on a basketball court well into the night shooting baskets. This powerful message says the practice sessions take up large amounts of time—and just as important, that they come first. The implication is that the time is taken away from other areas of life. This may even mean the time that would normally be given over to academic work.

Is this the oppositional culture that so many say inflicts the African American community? This theory about why young African Americans don't accept the mainstream norms has not been falsified and a lot remains to be done about it.

If African American student-athletes do not begin to assert themselves as students, they will fall in the same way that African American athletes in professional baseball have fallen—that is, they will no longer be the premier recruited athletes for intercollegiate sports such as football and basketball. Speaking to this topic more broadly, Harvard Professor Henry Louis Gates notes the following:

> The blind pursuit of attainment in sports is having a devastating effect on our people. Imbued with a belief that our principal avenue to fame and profit is through sports and seduced by a win-at-any-cost system that corrupts even elementary school students, far too many black kids treat basketball and football fields as if they were classrooms in an alternative school system. OK, I flunked English, a young athlete will say. But I got an A plus in slam-dunking. (Gates, 1991)

The theoretical and empirical reality of this assertion can be seen by looking at the National Basketball Association. In the past three years the NBA has shown that it will go to overseas markets for the players many of whom have either played on U.S. soil in the intercollegiate sport system or have been coached by American-born coaches who go overseas to find work.

These young African American males (and females) must begin to realize that their privileged positions are now being threatened and the only way to thwart this is to become better students. Likewise, the call for more African American coaches will also fall on deaf ears until the position is collectively assumed that there is a need to be more than supplicants at the door; African Americans must begin to contribute in the sport arena where it matters, and that is high-level decision making. Until that happens, the games African American males play will continue to look like the racial apartheid system that was dominant in the early social history of this country as it developed into the United States of America.

Ever since the first large-scale social experiments with public school integration in the 1950s, the issue of where and when African American students will play institutionalized sports has been hotly debated. Although the debates have changed somewhat, it remains that way today and still looks to be counterintuitive (Williams, 1998).

References

Ainsworth-Darnell, James and Douglas Downey. 1998. "Assessing the Oppositional Culture Explanation for Racial/Ethnic Differences in School Performance." *American Sociological Review*, 63:536–553.

Barash, David. 2002. "Evolution, Males, and Violence." *The Chronicle of Higher Education*, Section 2, B7–B9.

Braddock, Jomills II. 2000. "Athletics, Academics, and African American Males." Paper read at the symposium on African American Male Achievement, Hosted by Howard University.

Broussard, Chris. February 9, 2002. "Foreign All-Stars Lead Anticipated Invasion." *New York Times*.

Cantor, Nancy and Deborah Prentice. 1996. "Life of Modern-Day Student-Athlete: Opportunities Won and Lost." Paper read at the Conference on Higher Education, March 21–23, 1996, Princeton University.

Cosell, Howard and S. Whitfield. 1991. *What's Wrong with Sports?* New York: Simon & Schuster.

Davis, Timothy. 1992. "Examining Educational Malpractice Jurisprudence: Should a Cause of Action be Created for Student-Athletes?" *Denver University Law Review*, 69:57–96.

Edwards, Harry. 1997. "The End of the 'Golden Age' of Black Sports Participation?" *South Texas Law Review*, 38:1007–1027.

Edwards, Harry. 1984. "The Black Dumb Jock: An American Sports Tragedy." *College Board Review*, 131:8–13.

Edwards, Harry. 1982. "Common Myths Hide Flaws in the Athletic System." *The Center Magazine*, Jan/Feb, 17–21.

Early, Gerald. 1998. *Body Language: Writers on Sport*. Saint Paul, MN: Graywolf Press.

Ehrenreich, Barbara. 2001. *Nickled and Dimed: On (Not) Getting By in America*. New York: Henry Holt and Company.

Eschholz, Sarah, Ted Chiricos and Marc Gertz. "Television and Fear of Crime." *Social Problems*, 50:395–415.

Fox, Kevin. 2000. "Urban Space, Restrictive Covenants and the Origins of Racial Residential Segregation in a U.S. City, 1900–1950." *International Journal of Urban and Regional Research*, 24:616–633.

Gates, Henry Louis. 1991. "Delusions of Grandeur: Young Blacks Must Be Taught That Sports Are Not the Only Avenue of Opportunity." *Sports Illustrated*, 78.

Gavora, Jessica. 2002. *Tilting the Playing Field: Schools, Sports, Sex and Title IX*. San Francisco: Encounter Books.

Herrnstein, Richard and Charles Murray, 1999. *The Bell Curve: Intelligence and Class Structure in American Life*. New York: The Free Press.

Hochschild, Jennifer. 1995. *Facing Up to the American Dream: Race, Class, and the Soul of the Nation*. Princeton, NJ: Princeton University Press.

Hunt, Matthew. 1996. "The Individual, Society or Both? A Comparison of Black, Latino, and White Beliefs about the Causes of Poverty." *Social Forces*, 75:293–322.

Jensen, Arthur. 1969. "How Much Can We Boost IQ and Scholastic Achievement?" *Harvard Educational Review*, 39:1–123.

Kelley, Norman (ed.). 2002. *The Political Economy of Black Music*. New York: Akashic Books.

LaVeist, Thomas. 2002. "Consideration for the National Healthcare Disparities Report." Paper prepared for the Institute of Medicine, National Academy of Sciences, Committee on Guidance for Designing a National Health Care Disparities Report.

Merton, Robert K. 1936. "The Unanticipated Consequences of Social Action." *American Sociological Review*, 1:894–904.

Merton, Robert K. 1938. "Social Structure and Anomie." *American Sociological Review*, 3:672–682.

National Urban League. 2003. *The State of Black America*. New York: NUL Press.

Newman, Katherine. 1999. *No Shame in My Game: The Working Poor in the Inner City*. New York: Russell Sage Foundation and Alfred A. Knopf.

Ogbu, John. 1978. *Minority Education and Caste*. New York: Academic Press.

Ogbu, John. 1994. "Racial Stratification and Education in the United States: Why Inequality Persists." *Teachers College Record*, 96:264–298.

Oliver, Melvin and Thomas Shapiro. 1995. *Black Wealth/White Wealth*. New York: Routledge.

Pattillo-McCoy, Mary. 1999. *Black Picket Fences: Privilege and Peril among the Black Middle Class*. Chicago: University of Chicago Press.

Riggs, Randy. May 30th, 2002. "College Football Season's Dozen-Game Schedule Is Not Likely to Become the Norm." *Austin American-Statesman*.

Shockley, William. 1987. "Jensen's Data on Spearman's Hypotheses: No Artifact." *Behavioral and Brain Sciences*, 10:512.

Shulman, James and William Bowen. 2001. *The Game of Life: College Sports and Educational Values*. Princeton, NJ: Princeton University Press.

Shropshire, Kenneth L. 1996. *In Black and White: Race and Sports in America*. New York: New York University Press.

Shropshire, Kenneth L. 1996. "Merit, Ol' Boy Networks, and the Black-Bottomed Pyramid." *Hastings Law Journal* 47:455–472.

Smith, Earl. 1999. "Race Matters in the National Basketball Association." *Marquette Sports Law Journal*, Vol. 9, No. 2, 239–249.

Sperber, Murray. 2000. *Beer and Circus: How Big-Time College Sports Is Crippling Undergraduate Education*. New York: Henry Holt.

Suggs, Welch. September 21, 2001. "Graduation Rate for Male Basketball Players Falls to Lowest Level in a Decade." *Chronicle of Higher Education*, A34.

Whyte, William Foote. 1982. "Social Inventions for Solving Human Problems." *American Sociological Review*, 47:1–13.

Wilson, William J. 1987. *The Truly Disadvantaged: The Underclass, the Inner City, and Public Policy*. Chicago: University of Chicago Press.

Williams, Juan. 1998. *Thurgood Marshall: American Revolutionary*. New York: Three Rivers Press.

Wrong, Dennis. 1961. "The Oversocialized Conception of Man in Modern Sociology." *American Sociological Review*, 26:183–196.

Zimbalist, Andrew. 1999. *Unpaid Professionals: Commercialism and Conflict in Big-Time College Sports*. Princeton, NJ: Princeton University Press.

MUSCULAR ASSIMILATIONISM
Sport and the Paradoxes of Racial Reform

Patrick B. Miller

Frederick Douglass "Fritz" Pollard led the Brown University football squad to the Rose Bowl game at the conclusion of its thrilling 1915 gridiron campaign. Near the end of the following season the African American athlete became the star yet again in his team's stunning upsets over once-dominant Yale and the emerging powerhouse Harvard. The announcement would soon be made that Pollard had won All-American honors for his exciting charges through opposing defenses: three touchdowns on his first three carries in an early game versus Amherst; two scoring runs against a formidable Rutgers contingent; punt and kickoff returns, as well as pass-catching heroics, to turn the tide of the contest in New Haven; then a series of dramatic broken-field dashes and two more touchdowns leading to the win in Cambridge. In ensuing years Pollard's exploits figured prominently in launching the fledgling National Football League. Later still, sport historians, echoing journalists from his own era, would compare him to the legendary Jim Thorpe and Red Grange. But now, just hours after the conquest of Harvard in the late autumn of 1916, Pollard and his teammates were being treated to a spectacular rally on the Brown campus in Providence. At the point in the celebration when the students turned from their songs, chants, cheers, and yells to more sober, inspirational fare, campus dignitaries took the podium to proclaim the importance of the athletic victories in all their particulars.[1]

The president of the university, William Faunce, intoned that its recent successes meant "that Brown football had reached its manhood and can take care of itself." Concerning the school's headline performer, Faunce offered, as a compliment, the observation that "[T]here is no bigger white man on the team than Fred Pollard." Later, as the ceremonies concluded, Professor Courtney Langdon added his praise for the black athlete by saying that "the finest thing about the season when you come to think of it is the wonderful modesty of Pollard."[2] Other speakers gave voice that day to the usual football verities, but these comments stand out. The juxtapositions are significant, the palpable condescension of both assertions more revealing still. Manhood was won on the field of athletic competition, and if the black athlete showed talent in sport, he could be promoted for a time to white manhood. Yet while manhood asserts itself, modesty knows its place. In a few short sentences, Faunce and Langdon acknowledged, albeit obliquely, the potential utility of sport to alter race relations in the United States—then sharply modified the terms of that expansive proposition.

Significantly, the years of Pollard's athletic glory coincided with increasingly aggressive segregation of federal agencies by the Wilson administration, as well as government policies at the state level that ranged from indifference to contempt of the plight of Negro farmers and laborers. Even as many black Americans mourned the death of Booker T. Washington or the passing of Bishop Henry McNeal Turner in 1915, they were confronted with the appearance of D. W. Griffith's *Birth of a Nation* and the resurgence of the Ku Klux Klan. The number of recorded lynchings had diminished somewhat since the turn of the century, down to approximately one murder every five days on the fiftieth anniversary of Emancipation. Yet beyond those grotesque rituals of violence and slaughter, everyday acts of terrorism left both physical and psychic scars on the children and grandchildren of freedmen and women.[3] In response, African Americans protested and at the same time speculated about potential antidotes to the poisons of prejudice.

Set against the backdrop of tightening racial restrictions in the South and mounting hostility toward black people nationwide, the rise to prominence of an African American athlete, magnified in the spectacles of northeastern college football, then multiplied by the victories won and records set by black champions in other sports, was perceived by many apostles of uplift and racial progress as a significant opportunity to open the eyes of white America to the qualities of character African Americans brought to the sporting arena. In the most basic terms, black athletic success offered a measure of hope to those who sought to soften racial prejudice and advance the cause of social justice. According to the *New York Age*, "Mr. Pollard [was] doing a very great deal to help solve the race problem."[4] The history of what I call "muscular assimilationism" thus grew out of compelling assertions, communicated in the idiom of "manly sport," that showcased the efforts of African Americans meeting all the requirements of national pastimes.

The appeal of muscular assimilationism was as part of a broad-based dialogue that black activists endeavored to open with white America—in order to stop the dance of Jim Crow and replace that loathsome caricature with images of the skill, strength, and stamina that black athletes demonstrated in a variety of sports. From such a vision others might be fashioned, highlighting the success of African Americans in any endeavor they were allowed to enter on an equal footing. After the turn of the century, some racial reformers embraced the proposition that black achievement in athletic competition not only helped "uplift the race" toward mainstream standards and ideals, but would also cultivate pride in what blacks had already accomplished and what they promised to contribute to the American pageant of progress. What was more, the credo was intended to convert the dominant culture to egalitarian values. Muscular assimilationism first emerged as an article of faith; eventually it took the form of carefully articulated hopes and dreams, imagining the American social landscape as a level playing field.

Initial installments of the chronicle of black athletic achievement stood alongside efforts by racial crusaders to document the contributions of African Americans to the larger history of the United States, from the Revolutionary Era to the "Winning of the West" and beyond. 1915, it is important to note, was also the year that galvanized much of Afro-America in a campaign to keep *Birth of a Nation* out of the nation's theaters and the year in which Carter G. Woodson launched the Association for the Study of Negro Life and History. Only a few months later, Woodson would publish the first issue of the *Journal of Negro History*. Just as significant as such scholarly attempts to revise American history and memory were the proclamations in newspaper editorials and in gunfire that "New Negroes" would no longer tolerate the stereotypes of blackface minstrelsy and would fight back when confronted with racist violence.[5]

The gathering momentum of resistance to racism expressed itself in many ways. In the aftermath of World War I, the cultural renaissance identified with Harlem celebrated the substantial talents of black artists, intellectuals, and athletes not only in the creation of a "black bohemia," but also as affirmations of African American pride and dignity, readily demonstrated whenever they were permitted. The ex-heavyweight champion Jack Johnson remained an eminently controversial figure within the black community—principally for his sexual liaisons across the color line—but he held a substantial following among the Harlem literati and was portrayed by his friend James Weldon Johnson as someone who had not let himself be thwarted by mainstream prejudice and proscription. Yet if the literary New Negro often expressed elements of cultural nationalism, for the most part the athletic New Negro embodied the integrationist ideal. For the rest of the century the tensions compressed between these rival stances frequently burst forth in debates over the ends and means of racial reform. Assessing the benefits and costs of abiding by the rules established by the dominant culture has always figured prominently in the African American dilemma.[6]

The cultural front of black activism was inextricably linked to the politics of race in the United States, of course. Black artists and intellectuals had long made the case that what they created made a major contribution to the advancement of *all* African Americans.[7] In similar fashion, muscular assimilationism resonated deeply for the heirs of Frederick Douglass and the allies of W. E. B. Du Bois, who in their most hopeful moments sought models within mainstream culture for a truly democratic society that acknowledged merit wherever it was demonstrated and drew no distinctions of creed or color. When Pollard, Paul Robeson shortly after him, and ultimately a legion of talented and disciplined black champions began to make their way into the headlines of metropolitan daily newspapers, they elaborated the case for fair play and sportsmanship in the athletic domain. Those notions, the argument ran, could be extended to other realms—the classroom, the business deal, the political arena. If, however, such athletes were denied the chance to compete at the highest levels—as so many black prizefighters, jockeys, and baseball players had been at the turn of the century—then it was clear to anyone who had eyes to see that white America continued to betray the spirit of the Declaration of Independence and the founding principles of the republic.[8]

Cast in terms of equal opportunity, this embrace of the sporting creed corresponded with the ideology and politics of organizations such as the National Association for the Advancement of Colored People (NAACP) and became a significant element in the broader civil rights crusade. Under the editorship of Du Bois, and then of Roy Wilkins, the *Crisis* extolled the victories won on the playing fields as a means of subverting any notions of Negro inferiority. At the same time, the organ of the NAACP denounced prevailing patterns of exclusion and every act of discrimination in the sporting realm. Likewise, during the interwar years sportswriters such as Edwin Bancroft Henderson, Wendell Smith, and Sam Lacy chronicled with increasing eloquence and force black success in athletics, demanded equality and opportunity on diamond and gridiron, around the track oval and within the boxing arena, and decried every act of Jim Crow they discovered.[9]

It was this generation of sports journalists that most profoundly shaped the ideal of black athletic excellence helping to transform white culture and consciousness. In articles and editorials—published in the weekly black press, as well as in *Crisis, Opportunity* (journal of the National Urban League), and *The Messenger*—Edwin Henderson stood out as perhaps the foremost proponent of muscular assimilationism. Described by the historian David K. Wiggins as the "father of African American sport history," Henderson enlisted athletic achievements in the larger quest for liberty, just as he exalted black champions as "race men" alongside writers and artists and professors, lawyers, doctors, and entrepreneurs. At the same time, the expanding cohort of African American scribes in New York, Chicago, Pittsburgh, Washington, D.C., Baltimore, and beyond joined Henderson in pointing to the various "Gentleman's Agreements" that kept black athletes out of competition and likened those arrangements—in intersectional match-ups at the college level and in virtually all professional competition—to the laws that segregated schools and streetcars and deprived blacks of the essential rights of citizenship. During the interwar years especially, the muscular assimilationists mounted an impressive campaign of persuasion and protest, and eventually claimed some notable victories.

Yet the statements made at the rally in Providence just as clearly indicated the substantial limits white America might impose on black athletic achievements like Pollard's. That part of the story reveals how the exertions of black bodies—no matter in what fields they labored—have largely been devalued in prevailing thought and practice, ultimately rendered insufficient to sustain the claims made by African Americans for full participation in the social, cultural, and political life of the nation.

To highlight the contrast between "manhood" and "modesty" would be to link race and gender relations in the United States within longstanding hierarchies of privilege and subordination. Those terms, though, also shed considerable light on the framework used by many African American leaders to construct the civil rights appeal during the late nineteenth and early twentieth centuries. Both during the antebellum slave regime and throughout the era following Reconstruction, African Americans encountered severe limitations on any public assertions they might make in behalf of their dignity and sense of self-worth. By the turn of the century they were consigned to positions of subservience, a "proper sphere"—circumscribed by increasingly rigid segregation policies as well as by horrific reprisals when they defended their families and property or claimed their rights as citizens. The hundreds of lynchings and whitecappings occurring yearly in the postbellum South cannot be reckoned merely as tragic episodes; they also amounted to a long reign of organized terrorism. Whenever black men challenged the prevailing "racial etiquette," they did so at considerable peril.[10]

But in appropriating the discourse of manliness and emphasizing the ways that pride and prowess were customarily inscribed in athletic competition, racial reformers seized on an ideal that had long served to link individual character to the greatness of the nation. In athletic encounters such as boxing or track (or in many football match-ups), one man stood against another. The rules of the sport dictated the result, in part, but it was the talent of the athlete that ultimately shaped the outcome. When racial reformers invoked the competitive ideal, they effectively stood prevailing custom and protocol on its head. Such a stance represented an enormous departure from the Washingtonian creed, which at the turn of the century had encouraged southern blacks, at least, to withdraw from the kinds of contacts with white people that might endanger their lives. In context, what Washington advocated was an accommodationism that was also a strategic segregation. That kind of prudence had many critics both south and north of the Mason–Dixon Line, however. Du Bois was among the most famous of those critics, but the others included the Alabama sharecropper Ned Cobb, whose epic persistence and survival in the face of Jim Crow was always a matter of negotiating manhood and martyrdom. There were times to be wary about confrontation, he told his biographer many years later. But he was most proud in his recollections of the times he had felt compelled to push back—come what may.[11]

From a very different vantage, muscular assimilationism promoted "race men" in sport and thus posed no direct challenge to gender patriarchy at home or in American colonial projects abroad. Symbolically perhaps, any exertions on behalf of racial advancement can be seen as raising critical questions about social Darwinism and the increasingly rigid linkage of "race," nation, and empire at the turn of the century. Yet the new African American leaders were eager to place their claims about vigor and virility into larger debates regarding "manliness and civilization" or to boost black contributions to national strength and world leadership.[12] When black educators and social commentators embraced the notion of manly character expressed in sport, they were seeking ways to "prove equality" and to demonstrate "the same traits of courage" said to characterize the "dominant race." This was not a simple task, however. In practical terms, it required opportunities to display the talent and training of black athletes. Such occasions were scarce in a land where the distance between the races was both carefully measured and forcefully maintained.

In ideological terms, the black activists who crafted the assimilationist appeal relied on a complex of relations, in both elite and popular discourse, regarding the paths to social status and power. One of those could be traced back a century and more to Enlightenment and Victorian ideals concerning education—which, in turn, were characteristically resplendent in allusions to Greek and Roman antiquity. Here, the apostles of the athletic creed emphasized the importance of cultivating the body as well as the intellect to make "the whole man": *mens sana in corpore sano.* In part, such considerations of muscular moralism inspired the institutionalization of sporting competition in the majority of American colleges and universities just as they had in the public schools and at Oxford and Cambridge in England. More significant still, innumerable references within American history and lore, from frontier colonial heritage to log-cabin presidential campaigns of the antebellum era, underscored the connections between physical prowess, character, and command as the defining features of manliness and the requisites of cultural authority in the United States. By the end of the nineteenth century, sports metaphors had become commonplace. Describing the competitive impulses that underwrote "rugged individualism" as well as "social mobility," the litany of muscular values and virtues resonated with various tenets of the American civil religion well before Theodore Roosevelt enunciated the doctrine of the "strenuous life."[13]

In the imaging of character and opportunity in mainstream culture, moreover, the athletic creed—which so often infused political orations, business manifestos, the sermon, and the textbook—held that playing fields were laid out as level surfaces, that the starting line would be the same for all: "let the best man win." This dimension of the sporting ethos received considerable play during the Americanization movement of the Progressive era and beyond. One of its intended audiences—the millions of immigrant newcomers to the U.S.—was plied with athletic platitudes concerning initiative, hard work, perseverance, and the "melting pot" of the playing fields. Subsequently, memoir, fiction, and film have conjured vivid images of athletic heroism in terms of courage and honor as well as discipline and skill. For every hero of a Horatio Alger novel, the lore of athletics has produced many "real men" like Knute Rockne.[14] Apart from their dubious relation to the actual experiences of the mass of working people, immigrants, and African Americans—men and women alike—such myths and clichés not only testify to a sense of community imagined through ritual and spectacle; they also speak to the centrality of sport in modern American culture.

For those black Americans who aspired to the benefits of an inclusive social democracy (idealized though it was), one more feature of the doctrines of athleticism possessed considerable appeal. As it has been promulgated over the years, the sporting creed stresses that accomplishments on the field of play readily translate to success in other realms of achievement. Indeed, it avows that the qualities of character learned and demonstrated on the football gridiron or the baseball diamond are the same attributes that describe the great men of history. Numerous texts—printed, painted, photographed—depict generals and statesmen, religious leaders and inventors as guides to achievement, their biographies informing the notions of "progress" and "civilization." The energy and daring displayed by heroic athletic figures have served much the same function for generation after generation of participants and partisans who weave out of sports stories impressive fables about equality and opportunity in the United States. Many civil-rights crusaders, for their part, subscribed to such sentiments—or at least saw the strategic value embodied in them.

The idea of striving and success in the world of sports, and the campaign for racial reform it reinforced, was articulated by black commentators, both from the South and the North, from the turn of the century onward as an educational as well as a cultural desideratum. "Athletics is the universal language," an editorialist asserted in the Howard University campus newspaper in 1924. "By and through it we hope to foster a better and more fraternal spirit between the races in America and so to destroy prejudices; to learn and to be taught; to facilitate a universal brotherhood."[15]

Acting on this aspiration, many spokesmen for racial reform strenuously promoted the organization of sports in the historically black schools and colleges located mainly in the South. Operating behind the veil of segregation, aware of the need for circumspection, even educators of the old-school, Washingtonian persuasion believed that athletics served well the doctrine of uplift. Self-reliance and self-control, they emphasized, translated from athletics to a more prosperous, praiseworthy life. As early as 1901 the catalog of Wiley College proudly announced that "athletic sports are not only allowed, but encouraged." At this small school in Marshall, Texas, institutional policy stressed the notion "that the best education is that which develops a strong, robust body as well as other parts of the human makeup." In similar terms, Samuel Archer, a professor at Atlanta Baptist (later Morehouse) College, extolled sport for the qualities it inculcated. The conditions under which games were being played in the black colleges at that time, he argued, were "very favorable for the development of the strong and aggressive in union with the gentle and the just."[16]

To peruse the yearbooks turned out annually by historically black colleges and universities in the early twentieth century, or to read coverage in the black press of the great sporting traditions at Fisk, Talladega, Wilberforce, Bluefield—and then Grambling, Southern, Norfolk State, and Winston-Salem—is to learn that athletics played a significant role in the African American collegiate experience. Rituals fashioned by black undergraduates, like the revelry and rivalry that marked such contests as the Howard–Lincoln football game during the 1920s, demonstrate how fervently black collegians wanted to participate in national pastimes.[17]

But for commentators such as Henderson, the athletic creed always possessed an added dimension. One instance, stunning in its particulars, characterized his larger campaign. Of the seven players who had competed in the first football game between Biddle (later Johnson C. Smith) and Livingstone in 1892 and who were still alive in 1939, Henderson recorded, three were clergymen, one was a medical doctor, one a pharmacist, and another a professor at his alma mater. Some forty-six years after the inaugural gridiron contest between historically black colleges, the sole surviving member of the Livingstone squad was president of the college. These were exemplary individuals, Henderson pointed out; they were also among the best representatives of the race.[18]

Like the extraordinary talent displayed over the years in Negro League baseball, the achievements of even the most outstanding athletes at historically black colleges went largely unrecognized in the mainstream press. Some black activists, therefore, reserved their greatest enthusiasm for what could be won on the playing fields of the predominantly white colleges in the North. In this reckoning, for better and for worse, northern academia was presumed to be more progressive on the issue of race than was the professional arena. Henderson was both consistent and emphatic in mentioning the benefits—past, present, and future—of integration in collegiate athletics. The importance of blacks in white colleges should never be underestimated, he maintained: "colored boys fighting in gladiatorial arenas before hundreds of thousands of admiring whites have done much to soften racial prejudices."[19]

The heroic public image projected by the black athlete in the most prestigious centers of learning in the North—his picture placed in a student newspaper or yearbook, his contribution to collegiate tradition permanently inscribed on the walls of a gymnasium or stadium, his accomplishments narrated on a radio broadcast or proclaimed in a banner headline—these signs of success took their place alongside the boldest pronouncements calling for racial justice. As they had done in the past, Henderson argued, excellent athletes at predominantly white schools, if they "carry scholastic attainment and above all, be sportsmen of the admired type, would do more than anyone else to advance the cause of blacks everywhere. I doubt much," he continued, "whether the mere acquisition of hundreds of degrees or academic honors have influenced the mass mind of America as much as the soul appeal made in a thrilling run for a touchdown by a colored athlete." It was imperative, therefore, that "stellar athletes" continue to claim "headline space in metropolitan dailies." Henderson urged those who could "to make for Amherst, Michigan, Illinois, Penn, and Harvard to carve athletic marks. The battle may be harder but the glory will be larger for the individual and the race."[20]

Toward the goal of muscular assimilationism, writers like Henderson documented the impressive careers of numerous blacks who had made their name first as athletes, then as scientists or statesmen. Inspired by the historian Carter G. Woodson as well as by Du Bois, muscular assimilationists thus strove to exploit the possibilities of the athletic creed, hoping through their efforts to create a set of chronicles that linked African American biography to national history. Among the outstanding references were the stories of three graduates of M Street/Dunbar High School, which for many years was the first alma mater of the black elite of

Washington, D.C. All three won athletic honors and participated in student affairs at Amherst College during the mid-1920s, then went on to distinguished careers and impressive humanitarian efforts. Charles Richard Drew later earned international renown during the Second World War for perfecting a technique of storing blood plasma, thus saving countless lives. W. Montague Cobb conducted pathbreaking research in physical anthropology and comparative anatomy, helping to disprove the claims of "scientific" racism about inherent differences in the composition and workings of black and white bodies. And finally, William Hastie won acclaim as professor and later dean of law at Howard University before becoming a civilian aide to the Secretary of War during the early 1940s and then Governor of the Virgin Islands, and ultimately a United States Circuit Court judge.[21] To Edwin Henderson, among other racial reformers, the genealogy of these breakthrough accomplishments began with sport. The task at hand was to convert white America to that understanding.

Activists encouraged black youth to compete and to win, first to prove themselves as individuals, but also to promote the cause of the race. Carefully placing blacks within the contours of mainstream athleticism, the editor of *Opportunity* offered a short survey of the popular doctrine. "It is natural perhaps that a young and vigorous nation of pioneers should develop great respect and regard for physical prowess, for stamina and for that courage which finds expression in the heat of athletic competition," Elmer Carter wrote in 1933. "That the Negro was deficient in the qualities of which athletic champions are made was long one of the accepted shibboleths of the American people. That rare combination—stamina, skill and courage—it was commonly believed were seldom found under a black skin. Like many other myths concerning the Negro," Carter concluded with pride, "this myth is being exploded not by theory, nor by argument, but by performance."[22]

Not just metaphorically but in literal terms, the playing fields thus offered enormous promise for black activists as a strategy of appeal to "sportsmanship and fair play," broadly conceived. Athletic triumphs by "race men" bespoke the "fitness" of African Americans to become citizens of the republic in every sense. Those victories stood among the most prominent assertions of black pride and prowess that the majority of Americans would ever observe. Significantly, too, black triumphs in sports—and their celebration—held up a mirror to the rhetorical claims of mainstream culture to traditions of social justice. During the era when Jim Crow statutes and off-the-record "Gentleman's Agreements" consistently barred African Americans from athletic competition, observers of the playing fields could measure the distinction between sporting principles and practices in terms of hypocrisy and foul play, if not outright racism. Conversely, when a boxing championship or Olympic gold medal was acknowledged for all its worth, or when a pattern of desegregation in sport seemed to be emerging, African American commentators could applaud either longstanding ideals or the tendency of the times, always in the effort to create a more expansive culture, a more open society.

To a considerable extent, then, muscular assimilationism bespoke a remarkable subtlety of thought regarding the ways hallowed beliefs and symbols could be enlisted in the campaign to transform the dominant culture. It also testified to the assertiveness of "New Negroes," no longer willing to defer to the customs of the country or to deny a history of oppression. In a striking commentary on the heavyweight championship bout between Jack Johnson and Jim Jeffries in 1910, the Reverend Reverdy Ransom declared that in addition to black athletes, African American musicians, poets, artists, and scholars would "keep the white race busy for the next few hundred years . . . in defending the interests of white supremacy. . . . What Jack Johnson seeks to do to Jeffries in the roped arena will be more the ambition of Negroes in every domain of human endeavor."[23]

Nearly a quarter of a century later, the white president of Hampton Institute discussed the meaning of African American capability in terms and tone less defiant than Ransom's, though with an eye toward the same goal. In praise of the black champions of the 1932 Olympic Games— especially the sprinters Eddie Tolan and Ralph Metcalfe—Hampton's Arthur Howe insisted that their gold medals were not merely a "source of pride and inspiration" for African Americans. Those performances also symbolized "many less advertised victories . . . in more significant realms." Ultimately, for numerous advocates of the assimilationist ideal such triumphs challenged white society, in Howe's words, "to give the Negro his due in justice and opportunity."[24] To play into beliefs that the mass of Americans held sacred was to court their good graces, socially and culturally—or so racial reformers hoped.

Assertions of black pride and racial protest occurred in many forms and forums. Understandably, most muscular assimilationists targeted the sports pages, aiming at a simple and straightforward "proof of equality" through athletics. Yet at the same time, others aspired to strengthen black pride and to engage the vast disparity between African American achievement and racist custom in different venues and voices. Thus one could find several commentators who cast black sport in literary terms. Two poems, as striking in their stylistic differences as in their perspectives (self-conscious and assertive) on the ideology and practice of race relations, illuminate the several strands of the black athletic creed as it was advanced during the 1930s. Writing for the *Crisis*, Herbert Henegan immersed his poem in Northern European myths and symbols, then with a keen sense of irony used them to sink Teutonic pretensions. His description of the triumph of Eddie Tolan and Ralph Metcalfe in the 100-meter finals of the 1932 Olympic Games thus appropriates traditionally European-American heroic images in order to accentuate the achievements of exemplary black athletes. And from the vantage of a later era, Henegan's verse anticipates a more widespread response to the victories of Owens et al. at Berlin four years later.

Two swarthy ships
Sailing in the breeze
Like mighty Thors
Astride a blast of thunder
On they come, annihilating time
And space.
Upon a sable sea of cinders
See them fly—
Cutting calm waves of wind
Wind their sharp black prows
Leaving a helpless, trailing spray
Of Nordic foam.[25]

In contrast to such grand allusions, breathtaking in their assault on conventional racial hierarchy, the images projected in another verse—written in something akin to black vernacular—stand out for their cynicism and inclination to despair. If Henegan assessed one of the founts of African American self-worth, Harry Levette depicted the sources of black anxiousness, anger, and alienation in the face of the slow pace of change in American society. How else could his readers have responded to "Eddie Tolan Is the Fastest Human—But" as they scanned its lines in the pages of the various newspapers affiliated with the Associated Negro Press?

> *He's a "nigger" right on*
> *He can't run against white runners in Georgia*
> *He can't eat with white runners in Alabama*
> *He can't go to school with white runners in South Carolina*
> *He can't ride the train with white runners in Texas*
> *He can't sit beside a white runner in a street car in Florida*
> *He can't pray in a church with white runners in Tennessee*
> *He can't pose with white runners in Arkansas*
> *Because he's just a "nigger."*
> *Eddie's the "fastest human"—but*
> *Mistreatment shall be his portion as long as life shall last*
> *He's a "coon."*
> *Who cares if he ain't got nothin' to eat?*
> *He wants to be a doctor but money is scarce*
> *Who cares?*
> *Who'll give him a chance?*
> *Filipino, Japanese, Chinese, Mexican, Indian—Opportunity for All—*
> *But Eddie's a "nigger"*
> *Dirty, different.*
> *He can run like hell, but—he's a nigger right on.*
> *He wins honors for America, but nothing for himself*
> *He must plot right on, passing up eating places while he's hungry*
> *Begging for somebody to take his part so he can inch along.*
> *The better he does, the worse it hurts.*
> *Like Cullen, he can exclaim: "I who have burned my hands upon a star."*[26]

Henegen and Levette frame their notions of the role of sport in epic visions and everyday language, respectively—one a representation that revises some claims of "Western Civilization," the other a description that impels the reader to conceive of a black man who had in fact claimed "headline space in metropolitan dailies" but could not be served in most restaurants in the South or find a decent job. Taken together, the verses express a similar contempt of white hypocrisy as a response to black achievement; but they also imply that more "race men" would become champions, and that there might be different ways of communicating the relationship between African American excellence in sport and the shared desire among blacks to harvest the rewards of such accomplishments.

Other African Americans rose to prominence in the fields of medicine and science, jurisprudence and politics during the interwar years. Additionally, black artists and intellectuals transformed the larger culture: Zora Neale Hurston and Langston Hughes, Duke Ellington and Louis Armstrong, Aaron Douglas, Jacob Lawrence, and Romare Bearden ultimately ascended to prominent positions in the modernist canon. Yet even as they did so, for many black commentators the significance of athletics could not be overstated: more Americans read the sports pages than book reviews, everyone knew . . . and knows. Then as now, the same issues set the turnstiles at athletic arenas apart from the ticket offices at concert halls and museums. Thus in 1935, while the editor of the *Crisis* agreed with those who maintained "that a Negro historian or editor or philosopher or scientist or composer or singer or poet or painter is more important than a great athlete," he would also assert that none of those "worthy individuals" possessed more power or influence than the athlete. "Infinitesimal intellectual American" needed no instruction on race relations, he asserted optimistically:

> It is the rank and file, the ones who never read a book by Du Bois, or heard a lecture by James Weldon Johnson, or scanned a poem by Countee Cullen, or heard a song by Marian Anderson, or waded through a scholarly treatise by Abram L. Harris, Carter Woodson, Charles H. Wesley, or Benjamin Brawley. For those millions, who hold the solution of the race problem in

their hands, the beautiful breasting of a tape by Jesse Owens and the thud
of a glove on the hand of Joe Louis carry more "interracial education" than
all the erudite philosophy ever written on race.[27]

Such a litany and juxtaposition brilliantly encapsulated the paradoxical relation between black athletics and racial reform. The immediate response to the triumphs by Jesse Owens in the Berlin Olympics of 1936 was in fact rather ambivalent, owing to the champion's quick and rather quixotic turn to professionalism and his awkward involvement with both Democrats and Republicans during the presidential campaign that year. Still, the stopwatch and tape measure did not lie: Owens had won gold medals for the 100- and 200-meter dashes, the broad jump, and the 400-meter relay, setting four Olympic records. And for many black Americans as well as an increasing number of whites, these accomplishments constituted an impressive rebuttal to the claims of "Aryan" supremacy and the old racial order. What was billed as the Nazi Olympics had been largely transformed into the Owens Olympics, though an impressive array of black American males had stood upon the medals podium in the track-and-field venue: they had won every running event through 800 meters, as well as the high jump and long jump. Then again, as one historian of the Olympics has pointed out, while the German newspaper *Volkische Beobachter* carried a photo of Jesse Owens after his victories, the *Atlanta Constitution* did not, something more than irony shadowing that fact.[28]

The prevailing image of Joe Louis was much less ambiguous. Indeed, to view his victories from the perspective of the African American press was to witness the creation of another "black messiah," after the model of Frederick Douglass and before the idolization of Martin Luther King, Jr. One newspaper quoted an African American minister as saying: "He's doing more to help our race than any man since Abraham Lincoln." From a similar vantage, Adam Clayton Powell Jr., who was just then becoming a significant race leader in his own right, would state that with Louis' victories, "our racial morale took a sky high leap that broke every record from Portland to Pasadena. Surely the new day was just around the corner . . ."[29]

The inspiration blacks derived from the victories won by Joe Louis cannot be overstated. In contrast to Jack Johnson, who earlier provoked considerable controversy within Afro-America, Louis became a universal icon of race pride during the late 1930s. What is more, his ascendancy in the ring over such opponents as Primo Carnera and Max Schmeling made him a national hero—especially during the years when an increasing number of Americans wanted to project their own sense of might and manliness against the forces of fascism. Until U.S. troops actually entered combat, such elemental assertions were mounted on the athletic front; Joe Louis stood as a standard-bearer for both his race and his nation. Black Americans took pride in the image of Louis pounding away—with patriotism.[30]

Much of the praise echoed in verse and song. Black children created rhymes about Louis that would accompany their jumping rope. A host of musicians created songs as jazz, ballads, gospel, Tin Pan Alley, and the blues—by one recent count forty-three in all.[31] According to musicologist Paul Oliver:

> There are no blues devoted to the achievements of Paul Robeson, George Washington Carver (the Black scientist) or Ralph Bunche (Black politician and diplomat), though those figures would probably have been known to the more literate and especially the city-dwelling singers.... Not even Jesse Owens was commemorated in a blues, at any rate on record.... For the blues singer, Joe Louis was the singular inspiration of a man who had within his achievements all the drama, the appeal and the invincibility of the traditional ballad hero.[32]

Richard Wright wrote "King Joe," thirteen stanzas long. In it he drew on the animal characters of black folklore such as Brer Rabbit, and thus created a link between figures from the empowering lore within antebellum slavery and the modern sporting arena. Then, too, he referred to Louis's upbringing in Detroit and fashioned a compelling analogy between the boxer and the heroic figure of John Henry, avatar of black industrial labor in the new era:

> Old Joe wrestled Ford engines, Lord, it was a shame;
> Say Old Joe wrestled Ford engines, Lord, it was a shame;
> And he turned engine himself and went to the fighting game.

At another point, Louis's boxing prowess expresses not only race pride but also a means of veiling resentment:

Wonder what Joe Louis thinks when he's fighting a white man
Bet he thinks what I'm thinking, cause he wears a deadpan.

No less a personage than Count Basie set the lyrics to music, and Paul Robeson, singing blues for the first time—though by most accounts not very ably—recorded the song. Other musicians traced the champ's life from his rural origins in Alabama, to Detroit, then the early years of his career in the ring. Significantly, some of these songs were recorded within a day or so of a particular Louis triumph, helping to sum up the meanings of those victories for countless black Americans.[33]

To hear and read the comments of white Americans—observations emanating from street corners and sports pages as well as from the White House—that Louis brought credit to his race was for many black Americans to reinforce the notion that the assimilationist appeal was working. Other commentators may have been less exuberant about the meaning of Louis' feats, yet they too acknowledged his positive influence. Writing from London, Marcus Garvey asserted that there may have been better ways for black people to influence mass culture and extend their claims to whole lives within the American polity but conceded that Louis was making a powerful and positive impression on white people. Critically, though, many "race men" employed the same juxtaposition of intellectual and physical achievement that characterized the *Crisis* editorial of 1935 as well as many of Henderson's writings. Thus the *New York Daily Mirror* felt compelled to grant that "if Joe Louis beat Professor Einstein at his own game, whatever that is, white men would pay no attention. But when he knocks out a white man sixty pounds heavier than he is, white men do pay attention." Such a contrast of excellences and their effects is significant, although the implied tension between mind and body ultimately would add a knot to the paradox of racial reform in the United States.[34]

By numerous accounts, the radio broadcasts of Joe Louis in ritual combat during the 1930s and 1940s captured a swelling sense of pride and anticipation. The new medium clearly and forcefully underscored the meaning of athletics in the racial struggle, as the recollections of Malcolm X and Lena Horne—and for that matter, Jimmy Carter—eloquently attest.[35] Yet nowhere is the phenomenon rendered in such powerful terms as those that Maya Angelou used to describe what she heard as a child during the 1930s.

Angelou's portrait begins with the kitchen chairs and upturned wooden boxes that filled a small country store in Stamps, Arkansas, as folks gathered to hear the upcoming contest on the radio; her account mingles references to local ritual and racial theory, in addition to the fight itself. But in revealing the weight of Louis's burden as "race man," her remembrance also encapsulates the perceived power of sport to change society. An "apprehensive mood" characterizes the scene that frames Angelou's story, though on occasion it is "shot through with shafts of gaiety." Yet mid-bout, when the Brown Bomber is in peril, the despair of the crowd becomes palpable.

> *My race groaned It was our people falling. It was another lynching, yet another Black man hanging on a tree. One more woman ambushed and raped. A Black Boy whipped and maimed. It was hounds on the trail of a man running through slimy swamps. It was a white woman slapping her maid for being forgetful. If Joe lost we were back in slavery and beyond help. It would all be true, the accusations that we were lower types of human beings. Only a little higher than the apes. True that we were stupid and ugly and lazy and dirty and unlucky and worst of all, that God Himself hated us and ordained us to be hewers of wood and drawers of water, forever and ever, world without end.[36]*

Far more than Jack Johnson, Louis became a unifying force within the black community. Well before the career of Muhammad Ali, the image of Louis confronted white America with new meanings for blacks as citizens. What the heavyweight champion accomplished in the ring was projected into broader realms: throughout the late 1930s and 1940s, Louis reinforced the notion of the United States as superpower. During those years his power was also black power, strength and endurance readying itself for a larger struggle. Pride and hope shape culture and consciousness in subtle ways: "what can be" is often communicated through symbols and icons, and if Louis was the foremost athletic representative of a people seeking, in diverse and innovative ways, to transform American society, he was but one of many.

As successes of black athletes accumulated in most major sports, they seized the attention of fans across the racial divide. World records and Olympic championships stood out; so too did boxing titles in various weight divisions. Significantly, the stellar performances of African American baseball players might have been obscured by the segregation policies of the National and American leagues, if not for the fact that an increasing number of white athletes and fans were beginning to see for themselves that, individually and collectively, the stars of Negro baseball could be the equals of their counterparts in the major leagues. Annual all-star contests pitting the best black players against one another exhibited the astounding pitching feats of Satchel Paige, the speed on the base paths of "Cool Papa" Bell, the savvy of Oscar Charleston and William "Judy" Johnson, the intimidating power of Josh Gibson. Another showcase was the post-season: mixed competition between barnstorming teams of the best white ballplayers from the majors and the stars of the Negro leagues. Of the 445 contests on record between 1886 and 1948, black teams won 269 of them, prompting some of the most prominent athletes in the U.S.—Dizzy Dean and Hack Wilson, for instance—to laud the abilities of their African American rivals. Was Josh Gibson "the black Babe Ruth," someone would ultimately ask, or should the question be framed in a different way? Was Babe Ruth "the white Josh Gibson"?[37]

Add to these lessons in "interracial education" the significant presence of African American athletes on the collegiate gridiron during the thirties. To a considerable extent, William Bell of Ohio State, Willis Ward of Michigan, Bernie Jefferson of Northwestern, Oze Simmons of Iowa State, and Kenny Washington of UCLA, and a host of others stood as the successors to Fritz Pollard, their contributions often the difference between winning and losing seasons for their teams. In its own way, this phenomenon began to persuade university authorities, North and South, to discard Jim Crow contractual arrangements and

"Gentleman's Agreements," which for many years had made intersectional play a formidable stumbling block to interracial competition.[38]

Southern schools were compelled during the 1930s to consider in pragmatic terms not just the status of a high national ranking but also the potential income from a lucrative bowl game at the end of a season. Seeking greater exposure in match-ups against the best teams of the North, Midwest, and Pacific Coast ultimately meant that they needed to compete against the finest players on those squads, an increasing number of whom were African Americans. Thus black stars such as Ed Williams of NYU, who broke the color line against the University of North Carolina in 1936, and Wilmeth Sidat-Singh, who led Syracuse University against Maryland, and then Duke several years later, came to be factored into the calculus of interracial, inter-regional sporting competition. Though such advances in collegiate football occurred in a slow and halting manner in ensuing years, by the end of the decade athletic officials had begun inching toward a new expediency in the conduct of intercollegiate contests, in small ways breaking through the grid of rigid segregation. As Howard Zinn noted wryly during a later period of the civil-rights movement, for some white Southerners losing a college football game may indeed have been "a fate worse than integration."[39]

The key to these successes, racial reformers believed, was to win acknowledgment by white America that black athletic heroes deserved every opportunity to display their talents. The sporting realm thus represented one avenue of entry to the social mainstream. In some forums, this recognition actually seemed to be occurring. At the same time that the initial, tentative, forays into interracial competition were being played out, a number of the most widely syndicated white sports commentators joined their African American colleagues in calling for desegregated athletics. Such sportswriters as Heywood Broun, Westbrook Pegler, Jimmy Powers, Shirley Povich, and Ed Sullivan not only deplored the cowardice of the white athletic officials who maintained Jim Crow; they also began to portray black accomplishment in the hallowed terms of character and courage. In 1929, Broun had editorially skewered "the gutless coach of a gutless school" when Chick Meehan and New York University benched a black football player, Dave Myers, against the visiting University of Georgia football squad. During the following decade, a growing number of white sportswriters started to cross the bridge that the muscular assimilationists had fashioned for them; in writing about Joe Louis and other African American champions, they began to speak of discipline and skill and hard training, of "study, practice, study."[40]

In the aftermath of the Second World War and in the midst of the ideological and propaganda battles of the Cold War, national pastimes ultimately began to accommodate African American participation. The struggle for civil rights in the United States was clearly linked to the campaign for black liberation in Africa, as well as anti-colonialist efforts elsewhere around the globe. In the era of the newsreel, it was increasingly difficult for the nation's political leaders to explain the segregation of black and white men in uniform—whether in the armed forces or in major league baseball.[41] Desegregation of the military and the first breaches in the color line in professional sports both occurred in a series of events that seemed swiftly orchestrated to those who had not followed the years of groundwork laid by racial reformers such as Charles Hamilton Houston and the lawyers he trained at Howard University, by the many social scientists who "confronted the veil" in their studies of race relations and urban development, and by such muscular assimilationists as Edwin Henderson, Wendell Smith, and Sam Lacy.[42] Long before the mass movements of the 1960s, "the whole world was watching" as racial reformers in the United States assaulted the color line in constitutional law and on the cultural front.

The grandest breakthrough within the sporting realm occurred in 1947, when Jackie Robinson entered the ranks of major-league baseball. Almost instantly he joined Joe Louis as one of the idols of black communities, rural and urban. At the same time Robinson stood as a bridge between African American aspiration and the values and standards doted on by the mainstream culture: in the batter's box, on the base paths, ranging through the infield, he embodied both dauntlessness and enormous discipline. To watch Robinson play, and to admire other black athletes who followed, one chronicler of the game averred, "a man did not feel that he was taking a stand on school integration or open housing. But . . . to disregard color even for an instant, is to step away from old prejudices."[43] The day that Jackie Robinson took the field wearing the uniform of the Brooklyn Dodgers marked a major triumph for muscular assimilationists, whose goal of desegregation now became the ideal of full-scale integration. From their perspective, with "baseball's great experiment" one chapter in the history of sport ended, and another, far happier one began.

Shift the perspective, however, away from the daring stolen base by Robinson and the exciting touchdown run or drive to the basket by one of the African American athletes who helped desegregate the National Football League and the National Basketball Association. Or change the angle of vision away from editorials by white as well as black journalists pronouncing the comparability of accomplishment in sports, regardless of race. A very different set of conclusions might be drawn. In response to the efforts of racial reformers, many journalists and some academicians have sought to alter the terms of discourse about character and courage that had informed proud accounts of interracial athletic competition. Drawing on a long history of racial lore, as well as what were proclaimed as the findings of modern science, numerous white commentators on sport sought strenuously to diminish the influence of black athletes on American race relations. To write the notion of "natural ability" into the popular lexicon was fundamentally hypocritical to the rhetoric of the "level playing field." For each convert to the appeal of muscular assimilationism, other observers of sport have come forward to question or reject outright the applicability of the athletic ideal to race relations in the U.S. Within mainstream culture numerous image-makers have simply rested on stereotype, offering up an array of pernicious characterizations that seek to divorce excellence in sports from all the values and virtues inscribed in the creed. At the same time, many researchers were writing their results into the pseudo-science long before Jackie Robinson's athletic career and baseball's "great experiment." This situation persists to this day. Though racial reformers had hoped to engage white society, through sport, in a dialogue about egalitarian principles and practices, the victories they won have ultimately been partial ones, or Pyrrhic.

Well before the civil-rights campaigns of the 1950s and 1960s, the dominant culture began to accommodate black participation in carefully staged spectacles such as the national pastime. Yet the white counterpoint to black athletic accomplishment has all too often involved a calculated reinterpretation of the meanings of sport, revealing the racism that, though discredited time and again, has nevertheless shown few signs of retreat. These responses to the achievements of black athletes have effectively shifted the terms of debate from the democratic notions of a shared (athletic) culture to invidious distinctions based on blacks' innate talents in certain sporting activities. The stopwatch and tape measure do not lie, but neither do they interpret. And the influence of a particular set of representations remains, for the most part, the predicate of social power.

For the greater part of the last two centuries, manly independence, dignity, and courage loomed as the antitheses of the condition of servitude, a generalization that not only described the status imposed on the majority of blacks under slavery, or mandated a role for them, but that continued to be projected onto African Americans long after Emancipation had been proclaimed. Within this framework, the prevailing ideology included another standard of comparison, not historically contingent and therefore susceptible of change, but rather one that was fixed, immutable. It was against the supposed "natural" tendencies of black Americans that the majority could define and celebrate its own "cultural" achievements.[44]

The assessments in the 1916 rally speeches of Fritz Pollard's temporary rise to "white manhood" as well as of his "wonderful modesty"—his ability to take care of himself in sports, and yet more tellingly, what was conceived as his appropriate deportment in school and society—thus drew on a long tradition of imposition and containment, rooted in the desire to preserve white supremacy. To a significant extent, the response to the victories of other black athletes—down to our own time—would similarly deny the connection between the traits of manly character shown on the field of play and the requisites of responsibility in other domains.

The spectrum of white reaction to black prowess in sport has included race-baiting of the old school, of course. During the 1930s, for instance, the syndicated columnist Arthur Brisbane employed a "missing link" theory to explain the triumphs by African Americans in the Olympic Games, while other journalists described black stars as "glorified Pullman porters" and as the fleet "Sons of Ham." Grantland Rice, the famed spinner of sporting verse, once labeled Joe Louis a "Brown Cobra" and referred to his "blinding speed, the speed of the jungle, the instinctive speed of the wild."[45] How easily such images mingled with popular "scientific" and social scientific assertions is revealed in the pronouncement by one of the most influential track coaches in the country, who argued far beyond his observations of black performance in order to disparage the meaning of African American success in sport. "It was not long ago," wrote Dean Cromwell in 1941, that the black athlete's "ability to sprint and jump was a life-and-death matter to him in the jungle. His muscles are pliable, and his easy-going disposition is a valuable aid to the mental and physical relations that a runner and jumper must have."[46]

Such declarations never stood alone or without elaboration. In the ensuing years, the Harvard anthropologist Carleton S. Coon began his commentary on the black athlete's inherited advantages with a depiction of slender calves and loose-jointedness. He ended it with a striking analogy: the anatomical features that suited African Americans for certain sports, Coon observed, were characteristic of "living things (cheetahs, for instance) known for their speed and leaping ability." During the mid-1970s, two chroniclers of the history of college football still dwelled in the realm of gross stereotype, though by that time they had relocated their imaginings from the jungle to the palladium. Thus John McCallum and Charles Pearson would assert that "[b]ecause of their tap-dancer sense of rhythm and distinctive leg conformation, blacks excel as sprinters. It follows naturally that on the football field they stand out as broken field runners."[47]

Despite the efforts of the muscular assimilationists, a striking few observations have ranged beyond the essentials of black aptitude in athletics. In addition to the generalized portrayals of speed and strength advanced by authorities such as the Olympic coach Cromwell, a kind of "tracking" has emerged through the discourse on race and sport wherein many white educators have reduced African American social

contributions, or potential, to the arena. This can be seen in the argu-
ments made during the last dozen years of the twentieth century, when
several prominent sports figures contrasted black athletic ability with
"the necessities" required of good coaches and managers. The categorical
rift between African American successes in sports and the path to greater
opportunity in other careers has been only one theme of the work of
Dinesh D'Souza, Charles Murray, and Richard Herrnstein, but others have
promulgated the notion of an athletic "bell curve," a bio-determinism
asserting the genetic basis of a particular black physicality. During
the mid-1990s, J. Phillipe Rushton concocted numerous graphs and
charts in an attempt to link reproductive patterns (and size of genitalia),
performance on IQ tests, and such matters as marital stability and
administrative capability. The response to Rushton—as well as to Murray
and Herrnstein—was expansive and nearly instantaneous; those authors
sounded so much like the scientific racists and eugenicists of the turn of
the last century, and the sources of funding for their projects (as best as
could be ascertained) raised suspicions about both the science and politics
of much racial research. Still, the innatist turn of thinking later appeared
in a book that claimed to explain "why blacks dominate sports" and
why—supposedly because of the dictates of political correctness—"we are
afraid to talk about it." The "we" in the subtitle of Jon Entine's *Taboo* was
never specified. But much more is implied; although the author offered
no causal links between a specific biological inheritance and the fast
times registered by Kenyan long distance runners, for instance, he maintained that they must exist.[48]

While such insinuations might not immediately bring to mind the
odious correlations about race and society offered up almost a century
ago by Madison Grant and Lothrop Stoddard, at the very least they show
how the lines drawn between different forms of expressive culture so
often reveal enormous racial condescension and confinement. Yet again,
perhaps no one has sounded out such paternalism as movingly as Maya
Angelou did in the account of her graduation from middle school in the
late 1930s. As she depicts the invited speech delivered by a visiting politician, white condescension makes its best attempt to undermine the
meaning of the victories by such black cultural heroes as Joe Louis. And
she is appalled.

The politician spoke glowingly of the "newest microscopes and chemistry equipment" that were being ordered for the all-white school nearby, Angelou recollects. He then casually observed that "one of the first-line football tacklers at Arkansas Agricultural and Mechanical College had graduated from good old Lafayette Country Training School." Noting that a well-known artist would be coming from Little Rock to teach the white students, the speaker "went on to say how he had bragged that 'one of the best basketball players at Fisk sank his first ball right here at Lafayette Country Training School.'" Prefiguring the consternation felt by many student generations that followed her, Angelou delineates the narrow route from black education to "fitting" social roles that was being constructed for the most ambitious of African American youth. Ultimately, she exclaims:

> The white kids were going to have a chance to become Galileos and Madame Curies and Edisons and Gauguins, and our boys (the girls weren't even in on it) would try to be Jesse Owenses and Joe Louises. . . . Owens and the Brown Bomber were great heroes in our world, but what school official in the white-goddom of Little Rock had the right to decide that those two men must be our only heroes?[49]

That politician's speech, like the sports advertising campaigns of more recent vintage, clearly illuminates the hegemonic features of American popular culture—the means, sometimes subtle and sophisticated, of confining act and aspiration (or of rushing gratification). Over the years, in acquiescing to the desegregation of playing fields more readily and dramatically than it has accommodated black leadership roles in other occupations, white America has encouraged the channeling of the energy and ambition of black youth. But that very same concentration on athletics, frequently to the exclusion of other pursuits, has effectively narrowed the paths toward social mobility for many African Americans. To ghettoize achievement is obviously to place severe constraints on the assimilationist ideal.

In the end, prevailing social practices have also spoken to the contingent aspect of racialized responses to the African American experience in sport. It would not be black inferiority that was stipulated in the cases of track and boxing champions, then of the many heroes of court, diamond, and gridiron. In fact, the intention has been to circumscribe African American success. Occurring South and North, the phenomenon has been assessed by social scientists and racial activists alike as a refashioned ideology of limits rather than of potential. During the 1960s, the sociologist Harry Edwards was perhaps the first to liken organized sport to a plantation system, blacks having been acquired to supply the necessary labor. In recent years, a growing number of scholars have studied both the black presence in sporting competition and the representation of African American accomplishment on the playing fields; so in many ways Fritz Pollard's story remains enormously instructive.[50]

The vision of a substantial number of racial reformers had been to chart one African American's career trajectory from athlete to entrepreneur or lawyer, doctor, professor, or as in the case of Ralph Bunche, from football laurels to the Nobel Peace Prize. Then the task was to persuade white America that these instances fully spoke to the potential of all African Americans to fill important roles in the civic landscape. Dedicated to an idealized notion of athletic principles and practices, however, muscular assimilationism became bound to the paradox that the sport pages, largely reflecting the culture at large, have long formed a tight boundary around the demonstration of black aspiration and achievement. Ultimately, less equivocal images in other realms of endeavor—from Hollywood to Harvard, from the newsrooms in my hometown to the State Department and United Nations—suggest that the principal sites of racial change lay beyond the playing fields.

Notes

1. John Carroll, *Fritz Pollard: Pioneer in Racial Advancement* (Urbana: University of Illinois Press, 1992).
2. *Brown Daily Herald*, November 21, 1916, quoted in Carroll, *Fritz Pollard*, 106.
3. See Leon F. Litwack, *Trouble in Mind: Black Southerners in the Age of Jim Crow* (New York: Alfred A. Knopf, 1998); David Blight, *Race and Reunion: The Civil War in American Memory* (Cambridge, Mass.: Harvard University Press, 2001). See also James Allen, Hilton Als, John Lewis, and Leon F. Litwack, *Without Sanctuary: Lynching Photography in America* (Twin Palms Publishers, 2000). At the same time, the convict lease system in the South took a toll of one thousand black lives per year—the consequence of coerced labor in often hazardous conditions, malnutrition, exposure, and

institutional brutality. See David Oshinsky, *Worse Than Slavery: Parchman Farm and the Ordeal of Jim Crow Justice* (New York: Free Press, 1996); Alexander C. Lichtenstein, *Twice the Work of Free Labor: the Political Economy of Convict Labor in the New South* (New York: Verso, 1996).

4. *New York Age*, November 23, 1916, quoted in Carroll, *Fritz Pollard*, 103.

5. To that purpose, muscular assimilationists consistently made references to patriotism and sacrifice for the good of the nation, often assessing the boldness and bravery of athletes with the same vocabulary they used to describe those African Americans who had won honor for themselves and the race in armed conflict—from Crispus Attucks at the outset of the American Revolution, to the soldiers of the Massachusetts Fifty-Fourth and their ill-fated charge on Battery Wagner in 1863, to the "sable arm" of the U.S. military during the Spanish-American-Cuban-Philippine conflicts and again in the First World War. For a thorough discussion of African Americans' wartime contributions, see Bernard C. Nalty, *Strength for the Fight: A History of Black Americans in the Military* (New York: Free Press, 1986). On the revising of African American history, see Jacqueline Goggin, *Carter G. Woodson: A Life in Black History* (Baton Rouge: Louisiana State University Press, 1993); August Meier and Elliott Rudwick, *Black History and the Historical Profession, 1915–1980* (Urbana: University of Illinois Press, 1986). Among the many important studies of racial conflict, see William Tuttle, *Race Riot: Chicago in the Red Summer of 1919* (New York: Atheneum, 1970).

6. James Weldon Johnson, *Black Manhattan* (New York: Arno Press, 1968 [orig. 1930]). For appraisals of both "New Negro" assertions and the cultural controversies embodied in the 1920s, see David Levering Lewis, *When Harlem Was in Vogue* (New York: Vintage Books, 1982); Nathan Huggins, *Harlem Renaissance* (New York: Oxford University Press, 1971).

7. Alain Locke encapsulated this belief in his introduction to *The New Negro* (New York: Atheneum, 1983 [1925]): "In Harlem, Negro life is seizing upon its first chances for group expression and self-determination. It is—or promises at least to be—a race capital. . . . Without pretense to their political significance, Harlem has the same role to play for the New Negro as Dublin has had for the New Ireland or Prague for the New Czechoslovakia" (7). See also Kevin K. Gaines, *Uplifting the Race: Black Leadership, Politics, and Culture in Twentieth Century America* (Chapel Hill: University of North Carolina Press, 1996) on the issues of class and race in the discourse of uplift and assimilation. During the interwar years, many blacks characterized the NAACP as the National Association for the Advancement of *Certain* People.

8. It is significant, in this regard, that Douglass used the 4th of July as a touchstone for many of his assertions about black citizenship and loyalty within the national polity, or that he worked with the Republican Party for many years. Likewise, the emphasis of the NAACP on legal strategies and the transformation of constitutional law suggest the strategy pursued by many black intellectuals and commentators to hold a mirror to the shibboleths of American freedom and equality in order to expose its flaws, then to create frameworks for racial reform.

9. The term "assimilation" carries an enormous burden; it has long been subject to various interpretations. I use the term generally to mean the desire by black leaders

for inclusion in the mainstream culture as the end point of numerous social and political programs. These impulses can also be characterized as *integrationist*, and clearly the
campaigns to desegregate such sports as major-league baseball were enlisted as part of
a larger quest for equality—much in the manner of the court cases leading up to
Brown. Like the notion of the "melting pot," the term "assimilation" implies cultural
concessions—and more; it suggests that a group has not "arrived" until its acquisitions
and accomplishments resemble those of the receiving population, the social and cultural mainstream. For many years the social science literature on assimilation spoke
about structures and behaviors and did not fully engage what might be given up and
what might be gained, or for that matter the differences between the groups seeking to
be accepted. See Milton M. Gordon, *Assimilation in American Life: The Role of Race,
Religion, and National Origins* (New York: Oxford University Press, 1964). Some of these
issues are discussed in David Levering Lewis, "Parallels and Divergences: Assimilationist Strategies of Afro-American and Jewish Elites from 1910 to the Early 1930s" in
Bridges and Boundaries: African Americans and American Jews, ed. Jack Salzman, with
Adina Back and Gretchen Sullivan Sorin (New York: George Braziller, 1992), 17–35.

10. Litwack, *Trouble in Mind*; Joel Williamson, *The Crucible of Race: Black/White
Relations in America Since Emancipation* (New York: Oxford University Press, 1984);
Glenda Elizabeth Gilmore, *Gender and Jim Crow: Women and the Politics of White
Supremacy in North Carolina, 1896–1920* (Chapel Hill: University of North Carolina
Press, 1996).

11. Louis Harlan, *Booker T. Washington: The Making of a Black Leader, 1856–1901*
(New York: Oxford University Press, 1975); Harlan, *Booker T. Washington: The Wizard of
Tuskegee, 1901–1915* (New York: Oxford University Press, 1983); Theodore Rosengarten,
All God's Dangers: The Life of Nate Shaw (New York: Alfred A. Knopf, 1974).

12. Gail Bederman, *Manliness and Civilization: A Cultural History of Gender and Race in
the United States, 1880–1917* (Chicago: University of Chicago Press, 1995).

13. Clifford Putney, *Muscular Christianity: Manhood and Sports in Protestant America,
1880–1920* (Cambridge: Harvard University Press, 2001); Kathleen Dalton, *Theodore
Roosevelt: A Strenuous Life* (New York: Alfred A. Knopf, 2002); Edmund Morris, *The Rise
of Theodore Roosevelt* (New York: Modern Library, 1979); idem, *Theodore Rex* (New York:
Random House, 2001).

14. Many of those who have written about the European immigrant experience in
America have engaged the themes of social mobility and the assimilative potential
of sport, as well as the ways athletics has in some ways reshaped the sense of ethnic
community. See, for examples, Richard Sorrell, "Sport and Franco-Americans in
Woonsocket, 1870–1930," *Rhode Island History* 31 (Fall 1972): 117–26; Gary Ross
Mormino, "The Playing Fields of St. Louis: Italian Immigrants and Sport, 1925–1941,"
Journal of Sport History 9 (Summer 1982): 5–16; Tilden G. Edelstein, "Cohen at the Bat,"
Commentary 76 (November 1983): 53–56; Steven A. Riess, *A Fighting Chance: The
Jewish-American Boxing Experience* (Syracuse: Syracuse University Press, 1985): 230–252;
idem., *City Games: The Evolution of American Urban Society and the Rise of Sports* (Urbana:
University of Illinois Press, 1989): 93–123; idem., "Professional Sports as an Avenue of
Social Mobility in America: Some Myths and Realities," in Donald G. Kyle, ed., *Essays*

on *Sport History and Sport Mythology* (College Station, TX: Texas A&M Press, 1990): 83–117; Peter Levine, *Ellis Island to Ebbets Field: Sport and the American Jewish Experience* (New York: Oxford University Press, 1992); and George Eisen and David K. Wiggins, eds., *Ethnicity and Sport in North American History and Culture* (Westport, CT: Greenwood Press, 1994). One should also note in this regard that at the turn of the century, football was considered a prime means of acculturating Native Americans in the Indian boarding schools. For analysis of athletic rites of passage at schools such as Carlisle, see David Wallace Adams, *Education for Extinction: American Indians and the Boarding School Experience, 1875–1928* (Lawrence: University of Kansas Press, 1995), 181–191. Michael Oriard, *Reading American Football: How the Popular Press Created an American Spectacle* (Urbana: University of Illinois Press, 1998); Alan M. Klein, *Baseball on the Border* (Chapel Hill: University of North Carolina Press, 1993), 229–247; John Bloom, *To Show What an Indian Can Do: Sports at the Native American Boarding Schools* (Minneapolis: University of Minnesota Press, 2000). For other experiences, see Samuel O. Regalado, *Viva Baseball! Latin Major Leaguers and Their Special Hunger: A Tale of Two Laredos* (Princeton: Princeton University Press, 1997). See also Regalado, "Baseball along the Columbia: The Nisei, Their Community, and Their Sport in Northern Oregon," in John Bloom and Michael Willard, eds., *Sports Matters: Race Recreation and Culture* (New York: New York University Press, 2002), 75–85; idem., "Incarcerated Sport: Nisei Women's Softball and Athletics during the Japanese American Internment Period," *Journal of Sport History*, 27 (Fall 2000): 431–444; idem., "'Play Ball!' Baseball and Seattle's Japanese American 'Courier League,' 1928–1941," *Pacific Northwest Quarterly* 87 (Winter 1995–1996), 29–37.

15. Howard University *Hilltop*, April 29, 1924.

16. Wiley College Catalog, 1901, 16–17, quoted in Michael Heintze, *Private Black Colleges in Texas, 1865–1964* (College Station: Texas A&M University Press, 1985), 171; Samuel H. Archer, "Football in Our Colleges," *Voice of the Negro* 3 (March, 1906), 199–205. See also Patrick B. Miller, "To 'Bring the Race along Rapidly': Sport, Student Culture, and Educational Mission at Historically Black Colleges during the Interwar Years," *History of Education Quarterly* 35 (Summer 1995): 111–133. Like the colleges, the segregated YMCAs of the South promoted athletics and physical activity as sources of social discipline. Although the subject of sport does not loom large in her treatment of the "Y" movement, Nina Mjagkij's *Light in the Darkness: African Americans and the YMCA, 1852–1946* (Lexington: University of Kentucky Press, 1993) describes the institutional context for such developments.

17. See Miller, "'To Bring the Race Along Rapidly'"; Ocania Chalk, *Black College Sports* (New York: Dodd, Mead, 1976).

18. See Henderson, *The Negro in Sports*, 98, 270, 271.

19. Edwin B. Henderson, "Sports," *Messenger* 8 (June 1926): 181. See also Henderson, "The Colored College Athlete," *Crisis* 2 (July 1911): 115–119; Ira F. Lewis, "Our Colleges and Athletics," *Competitor* 2 (December 1920): 290–292; *Pittsburgh Courier*, December 1, 1923.

20. Henderson, "Few Headliners in Northern Colleges," *Messenger* 9 (February 1927): 52.

21. For information on the these figures, see *New York Amsterdam News*, December 24, 1924; Henderson in *The Messenger* 5 (May 1927), 148; *Norfolk Journal and Courier*, G. James Fleming and Christian Burckel, eds., *Who's Who in Colored America* (Yonkers-on-Hudson, NY: Christian E. Burckel and Associates, 1950); *Amherst College Biographical Record* (Amherst, MA: Amherst College Press, 1963); Chalk, *Black College Sports*, 164–165, 285–287. Concerning the significance of M Street/Dunbar High School, see Mary Church Terrell, "History of the High School for Negroes in Washington," *Journal of Negro History* 2 (July 1917), 259–260, and Thomas Sowell, "Black Excellence: The Case of Dunbar High School," *The Public Interest* 35 (Spring 1974), 3–21. Like the dozens of black captains of predominantly white college teams Henderson had traced—seventeen in track and field between 1921 and 1939, five in football, nearly a dozen more in baseball, basketball, tennis, cross country, and fencing—and the scores of other African American collegians who later won distinction in education, religion, medicine, business, law, and civic affairs, these athletes became the standard against which muscular assimilationists wanted to be judged by white America. See Henderson, *The Negro in Sports*, 98, 270, 271. Two noteworthy biographies that make references to sports as background are Spencie Love, *One Blood: The Death and Resurrection of Charles R. Drew* (Chapel Hill: University of North Carolina Press, 1996) and Brian Urquhart, *Ralph Bunche: An American Odyssey* (New York: W. W. Norton, 1993).

22. Elmer Carter, "The Negro in College Athletics," *Opportunity* (July 1933): 208.

23. Ransom quoted in Lawrence Levine, *Black Culture and Black Consciousness: Afro-American Folk Thought from Slavery to Freedom* (New York: Oxford University Press, 1977), 431. "That Mr. Johnson should lightly and carelessly punch the head off Mr. Jeffries," contended the *New York World*, "must have come as a shock to every devoted believer in the supremacy of the Anglo-Saxon race."

24. Arthur Howe, "Two Racers and What They Symbolize," *Southern Workman* (October 1932): 387.

25. *The Crisis* 40 (November 1933): 262.

26. Poem from the *Minneapolis Twin Cities Herald*, August 27, 1932. See Tuskegee Institute News Clipping File, Reel 42, p. 993 (1932).

27. *The Crisis* (August 1935): 241.

28. See William J. Baker, *Jesse Owens: An American Life* (New York: Free Press, 1986), 122–145.

29. Quotes in Wilson Jeremiah Moses, *Black Messiahs and Uncle Toms: Social and Literary Manipulations of a Religious Myth* (University Park: Pennsylvania State University Press, 1982), 158–159.

30. The fight between Louis and Carnera was of special importance to African Americans, for it was during the summer of 1935 that Mussolini was mobilizing Italian troops to invade Ethiopia. As John Hope Franklin writes, "Almost overnight even the most provincial among black Americans became international-minded. Ethiopia was a black nation, and its destruction would symbolize the final victory of whites over blacks." Franklin and Alfred A. Moss, Jr., *From Slavery to Freedom: A History of African Americans* (New York: McGraw Hill, 1994), 433. See also William R. Scott, *The Sons of*

Sheba's Race: African-Americans and the Italo-Ethiopian War, 1935–1941 (Bloomington: Indiana University Press, 1993); and Joseph E. Harris, *African-American Reactions to War in Ethiopia, 1936–1941* (Baton Rouge: Louisiana State University Press, 1994). This calculation became even more significant when black athletes proved victorious in international competition; when Jesse Owens dashed to glory for the United States at the 1936 Berlin Olympics, for instance, or when Joe Louis pounded the German boxer Max Schmeling to the canvas in their dramatic confrontation of 1938. Accompanying the observations that Owens and Louis brought "credit" to their race were exhortations—and with their victories, exclamations—that those athletes had become *national* heroes. With an increasing number of sporting accomplishments as a backdrop, civil-rights activists endeavored to alter prevailing social arrangements on the home front, arguing through essay and editorial that talented black athletes were capable of engaging white America in a wide-ranging dialogue about the egalitarian principles and practices that supposedly distinguished the United States from other nations. Not surprisingly, this appeal to democratic ideals on and beyond the field of play reached its apogee during the 1930s and 1940s, when the evils of fascism and totalitarianism loomed ever larger in the American consciousness.

31. William H. Wiggins, Jr., "Reflections on the Joe Louis Recordings," liner notes for *Joe Louis: An American Hero* (CD recordings compiled by Rena Kozersky, Rounder Records, 2001). See also David Margolick, "Music: Only One Athlete Has Ever Inspired This Many Songs," *New York Times*, February 25, 2001.

32. Paul Oliver, *Aspects of the Blues Tradition* (New York, 1970), 146, 149. Lawrence Levine offers the cultural context for such celebrations in *Black Culture and Black Consciousness*, 420–440.

33. Chris Mead, *Champion: Joe Louis, Black Hero in White America* (New York: Penguin, 1985); Richard Wright, "Joe Louis Uncovers Dynamite," *New Masses* (October 8, 1935), reprinted in Ellen Wright and Michel Fabre, eds., *The Richard Wright Reader* (New York: Da Capo Press, 1997), 32–34; Wright, "High Tide in Harlem: Joe Louis as a Symbol of Freedom," *New Masses* (July 5, 1938): 18–20. See also David K. Wiggins and Patrick B. Miller, *The Unlevel Playing Field: A Documentary History of the African American Experience in Sport* (Urbana: University of Illinois Press, 2003).

34. When Louis was invited to the White House, President Franklin D. Roosevelt stressed the importance of the upcoming fight against Schmeling: democracy *versus* fascism. Though many African Americans could perceive the irony—Washington, D.C., remained a segregated city—at the same time they hoped that Louis might serve to turn the tide of public opinion toward better race relations. See Moses, *Black Messiahs and Uncle Toms*, 158–159. For more on the response to Louis, see *Joe Louis Scrapbook*, Schomburg Center for Research in Black Culture; Chris Mead, *Champion*, 188–206; Capeci and Wilkerson Capeci, Dominic J., Jr., and Martha Wilkerson, "Multifarious Hero: Joe Louis, American Society, and Race Relations during World Crisis, 1935–1945," *Journal of Sport History* 10 (Winter 1983): 5–25; Anthony O. Edmonds, "The Second Louis–Schmeling Fight: Sport, Symbol, and Culture," *Journal of Popular Culture* 7 (Summer 1973): 42–50; idem., *Joe Louis* (Grand Rapids, MI: William B. Eerdmans, 1973); William H. Wiggins Jr., *Joe Louis: American Folk Hero* (Bloomington, IN: Phi Delta Kappa

Educational Foundation, 1991); Thomas Hietala, *The Fight of the Century: Jack Johnson, Joe Louis and the Struggle for Racial Equality* (New York: M. E. Sharpe, 2002); Jill Dupont, "The Self in the Ring, the Self in Society: Boxing and American Culture from Jack Johnson to Joe Louis" (Ph.D. dissertation, University of Chicago, 2000).

35. Malcolm X, for his part, remembered that in East Lansing, Michigan, after one Louis victory, blacks "went wildly happy with the greatest celebration of pride our generation had ever known." *The Autobiography of Malcolm X* (New York: Grove Press, 1965), 23. In his campaign autobiography of 1975, Carter related how blacks who worked for his father crowded near the family radio to hear the broadcast of the second Louis–Schmeling bout in 1938. After Louis "almost killed his opponent" midway through the first round, Carter recalled: "There was no sound from anyone in the yard, except a polite 'Thank you, Mister Earl,' offered to my father. . . . All the curious, accepted proprieties of racially-segregated society had been carefully observed. . . . Then, our several dozen visitors filed across the dirt road, across the railroad track, and quietly entered a house about a hundred yards away out in a field. At that point, pandemonium broke loose inside that house, as our black neighbors shouted and yelled in celebration of the Louis victory." Jimmy Carter, *Why Not the Best* (Nashville: Broadman, 1975), 36–37.

36. Quoted in Levine, *Black Culture and Black Consciousness*, 435.

37. The statistics concerning the off-season exhibition games derive from John Holway, *Voices from the Great Black Baseball Leagues* (New York: Da Capo, 1975), xvi. In *Blackball Stars: Negro League Stars* (Westport, CT: Meckler, 1988), xii. Holway offers a slightly different figure. I am grateful to Jerry Malloy for pointing these figures out to me. Regarding black baseball generally, see also Robert Peterson, *Only the Ball Was White*; Donn Rogosin, *Invisible Men: Life in Baseball's Negro Leagues* (New York: Atheneum, 1983). Harold Seymour, Geoffrey Ward, and Ken Burns, *Baseball: An Illustrated History* (New York: A. A. Knopf, 1994), 129, offers different won-lost records (309–129) for the Negro League teams.

38. See Patrick Miller, "Slouching Toward a New Expediency: College Football and the Color Line during the Depression Decade," *American Studies* 40 (Fall 1999): 5–30.

39. Howard Zinn, "A Fate Worse than Integration," *Harper's Magazine* 219 (August, 1959), 53–56. See Jules Tygiel, *Baseball's Great Experiment: Jackie Robinson and His Legacy* (New York, Oxford University Press, 1983). On professional football, see Charles K. Ross, *Outside the Lines: African Americans and the Integration of the National Football League* (New York: New York University Press, 1999); Thomas G. Smith, "Outside the Pale: The Exclusion of Blacks from the National Football League, 1934–1946," *Journal of Sport History* 15 (Winter 1988): 255–81; idem., "Civil Rights on the Gridiron: The Kennedy Administration and the Desegregation of the Washington Redskins," *Journal of Sport History* 14 (Summer 1987): 189–208. On the long history of the efforts to desegregate intercollegiate sport, see Charles H. Martin, "The Rise and Fall of Jim Crow in Southern College Sports: The Case of the Atlantic Coast Conference," *The North Carolina Historical Review* 76 (July 1999): 253–284; idem., "Jim Crow in the Gymnasium: The Integration of College Basketball in the American South," *International Journal of the History of Sport* 10 (April 1993): 68–86; idem.,

"Racial Change and Big-Time College Football in Georgia: The Age of Segregation, 1892–1957," *Georgia Historical Quarterly* 80 (1996): 532–62; idem., "Integrating New Year's Day: The Racial Politics of College Bowl Games in the American South," *Journal of Sport History* 24 (Fall 1997): 358–77; idem., "The Color Line in Midwestern College Sports, 1890–1960," *Indiana Magazine of History* (2002): 85–112.

40. See "It Seems to Heywood Broun," *The Nation* 129 (November 6, 1929), 514. See Mead, *Champion* 74, on the declining use of stereotype, 266–267, and on Pegler, who rejected "the freak theories and pseudo-scientific speculation that inevitably attend a Negro's rise. It is a doubtful compliment to a Negro athlete who is qualified to attend a college to attempt to account for his proficiency in on the field by suggesting that he is still so close to the primitive whenever he runs a foot-race in a formal meet between schools his civilization vanishes and he becomes again for the moment an African savage in breachcloth and nose ring legging it through the jungle."

41. See Penny M. Von Eschen, *Race Against Empire: Black Americans and Anticolonialism, 1937–1957* (Ithaca, N.Y.: Cornell University Press, 1997); Brenda Gayle Plummer, *Rising Wind: Black Americans and U.S. Foreign Affairs, 1935–1960* (Chapel Hill: University of North Carolina Press, 1996); Thomas Borstelmann, *The Cold War and the Color Line: American Race Relations in the Global Arena* (Cambridge, Mass.: Harvard University Press, 2001). See also Damion Thomas, " 'The Good Negroes': African-American Athletes and the Cultural Cold War, 1945–1968" (Ph.D. dissertation, University of California–Los Angeles, 2002).

42. Genna Ray McNeil, *Groundwork: Charles Hamilton Houston and the Struggle for Civil Rights* (Philadelphia: University of Pennsylvania Press, 1983); Jonathan Scott Holloway, *Confronting the Veil: Abram Harris, Jr., E. Franklin Frazier, and Ralph Bunche, 1919–1941* (Chapel Hill: University of North Carolina Press, 2002).

43. Roger Kahn, quoted in Jules Tygiel, *Baseball's Great Experiment*, 344.

44. From the early Republican Era down to our own time, manliness has been defined in opposition to sensibilities and attributes supposedly feminine, such as modesty. Set against conventional notions of female domesticity, manhood claimed dominion over the public sphere; within the dominant discourse, the attributes of manliness likewise set whiteness apart from and above blackness.

45. Henderson, "The Negro Athlete and Race Prejudice," *Opportunity* 14 (March 1936): 78. Rice quoted in Chris Mead, *Champion*, 62–63. After the Carnera fight, Rice wrote:

"For he is part of years long lost, back on an age-old beat
Where strength and speed meant life and love—and death ran with defeat.
For those who slugged the dinosaur, or lived on mammoth's meat.
There was a day when brawn and might were all they cared to know;
There was a day when fang and claw made up the ancient show—And so today we slip
our cash to Bomber Joe. . . ."

46. Dean Cromwell and Al Wesson, *Championship Techniques in Track and Field* (New York: Whittlesey House, 1941), 6. Compare this with statements that the Nazi

architect and functionary Albert Speer attributed to Adolf Hitler: "People whose antecedents came from the jungle were primitive . . . . Their physiques were stronger than those of civilized whites. They represented unfair competition and hence must be excluded from future [Olympic] games." Albert Speer, *Inside the Third Reich* (New York, 1971), 114, quoted in John Hoberman, "Toward a Theory of Olympic Internationalism," *Journal of Sport History* 22 (Spring 1995): 26.

47. Coon quoted in David K. Wiggins, " 'Great Speed But Little Stamina': The Historical Debate over Black Athletic Superiority," *Journal of Sport History* 16 (Summer 1989): 167. David Wiggins's work on scientific racism in sport was pathfinding in many ways; John McCallum and Charles H. Pearson, *College Football, USA, 1869–1973* (New York, 1973), 231.

48. J. Phillippe Rushton, *Race, Evolution, and Behavior: A Life Historical Perspective* (New Brunswick: Transaction Publishers, 1995); Jon Entine, *Taboo: Why Black Athletes Dominate Sports and Why We're Afraid to Talk about It* (New York: Public Affairs, 2000). Among the critiques have been Richard Lewontin, "Of Genes and Genitals," *Transition* 69 (Spring 1996): 178–193; Patrick B. Miller, "The Anatomy of Scientific Racism: Racialist Responses to Black Athletic Achievement," *Journal of Sport History* 25 (Spring 1998): 119–51; Paul Spickard (review of Entine), *Journal of Sport History* 27 (Summer 2000): 338–400; Mark Dyreson, "American Ideas about Race and Olympic Races from the 1890s to the 1950s: Shattering Myths or Reinforcing Scientific Racism?" *Journal of Sport History* 28 (Summer 2001): 173–215.

The historians of science who have made the most telling rebuttals to the new scientific racists include Jonathan Marks, *Human Biodiversity: Genes, Race, and History* (New York: Aldine De Gruyter, 1995); idem., *What It Means to Be 98% Chimpanzee: Apes, People, and Their Genes* (Berkeley: University of California Press, 2002), especially Ch. 6; Joseph L. Graves, Jr., *The Emperor's New Clothes: Biological Theories of Race at the Millennium* (New Brunswick: Rutgers University Press, 2001); William H. Tucker, *The Science and Politics of Racial Research* (Urbana: University of Illinois Press, 1994); idem., *The Funding of Scientific Racism: Wickliffe Draper and the Pioneer Fund* (Urbana: University of Illinois Press, 2002).

49. Angelou, *I Know Why the Caged Bird Sings* (New York: Random House, 1970), 174.

50. Harry Edwards, *The Revolt of the Black Athlete* (New York: Free Press, 1970); Henry Louis Gates, Jr., "Delusions of Grandeur," *Sports Illustrated* (August 19, 1991): 78; Hoberman, John. *Darwin's Athletes: How Sport Has Damaged Black America and Preserved the Myth of Race* (Boston: Houghton Mifflin, 1997). For extensive discussions of these issues, see Wiggins and Miller, *The Unlevel Playing Field*, especially Parts 7 and 8.

THE UNEVEN VIEW OF AFRICAN AMERICAN BALLERS

C. KEITH HARRISON AND ALICIA VALDEZ

INTRODUCTION

At Michigan State University in 1972, several African American leaders—students, faculty, administrators, and researchers—came together in protest of the Big Ten Conference. The protest was motivated by a report titled "The Status of Blacks in the Big Ten Athletic Conference: Issues and Concerns" (Kirk and Kirk, 1993), and followed a myriad of protests at other universities across the nation over the structural exclusion of African American needs and wants. For example, many protests erupted based on the exclusion of black hairstyles such as the "afro," the lack of African American coaches in intercollegiate athletics, and the lack of African American female involvement on the pom-pom teams (Kirk and Kirk, 1993).

The report that spurred the protest at Michigan State dealt with three critical issues: the racism experienced by African American athletes, the lower graduation rate for this population of student-athletes, and the lack of African Americans in positions of power such as coach or administrator (Kirk and Kirk, 1993). These issues are both relevant and problematic, as they are yet to be resolved and have been only minimally addressed over the last thirty years. What has interrupted or stalled the process in addressing these problems with viable solutions?

This research will attempt to illuminate the spectrum of problems surrounding the poor academic performance of African American male student-athletes, and to provide solutions to increase the frequency of academic success for these aforementioned athletes.

The poor academic performance of African American student-athletes has been attributed to several intrinsic and extrinsic variables

(Adler and Adler, 1987; Chavous, 2000). Much research has been done on the contributors in positions of power, such as a coach and/or administrator (Kirk and Kirk, 1993). These issues are indicators of poor academic performance (Adler and Adler, 1987; Chavous, 2000). However, solutions to the problems that have persisted over time have been either nonexistent or ineffective.

Further, the image of African American student-athletes and the stereotyping that contributes to that image are still ingrained within collegiate sports (Davis, 1995). The racism in intercollegiate athletics has shifted from being more overt to covert in today's educational and societal institutions. Along with stereotyping and racism, myths of the African American student-athlete consume media images as well (Kirk and Kirk, 1993).

The African American student-athlete is a unique type of college student. Several concerns arise when they arrive on predominantly white campuses. The most critical point to address is how to increase the frequency of the academic message (graduating from college) for African American male student-athletes. They are consistently bombarded with lowered expectations from peers, faculty members, and society as a whole who have preconceived notions about their academic abilities (Harrison, cited in Polite and Davis, 1999). These lowered expectations continue to cause self-internalization of non-academic messages, attitudes, and images. Creating a successful academic image of African American male student-athletes will help to promote the acceptance of a new label, "scholar-baller," for this unique group in the college environment (Harrison and Lampman, 2001). The word "baller" is a term from popular culture that refers to the status of professional athletes, entertainers, or criminals. This term refers to the perception of prestige limited to these three identities. A scholar-baller refers to a student who has both the responsibility of studying and participating in revenue-producing intercollegiate athletics. This student-athlete maintains the athletic identity by remaining popular on campus. This term utilizes "baller" in regards to the perception of prestige versus the role as criminal and entertainer.

Through proper marketing efforts, the educational component may change the public perception of the student-athlete. This thesis focuses on two central research questions: First, what is the current image of the baller? Second, how do we increase the frequency of academic success to better market the educational component of the student-athlete experience so that scholar-baller is an acceptable label?

Historically, the commercialization of college sports led to the huge increase in participation of African American student-athletes in college athletics. This commercialization enhanced pressure on universities to win, which entailed recruiting the best athletes regardless of color (Davis, 1995). This also meant that African American student-athletes were recruited predominantly into revenue-producing sports where winning counted the most. Predominantly white universities reaped the benefits of winning national titles and championships by allowing African American student-athletes on their revenue-producing teams (Davis, 1995). Ending discriminatory and racist practices to allow students of color to participate in intercollegiate athletics did not change the reality of racism for other African Americans in society (Kirk and Kirk, 1993). Sport has often been considered ahead of society: the notable example is that Jackie Robinson of the Brooklyn Dodgers integrated Major League Baseball (MLB) seven years before the U.S. Supreme Court ordered an end to segregation in the school systems (Brown v. Board of Education). Dr. Harry Edwards (a sport sociologist) parallels the relationship between society and sport:

> *The first principle of sport sociology is that sport inevitably recapitulates the character, structure, and dynamics of human and institutional relationships within and between societies and the ideological values and sentiments that rationalize and justify those relationships. (Edwards, cited in Davis, 1999, p. 898)*

Some African American student-athletes used the opportunities allotted to them to improve the social and economic status of people of color (Kirk and Kirk, 1993). An example of this concept would be the 1968 Olympic protest by track and field stars Tommie Smith and John Carlos. However, these opportunities and benefits came with several consequences and stigmas detrimental to the African American image.

As Davis (1995) explains, "Increased access stemming from self-interest has not, however, resulted in a transformation of the underlying cultural attitudes and values that helped to produce overt discrimination against the African American college athletes."

Some research contends that the perception of equality is different between blacks and whites in regards to the impact of race in collegiate sport (Davis, 1995). In other words, since Jackie Robinson integrated baseball and the demographics in football, basketball, and baseball have become more diverse, the dominant assumption by a casual observer is that equality has been reached. This observation overlooks the minimal numbers of African Americans and other citizens of color in leadership positions such as owner, head coach, or sportscaster. Many white Americans assume that allowing black athletes to participate has eliminated all racial barriers in college sport; African Americans do not buy into this notion. This ideology stems from the "illusion of integration" where African American athletes dominate in the top revenue-producing sports, football and basketball (Davis, 1995). Even though many different collegiate sports have African American male participants, basketball and football are the most visible by being the top revenue-producing college sports (Harrison, 1998).

African American student-athletes in revenue-producing sports have consistently fallen into the bottom of many academic categories such as lowest Grade Point Averages (GPAs) in college, lowest graduation rates, and least prepared for college (Benson, 2000). In 1998 the NCAA Division I graduation rate for all student-athletes was 57 percent, 60 percent among white male football players, and only 40 percent among black male football players (Benson, 2000). Further, the U.S. Department of Education indicates that approximately 75 percent of high school graduates who enroll in college full-time immediately after graduation (and continue full-time at the same institution) will receive a bachelor's degree within five and a half years (Knight Commission Report, 2001). In comparison, in the year 2000, the NCAA reported that 48 percent of Division 1-A football players and 34 percent of Division 1-A basketball players earned degrees. The group hit hardest by these low numbers is African

Americans: only 42 percent of black football players in Division 1-A graduate, compared to 55 percent of white football players (Knight Commission Report, 2001).

In basketball, Derrick Z. Jackson, a columnist for the *Boston Globe*, analyzed the graduation rates of African American players on the sixty-four teams in the 2001 NCAA men's basketball tournament. He found that twenty-six of those teams graduated fewer than 35 percent of their African American players. Seven teams had African American graduation rates of zero (Knight Commission Report, 2001).

Some research uses basic demographic and environmental data as an explanation for poor academic achievement. For instance, African American males are more likely to come from single-parent homes with only a mother (Wilson, 1996). Their family experiences typically include economic adversity and substandard housing. Further, many African American children are raised by a relative other than a parent and have an absent or negative male role model (Harris, 1999). These factors have been shown to help explain the discrepancy between African American and white students' overall college achievement (Chavous, 2000).

CAMPUS ADJUSTMENT

Research on African American students at predominantly white colleges and universities shows that African American students often encounter difficulty socially and academically (Chavous, 2000). Poor academic achievement has been attributed to the adjustment to campus culture at such universities (Chavous, 2000). One critical background factor important to the college adjustment of African American students is the difference between the high school and neighborhood environment and the college environment (Chavous, 2000). White students who report coming from more racially homogenous environments within the college environment have reported an easier college adjustment than students from more racially heterogeneous environments. This pattern is repeated among African American students at historically black colleges and universities, who report an easier college adjustment due to the norms of the dominant cultural group on that campus. James Duderstadt (2000) writes:

> One of the most sensitive issues in intercollegiate athletics concerns race. Basketball and increasingly football are dominated by talented black athletes, whose representation in these sports programs far exceeds their presence elsewhere in the university. To be sure, sports provide many minority students with opportunities to attend and benefit from a college education. (Duderstadt, 2000, p. 213)

The campus environment can be very isolated for student-athletes of color, and due to social stratification there is frequently little contact between student-athletes of color and the predominately white university campus (Allport, 1954). Although Gordon Allport does not specifically address the category of student-athletes, the concepts do apply. Harry Edwards (1989) discusses the history of segregation in the American school system (Edwards, 1989). Often, the only academic development promoted for student-athletes regards eligibility (King and Springwood, 2001).

Research has indicated that a student's beliefs about race and self are factors in their social and academic outcomes at predominantly white universities (Chavous, 2000). Mainstream or dominant views of African American students on traditionally white campuses, and lack of connection to African American culture, persist to the detriment of African American students academically and socially on campus (Chavous, 2000). Harrison (1998) found in one study that African American male student-athletes internalize negative stereotypes and low expectations often experienced after their arrival on predominantly white campuses (Harrison, cited in Polite and Davis, 1999). Harrison also contends that these social constructions are based on a campus culture that often isolates, exploits, and objectifies African American males (Polite and Davis, 1999). Individuals who for the first time enter a new setting, must adapt to the setting. The level of familiarity that an individual has with the environment before entering the new setting is critical in successful adaptation (Chavous, 2000). If African American male student-athletes are not familiar with the predominantly white environment before entering a predominantly white college and university, the adaptation process to the social and academic life of campus will likely not be successful (Chavous, 2000).

Moreover, some research indicates that black students' academic performance differs from their performance at historically black colleges and universities (HBCUs) (Polite and Davis, 1999). This may further indicate the structural barriers that inhibit black students' cultural adjustment at predominantly white universities. These students have lower grade point averages than their peers at HBCUs (Polite and Davis, 1999).

Some suggest that black students at HBCUs receive more academic and social support. In contrast, predominantly white institutions fail to meet the needed social support for African American males (Polite and Davis, 1999). Research has shown that black males at predominantly white universities have more negative feelings about college. Students and student-athletes in this situation feel that they are unfairly treated, experience demoralization in academics, and think less of their academic ability (Polite and Davis, 1999).

SELF-IDENTIFICATION IN THE CAMPUS ATHLETIC ENVIRONMENT

Another issue related to academic performance is the status of athletes at universities, characterized by Adler and Adler (1987) as "institutional powerlessness." For instance, some coaches control all aspects of the athlete's life (Adler and Adler, 1987): they influence the athlete's personal time, academic schedules, and playing role on the team. Regardless of a player's expectations, he must abide by the coach's goals and expectations to remain on the team (Adler and Adler, 1987). Student-athletes, in turn, make assumptions that if they fail academically, coaches will fix the problem (Adler and Adler, 1987). This lack of responsibility on the part of the student-athlete is created in part by a lack of expectation of academic investment by the coaches. The irony of trying to make a system more convenient for student-athletes has actually distanced them from the academic responsibilities of college.

Adler and Adler (1987) further found that players during their first school year are cognizant of their lack of control over course selection, but still comply with the process (Adler and Adler, 1987). An assistant coach picks out the classes and registers the student-athletes without their consultation and also buys their books, drops or adds classes, and contacts professors if they are going to be absent (Adler and Adler, 1987). This results in many student-athletes not developing the knowledge of, or even interest in, academic skills and responsibilities, and distances them from the faculty and their non-athlete peers. Student-athletes also are often segmented into academic majors that require less rigor and time commitment from the student-athlete (Harrison and Lampman, 2001). A lot of time spent traveling for their sport commitments leads to a tremendous amount of on-campus and classroom time missed by the student-athlete (Harrison, in review). These absences are excused and clearly portray the image that academics take a "back seat" to athletic commitment.

Kirk and Kirk (1993) contend that loneliness and isolation often occur for African American student-athletes because coaches and athletic personnel shelter them from the general student body at critical points of adjustment (Kirk and Kirk, 1993). Moreover, research conducted by Ellickson (1990) indicated that participation in college athletics "saps" the energy needed to perform well academically. Thus, several factors in the university structure influence academic engagement on the part of the student-athlete.

Benson has conducted research on academic inadequacy by evaluating stories from African American student-athletes (Benson, 2000). Some of the narratives collected reveal the feeling of "institutional powerlessness." For example, one student responded, "I would have done a whole lot better if it weren't for coming in and having a group of people say, 'this is the minimum you need to do,' and holding your hand here, and holding your hand there. . . . They were already expecting me not to do well, so why would I want to do more?" (Benson, 2000, p. 225). Benson describes another participant in this way: "the easy classes he was given by his advisor delivered the message that he could scale down his personal expectations, even though he thought college would be hard when he was a senior in high school" (Benson, 2000, p. 226). These narratives illustrate the link between structural practices in the athletic process and poor academic performance of student-athletes (Benson, 2000). When considering solutions for this poor academic performance, one must not assume that the individual student-athlete is wholly responsible.

Kirk and Kirk (1993) explain that athletic counselors should not only understand the social, cultural, and developmental factors affecting African American student-athletes but should also be cognizant of techniques and theoretical approaches that are beneficial to this population. One example given by Vontress concludes that counselors need to be cognizant of their use of "language, behavior, attitude, self-disclosure, and personalism" (Vontress, 1971). Vontress also contends that African American student-athletes relate best to theoretical approaches such as existentialism, gestalt, client-oriented counseling, reality counseling, rational emotive therapy, and behaviorism (Kirk and Kirk, 1993; Vontress, 1971).

ATHLETE PEER SUBCULTURE AND ROLE IDENTITY

Some researchers contend that the life of a student-athlete is a culture of its own with unique developmental needs (Engstrom and Sedlacek, 1991). This culture is influenced and perpetuated by coaches, teammates, alumni, the media, and the general university community (Engstrom and Sedlacek, 1991). A major influence comes from the athlete peer subculture, which the student-athlete consumes on a daily basis.

Adler and Adler (1987) contend that the athlete peer subculture consists of five mechanisms that conflict with academics. These include: (1) discouraging the athletes from putting an effort into academics; (2) providing them with distractions that inhibit them from studying; (3) providing them with role models who seem to be making it through college without an identity-salient academic role; (4) discouraging them from seeking out and associating with other students on campus who could have provided greater academic role modeling; and (5) providing excuses and justifications that legitimate their academic failures (Adler and Adler, 1987).

Compounding this athlete subculture, role conflicts between academics and athletics are created. College athletics dominate the student-athlete identity on campus in social and academic situations (Adler and Adler, 1987). Student-athletes are constantly recognized (or identified) as athletes, which becomes their most salient identity, with academics becoming of lower importance (Adler and Adler, 1987). As labeling theory suggests, this recognition by others leads to the student-athlete identifying athletics as the master identity, therefore reducing the importance of their academic role (Becker, 1963).

A label externally attached to a person creates a definition of the person based on personal perceptions (Becker, 1963). The label of "athlete" in relation to the student-athlete is problematic because of the emphasis on "athlete" at the expense of "student" (Comeaux and Harrison, in press). Adler and Adler (1987) contend that, with the growth of the athletic role, the athlete peer subculture is also further endorsed.

Role reinforcement is also critical in the role identity choice between athlete and student. College athletes receive little positive reinforcement for academic accomplishments, but receive positive reinforcement for their athletic achievements. Adler and Adler (1987) contend that without much positive reinforcement an individual is less likely to put effort into the self-identity of the particular role not being reinforced.

STEREOTYPES AND THE CONNOTATIONS OF THE "ATHLETE" LABEL

The identity and academic performance of African American male student-athletes are greatly influenced through the perpetuation of stereotypes in which they are viewed only as "super-athletes" (Brooks and Althouse, 2000). Student-athletes are visualized as "superior beings" and become objects of admiration by the public at large and the university campus (Harrison, in review). Davis (1999) writes, "All too often black men are cast as super-athletes, super-entertainers, and super-criminals, because of their innately athletic, rhythmic, humorous, and violent character" (p. 899). The most prevalent stereotype African American athletes continue to face is that of intellectual inferiority to their white counterparts (Brooks and Althouse, 2000).

The "dumb jock" myth is a stereotype that has persisted over time. Kirk and Kirk (1993) cite from a *USA Today* poll in which many respondents felt that positions such as quarterback and pitcher require thinking and leadership, skills not usually attributed to African Americans (Kirk and Kirk, 1993). Further, both black and white respondents listed leadership as the highest attribute of white athletes. This attribute was followed by several others in the following order: thinking, instincts, strength, and speed. These skills were listed in the exact opposite order for black athletes (Myers, 1991). Many of these stereotypes have caused a decreased ability for African American male student-athletes to define themselves academically on college campuses (Brooks and Althouse, 2000). The "dumb jock" myth is supported by the structural inequities in institutions of higher education where student-athletes are consistently faced with lowered expectations. A myriad of factors contribute to this myth that is not wholly created through self-internalization.

Stereotypes contribute to the formulation of racial identities that are often key in defining perceptions of the character and abilities of African American student-athletes. These stereotypes are linked to a person's ability to perceive "actual qualities and capabilities" of African American athletes being stereotyped (Davis, 1995), and often contribute to the lack of acknowledgment of the hard work and dedication required to participate in intercollegiate athletics. If society attributes their success only to physical ability, intellectual inferiority becomes salient as well (Davis, 1995). Edwards (1971) states, "Athletic skills are essentially culturally linked capabilities. It is racism, not genes, that explains the domination of black athletes" (p. 38).

Myths often perpetuated about the African American male experience in college athletics persist over time and become salient for these individuals. One such myth is that sport is a vehicle for social mobility.

Two major contentions exist in the literature. Some researchers contend that sport is a vehicle for social mobility as it allows African Americans opportunity to attend a university (Kirk and Kirk, 1993; Edwards, 1971; Harris, 1997). Others, such as Sailes (1990), present the notion that an African American male can be successful in sport, especially if they reach "super-star" status, receiving many rewards for this achievement such as social prestige, recognition, and status (Kirk and Kirk, 1993). However, Sailes puts forth that, "Over 75 percent of Black athletes playing NCAA Division I basketball and football never graduate and fewer than 1 percent ever sign a professional sports contract" (Sailes 1990).

Sailes's research recognizes the opportunity afforded to African American athletes, but recognizes the reality of this opportunity and its fallacy in terms of "true" social mobility for African American males (Sailes, 1990). Hartmann (2000) affirms the idea that sports are one of the most integrated institutions in the United States. However, it is problematic when sport reproduces images and social practices that are obviously racialized. Further, sport should be used to transform these images, not reproduce them (Hartmann, 2000).

A second myth discussed by Kirk and Kirk (1993) is that sport has helped to decrease racism. As with the myth of social mobility, the media often portray the lives and athletic accomplishments of successful black athletes in ways that promote the myth that sport has alleviated racial prejudice (Kirk and Kirk, 1993). However, Kirk contends that behind the media misconception of racial harmony lies a truth of "overt and subtle racism" (Kirk and Kirk, 1993). Chu, cited in Kirk and Kirk (1993), states:

> *Sports, it is presumed, has done something for Blacks. Much of this thinking has unfortunately been anecdotal, journalized and unsystematic. Sport sociology literature contains empirical evidence of the existence of institutionalized discriminatory practice (in the areas of recruitment policy, position assignment, performance expectation, reward, authority structure and salary) in collegiate and professional circles. Some of these racist practices are more or less directly demonstrable; others are more subtle, requiring inferential leaps. (Kirk and Kirk, 1993, p. 104)*

Engstrom and Sedlacek (1991) state that for years the university system has been a system of collective actions that have contributed to negative outcomes for student-athletes. Many myths and stereotypes about athletes have persisted over the years, such as those of the "campus hero" or the "campus idiot." As mentioned above, the dumb jock myth is particularly prevalent for the African American male student-athlete (Engstrom and Sedlacek, 1991).

Negative attitudes toward student-athletes in the campus environment can come from many different constituents. Research conducted at an NCAA Division II school found evidence that faculty, in general, have negative perceptions and stereotypes of male student-athletes (Baucom and Lantz, 2001). Some prejudices found in this study deal with issues of perceived preferential treatment of male student-athletes in regards to academic admissions, financial support, academic services, and coverage by the campus newspaper (Baucom and Lantz, 2001). For example, in this same study the particular university had a graduation rate for student-athletes of 52 percent. Although this number was 12 percent above the national average for Division II schools in 1998, Baucom (2001) contends that faculty still hold prejudices about poor academic performance of student-athletes.

Further, Engstrom and Sedlacek (1991) conducted research that indicates that non-athlete peers express negative attitudes toward student-athletes, particularly in academics. One finding indicated that students were more suspicious and did not believe that student-athletes have the academic ability to obtain an A in class without special help (Engstrom and Sedlacek, 1991). Other findings showed that students had negative responses to student-athletes being their lab partner and to tutorial and advising services allotted to the student-athletes (Engstrom and Sedlacek, 1991).

Additional tutoring and advising services are viewed as "extra help" to the student-athlete and as implying they are less academically prepared or are receiving special privileges that unfairly prepare them more than the general student body. This research may indicate a lack of awareness of the different needs of student-athletes, or even lack of appreciation for the athletic commitment (Engstrom and Sedlacek,

1991). This study shows how the student-athlete is subject to many stereotypes and prejudice from the student body at large.

Social psychologists have shown that when individuals perceive themselves the target of a negative stereotype, they will make self-serving prophecies about themselves (Stone, 2001). This defense mechanism against negative stereotypes has an unintended effect of leading to behaviors that confirm instead of reject the negative belief (Stone, 2001). Recent research on Stereotype Threat Effect shows that when a stereotype becomes salient for evaluating a group, the individual group members become so preoccupied with performing well and breaking the negative stereotype, that they ultimately conform to it instead (Stone, 2001).

Consequently, the Stereotype Threat Effect may contribute to the self-channeling by black men toward sports. Research has shown that minorities tend to underachieve in school in comparison to white students (Steele, 1997). Negative stereotypes may contribute to their belief that they cannot be successful academically. This impedes both their motivation and effort in the educational realm, and may further enhance their motivation to be successful at sports, which has been purported as the only valued option (Steele, 1997).

Sports play a significant role in eliciting racial attitudes that may be detrimental to the African American student-athlete by contributing to the perpetuation of stereotypes. Jay Coakley, a well-known sports sociologist, comments that, "At an even deeper level, sports are sites in cultures where people formulate and put into action ideas about skin color and cultural heritage that they then carry over into the rest of society" (Coakley, cited in Davis, 1999, p. 899).

IMAGE OF THE AFRICAN AMERICAN STUDENT-ATHLETE

There are limited images of the African American male and athlete that have both been self-generated and media-perpetuated. The term "cool pose," coined by psychologist Richard Majors, represents a black male expressive style that stemmed from a need to cope with racism (White,

1999). Cool pose refers to a combination of physical postures, clothing styles, specific social roles and behaviors, styles of walk, content and flow of speech, dances, handshakes, and attitudes that are used to symbolically represent black masculinity (White, 1999). This "coping style" is often used as a mechanism to enhance the black male's sense of pride and dignity. White contends that cool pose give black males a sense of individual power in a society that offers African American males limited options (White, 1999). This expressive style also extends into sport: end-zone dances and slam-dunks are two examples of this style (Andrews, 1997).

Majors explains that cool pose is a response to racial oppression. It combats a negative status image in American society: black males create a symbolic universe of behavior, scripts, and postures that represent creative self-expression (White, 1999). Although the intention of "cool pose" is to boost their image, it also inhibits black males by making them less marketable in mainstream society in terms of finding employment. Cool pose also inhibits the ability of black males to view themselves and to be viewed by others as productive members of society.

It seems, however, that white America still embraces the black male image in particular identities and roles. The image of the black male athlete has become dominant in mainstream popular culture (Childs, 1999). White America has a history of being obsessed with the black body, especially black sexuality. Childs explains that historically, the black male has been viewed as a "primitive, aggressive beast with an insatiable sexual appetite, especially when it came to White women" (Childs, 1999). As an extension of these images, black men have been labeled as physically superior. These images of the black male influenced race relations between blacks and whites and became justifications for discrimination throughout American history. Dyson (1993) contends that today's acceptance of the black male image is just an extension of the stereotypes of a "primitive" black man, but the image has been re-created as a commodity that makes money.

These stereotypical images are reinforced by the media on several levels. Sports magazines and television announcers often use words that describe the physicality of black athletes instead of acknowledging the intellectual strength it takes to be successful in athletics (Childs, 1999). A recent Hanes commercial featuring Michael Jordan again represents the over-sexualized image of the black male. The athletic and sexual role of black men has become ingrained and accepted in popular culture. Black athletes receive payment for commercial and product endorsements, their styles are often mimicked by youth, many have large fan followings, and many are also revered as sex symbols (Childs, 1999).

However, the reinforcement of these images can also have a negative effect on the mentality of black males who begin to buy into the myths. Edwards (1979) suggests that black masculinity is "hustled" by white patriarchy, and the black male role is like a pawn for masculine institutions such as athletics and prisons (Edwards, 1979). Gates (1996) contends that the black community tends to gain an understanding of itself based on the images and narratives created by white "authorities" (Gates, 1996). Pressure becomes self-imposed by the black community to excel in physical activities, often to the detriment of academics (Childs, 1999).

African American males have become increasingly visible in revenue sports, and young African Americans tend to focus on developing skills only in those sports (Harrison, 1998). Coakley (2001) contends that because these African American males have not seen the payoffs connected to education, they tend to conclude that playing sports is a feasible means for social mobility. Until images are available that relay the educational payoffs, young African American males will continue to channel themselves into limited roles such as revenue producing sports (i.e., basketball and football).

In his article "The Assassination of the Black Males Image in Sport," Harrison (1998) explains that there are six factors that contribute to the channeling of young black males in sport, which he has coined "Popular Culture Credo." These factors include: (1) No historical foundation or knowledge of past athletes and their motivations for initial athletic participation; (2) Monolithic Media Adoption, where young black males accept the images presented about them in the media (i.e., athletes, entertainers, and criminals); (3) Identity Internalization, the limited belief of what one can become in life; (4) Role Models Missing in Action, the lack of exposure to positive African American males not perceived as "sellouts" or "Uncle Toms"; (5) School Is Not Cool, a belief that school is for white people, or that learning is a sign of weakness, not prowess; and 6) Goal Setting: Either/Or vs. Either/And, the reality (which is not popular) of picking a career other than sport (Harrison, 1998).

When African Americans finally were allowed to attend predominantly white universities, their motivations were highly academic and intellectual (Harrison, working paper). These student-athletes utilized sport as a means to gain access to the educational components of the university. This image is very different from that of today's African American male athletes, many of whom view athletics as their number one priority. The media has also created limited identities for African American males, as the images promoted for them tend to be athletes, entertainers, or criminals (Hawkins, 1998). These images become engrained in the mentality of many young African Americans and, after they have internalized these images, little effort is made to choose different academic or career-oriented paths.

Further, African American males lack role models that represent black masculinity through images other than athlete, entertainer, and criminal. Images of the approximately thirty-two thousand black physicians and lawyers in the U.S. are not prevalent in mainstream popular culture media. There are only about thirty-five hundred professional athletes in revenue-producing sports (Coakley, 1999, 2001). This lack of intellectual black male images also promotes the ideology that "school is not cool," and academic achievement becomes a rejected identity. Not only that, but many young African American athletes do not believe that they can be both a "baller" and a "scholar." The phenomenon of picking just one becomes salient, and as the media promotes the baller more than the scholar, the choice to be a baller is more readily chosen (Comeaux and Harrison, in press).

Several problematic issues arise with the existence of mythical black male images. African American coaches and administrators are often absent from intercollegiate and professional athletics (Hoberman, 1997); this reinforces the perception or belief that African Americans lack of intellectual ability to hold positions of power. More importantly, black and white athletes have conflicts as well, due to the pervasive image that black males are better athletes and white males are more intelligent at the expense of white athleticism. Further, white sport fans who consistently cheer and celebrate the black athlete often still engage in racist behaviors and dialogue (Hoberman, 1997).

The image of the black athlete has a history in our society. One example is the Jim Crow era that was founded on a principle of racial superiority. African Americans were viewed as inferior and inhuman (Davis, 1995). This ideology was based on stereotypes of physical characteristics of African Americans (such as strength and stamina) such as strength and stamina and their perceived intellectual inferiority. For example, whites believed that African American athletes could not follow structured sports rules with "sophisticated whites" (Davis, 1995).

The Harlem Globetrotters of the 1940s reinforced this notion with the image they portrayed. The Harlem Globetrotters were often comedic and interrupted the game to taunt the crowd, the other team, and even the game officials (King and Springwood, 2001). This behavior led to an image of African American athletes as not being serious and helped to elicit justifications for their exclusion from organized sport. The success and failures of African American athletes were attributed to their physiology versus their psychology.

As mentioned earlier, today's images of African American athletes are products of more covert racist practices. The old notions of intellectual inferiority and physical superiority are denied by white consciousness and exist in more subtle forms (Davis, 1995). This same ideology exists for white athletes as well. Their athletic success is often attributed only to their "intellectual resourcefulness" and not athletic ability. This construct is problematic in that the overt racism is falsely stereotyping both black and white athletes (Davis, 1995).

The popular media plays a critical role in the image reinforcement of athletes. Stereotypes of white and black athletes are pervasive throughout print media and advertising. Too often these images falsely stereotype and influence the role identities of the athletes themselves and those placed upon them by others. Contact between white and black people is still highly limited (Edwards, 1989), and the media becomes a salient source of information and image transfer between whites and blacks.

Within sports there remains a "racial hierarchy" that show whites dominating management and ownership (Childs, 1999). This creates the disparity in contact between whites and blacks. Sport does not yet avail itself of favorable conditions via the contact hypothesis (discussed in the pages that follow) to alleviate racial prejudices. The media also still reinforce the unequal status of blacks and whites in the United States. Dates and Barlow (1993) suggest that white Americans are given a false impression of black life, art, and culture (Dates and Barlow, 1993). These false images concurrently help to shape public opinion on race issues that increase the cultural gap between white and black America (Dates, 1993). In order to change the negative images of the black male, the media must help to promote the ideology of equality.

Several theories are applicable in evaluating the image reinforcement of revenue-producing African American male student-athletes. A few are more relevant than others, including Labeling Theory, Stigma Theory, and the Contact Hypothesis.

Howard Becker contributed to the theory of labeling in *Outsiders: Studies in the Sociology of Deviance* (1963). A label is a definition that is externally attached to a person by an audience which then creates this definition based on its perceptions of the person (Becker, 1963). The process by which labels are created and applied to people or groups by an audience is the "labeling process" (Goffman, 1959). The label of "athlete" in relation to student-athlete retention is problematic because of the emphasis on "athlete" at the expense of "student" (Comeaux and Harrison, in press). As in the earlier discussion of role identification, student-athletes are often referred to as "athletes" only and not recognized as much for their student status. In other words, the term "athlete" has developed a meaning of its own throughout history by the individuals who are labeled and by institutional forces such as sport, society, and American higher education. Often these institutions socialize a cultural bias towards athletics (Smith, 1988).

The "athlete" label is further complicated by its pseudo-term in popular music, sports, and entertainment culture the "baller" (Comeaux and

Harrison, in press). The term can be used as a noun, adjective, or verb (Boyd and Shropshire, 2000). The "baller" label is considered desirable at the amateur level of intercollegiate athletics in terms of popularity on campus and recognition nationwide (Comeaux and Harrison, in press). The commercialization of college athletics, incorporating the selling of student-athletes' jerseys, television and radio exposure, and possible opportunities for playing at the professional level, often influences the label of "baller" for college athletes (Comeaux and Harrison, in press).

There are possible consequences when labels are applied to a person or group. When someone is labeled and identified as "deviant" by an external audience, it may lead to negative reactions from the audience (Harrison and Lampman, 2001). When negative reactions persist they may affect the emotional state of the alleged deviant, which may intensify deviant activity of the labeled individual (Harrison and Lampman, 2001).

Labels are applied by individuals based on their subjective perceptions. Therefore, certain groups may be inappropriately labeled even in the absence of guilt (i.e., scholar-ballers who are academically invested student-athletes but still popular and not considered "nerds, geeks, busters, or sellouts"). The status of "who" individuals are can influence how they are labeled as much as what they do. An example would be the status on campus of a high-profile athlete or "baller" (Harrison and Lampman, 2001). In the labeling process, characteristics of the person being labeled are more important than characteristics of the supposed act (Becker, 1963; Goffman, 1959). For example, student-athletes who are academically invested may be labeled as athlete only and a person's perception of the label may be a false stereotype. In addition, self-internalization can result for African American students from peer-group pressures involving academic achievement, with those successful labeled as "acting white," "being a buster," "a sellout," or an "Uncle Tom." African American students must deal with the fear that if they perform well in school they will have problems conforming to their peer group (Ogbu and Matute-Bianchi, 1986).

Gordon Allport's Contact Hypothesis suggests that the majority of attitudes that a person has are formed based on conversations with his/her family (Allport, 1954). The Contact Hypothesis also states that when groups interact and the context of these interactions is favorable, prejudice is reduced (Allport, 1954). There are five favorable conditions: (1) equal status between the members of the various ethnic groups, (2) supporting social climate to promote the intergroup contact, (3) intimate rather than casual nature of contact, (4) pleasant and rewarding contacts, (5) common goals (Allport, 1954). Contact will decrease negative attitudes held towards the stigmatized group if these conditions are met. This framework may suggest that in collegiate sports the disparity between the equality of the athlete and fan, athlete and coach, athlete and faculty, or athlete and administration may not be a favorable condition to reduce prejudice. African American student-athletes are not readily in contact with white constituents in the campus environment (Chavous, 2000), which is not conducive to the reduction of prejudice using the contact hypothesis.

For members of the athletic population of revenue-producing sports, stigma is not reduced due to lack of contact. Stigma Theory, suggested by Goffman in *Stigma: Notes on the Management of Spoiled Identity* (1971), suggests that the college campus is a setting conducive to the establishment of categories, labels, and stigmas (Harrison, working paper). The basic principle behind stigma theory comes from the Greeks who used the term stigma to refer to bodily signs designed to expose something unusual and bad about the moral status of the signified (Harrison, working paper). Goffman explains this framework by noting:

> *While the stranger is present before us, evidence can arise of his possessing an attribute that makes him different from others in the category of persons available for him to be, and of a less desirable kind—in the extreme, a person who is quite thoroughly bad, or dangerous or weak. He is thus reduced in our minds from a whole and usual person to a tainted, discounted one. Such an attribute is a stigma, especially when its discrediting effect is very extensive; sometimes it is also called a failing, a shortcoming, a handicap. It constitutes a special discrepancy between virtual and actual social identity. (Goffman, 1963, p. 3)*

Stigma theory will be used to evaluate how the campus environment and its constituents perceive African American male student-athletes on a traditionally white campus. Examining these stigmas may help to decipher specific attitudes that contribute to the negative stigma of the student-athlete experience for African American males.

METHODS

Visual elicitation is a technique of interviewing in which photographs are used to stimulate and guide a discussion between the interviewer and the researcher(s) (Snyder and Kane, 1990). This method has been used extensively by anthropologists but infrequently by sport science scholars (Curry, 1986). Considering the salience of cultural artifacts and images in sport, the use of photographs is pertinent to study the attitudes and meanings of people associated with sports (Gonzalez and Jackson, 2001).

As argued by Johnson, Hallinan, and Westerfield (1999), "photographs may be used as a research tool to evoke thoughts, reactions, and feelings from individuals about some aspect of social life" (256). Cauthen, Robinson, and Karaus (1991) claimed, "The use of pictures is the best because it allows the most latitude in determining the content of the stereotype" (105).

This paper seeks to analyze the graduation rate of African American male student-athletes with a mixed-method approach: "These are studies that are products of the pragmatist and that combine the qualitative and quantitative approaches within different phases of the research process" (Tashakkori and Teddlie, 1998, p. 19). It is hoped that this approach will reveal empirical answers that are meaningful, reliable, and solid (Tashakkori and Teddlie, 1998).

DATA ANALYSIS

Quantitative

Using the Statistical Package for the Social Sciences (SPSS), a cross tab and chi square test were run to discern differences between African Americans and whites on a number of background variables. These background variables include number of hours of television watched a day in both college and in high school; the type of community participants grew up in; and the percentage of African Americans in the participants' high school and neighborhood. The sample was broken into two groups, African Americans and whites. A series of t-tests were run to examine the statistical significance of differences between these groups on a number of items which measured the participants' attitudes related to socioeconomic status (SES), gender, race, and effects on student-athletes' graduation rates.

Qualitative
Narratives were transferred and coded from the Graduate Image Instrument (GII hereafter) by two trained researchers and one trained graduate student. Themes were logically coded and categorized based on previous studies, related research literature of student-athletes, and patterns of participants.

Hierarchical content analysis, as suggested by Patton (1990), was utilized in the analysis. Following transcription, each investigator read each participant's transcript in order to get a sense of the student's experiences. Each investigator independently identified raw-data themes that characterized each participant's responses. Then the investigative team met to begin discussing the transcripts. The primary purpose of this meeting was to interpret and identify major themes. Raw-data themes were utilized in conducting an inductive analysis in order to identify common themes or patterns of greater generality. Themes were derived from all of the transcripts and attempts were made to interpret commonalities among the experiences described in each of the transcripts (Patton, 1990). Major themes and sub-themes were identified across transcripts and support for each theme was located in each of the transcripts (Patton, 1990).

Participants
In the fall of 2001, data were collected from 273 students in an introductory communications class at a large midwestern university. The majority of the sample was female (70 percent) and nineteen years of age or younger (73.6 percent); the remaining 26.4 percent were between the

ages of twenty and twenty-two. The racial distribution was as follows: 78 percent were white, followed by 11.7 percent Asian, 6.6 percent African American, 1.8 percent Hispanic, and 1.8 percent other. Participants received one point extra credit from their instructor for participating in the study.

Survey Instrument/Questionnaire

The GII contained 32 items. This instrument was constructed with experts in the field of sport sociology and higher education. The majority of the items on this instrument were structured and measured using a five point Likert scale. The responses were coded as 1 = Strongly Agree, 2 = Agree, 3 = Neutral, 4 = Disagree, 5 = Strongly Disagree. For example one item read, "University students graduate on time." A second item read, "Male students graduate on time."

Reliabilities were run on the items and alphas were obtained. The items measured perceptions of student athletes and non-athletes on SES, race, and gender. The following are the results of the internal consistencies:

(1) SES effects student athletes rate of graduation (3 items, a = .61)
(2) SES effects non-student athletes' rate of graduation (3 items, a = .81)
(3) African American male football and basketball players graduate on time (2 items, a = .93)
(4) White male football and basketball players graduate on time (2 items, a = .90)
(5) African American women track and basketball players graduate on time (2 items, a = .92)
(6) White women track and basketball players graduate on time (2 items, a = .93)

There are thirty-one items and one open-ended question.

Procedure

The GII was distributed to students in one very large introductory communication class. Students had approximately 20 minutes to fill out the questionnaire. The data was collected by trained research assistants. Hypotheses are as follows:

(1) White students' perceptions will differ from African American students' perceptions of whether African American male football and basketball players graduate on time.
(2) White students' perceptions will differ from African American students' perceptions of whether white male football and basketball players graduate on time.

FINDINGS AND RESULTS

Demographics
On average, students reported watching up to three hours a day of television while in high school and only two hours of television a day while in college. African American students watched significantly more television a day both in college and in high school than whites. In high school African Americans reported watching up to four hours of TV a day while whites watched three ($t = .2.69$, $p < .05$). In college African Americans reported watching up to three hours of TV a day while whites reported watching two hours a day ($t = -3.4$, $p < .05$). About 15 percent of the sample played intercollegiate sports.

The majority of the students in the sample grew up in the suburbs, followed by large urban cities, small cities, small towns, and rural communities. Even more interesting is the racial distribution by type of community. A chi square test indicates that race differed significantly by type of community. A little over 60 percent of whites reported growing up in the suburbs, while 57 percent of African Americans grew up in large urban cities. The differences in the types of communities where whites and African Americans reside were statistically significant ($x^2 = 40.11$, $p < .01$).

On the other hand, only 7 percent of African Americans reported that their high schools had zero African American students while 23.7 percent of whites said their high school had zero African American students ($x^2 = 67.72$, $p < .01$). A similar pattern was found among neighborhoods.

African Americans were significantly more likely than whites to grow up in neighborhoods that were more African American ($x^2 = 85.29$, p $<$ .01). These data are strong indicators of Allport's contact hypothesis and the lack of exposure that blacks and whites have traditionally had to one another.

HYPOTHESES AND QUANTITATIVE RESULTS

Students were asked questions regarding their perceptions of college student-athletes and graduation, and two hypotheses were examined.

H1: White students' perceptions will differ from African American students' perceptions of whether African American male football and basketball players graduate on time.

H1 Results: White students' perceptions did not differ significantly on whether African American male football and basketball players graduate on time.

H2: White students' perceptions will differ from African American students' perceptions of whether white male football and basketball players graduate on time.

H2 Results: White students' perceptions did not differ from that of African Americans about white male football players graduating on time. However, whites were more likely to feel neutral about the statement, "white American basketball players graduate on time" while African Americans were more likely to agree with it (t = 1.8, p $<$ .10).

Over 35 percent of African Americans reported that their high school was 50 percent African American or more while only 6.7 percent of whites reported their high school was 50 percent African American or more. Whites were significantly more likely to agree that students from lower economic classes graduate on time than African Americans, who felt more neutral about the issue.

Whites were significantly more likely to feel neutral about the statement "white basketball players graduate on time"; African Americans were more likely to agree with it. White students were significantly more likely to feel neutral/agree with the statement "women African

American players graduate on time," while African American students were more likely to agree/agree strongly with the statement.

The following major themes emerged from the open-ended questions. These themes describe the perceptions, attitudes, and feelings concerning the visual representation of the graduation of student-athletes. The themes include Balance the Commitment, Dumb Jock Myth, Leaving School Early, Breaks Stereotypes, and Role Model.

The theme of Balancing the Commitment between athletics and academics emerged more than all others with 33 percent of African American respondents; 41 percent of whites responded the same. This theme had several sub-categories such as time management, hard work, and dedication:

> *This man was very focused and determined. He must have worked hard because of the time restraints of balancing sports and school (137).*
>
> *I think this is very impressive that this person managed playing football, an accounting major and finishing in four years at once. Not to mention, he probably knew he had a chance at the NFL and wanted to get a degree in a difficult field anyway. He must be a very driven and dedicated individual (025).*

The second theme is Dumb Jock Myth. This theme emerged 24 percent of the time for white respondents and not at all for African American respondents. This was the second most prevalent theme from white respondents. This result may indicate that white respondents more than African American respondents view African American male student-athletes as dumb jocks and intellectually inferior:

> *When I first looked at this picture I saw a rare exception to the norm that this black man graduated on time with a legitimately challenging degree such as accounting. I can't help thinking about all the private tutoring and extra help that went in to him receiving his degree. Although he may just be a smart, athletic black man, I see him as someone who got in to the university based on either his athletic abilities or affirmative action. I am embarrassed to have written what I just did, but unfortunately, these are my personal perceptions (169).*

The third theme of Leaving School Early to participate in professional sports emerged in both African American and white narratives. Both brought this theme up 11 percent of the time. This theme plays on the notion that African American male student-athletes would leave school early to try and play professional sports instead of finishing their degree and then attempting to advance to the next level. However, most of the narratives felt that it was positive that the student-athlete did not leave school early:

> I think he has accomplished a major goal and has done something unique in society. He has completed college before going on to play professional football (156).
>
> I am impressed that this young man stayed in school and got his degree in accounting before heading to the NFL. It seems that most of the stories I hear about student athletes say that athletes will drop out of school to play professional sports, and I think it is important for athletes, or anyone, to have a degree to fall back on in case things do not go as planned (065).

In the fourth theme, that the image Breaks Stereotypes, 27.7 percent of African American respondents expressed that the image of the African American male student-athlete graduating breaks the stereotypical image. This theme emerged for white respondents only 7 percent of the time. This may be a reflection of the previous theme, Dumb Jock Myth. Most white respondents still promoted the stereotype of Dumb Jock and therefore, the theme for Breaks Stereotypes seems to not be very relevant:

> I think that this picture represents the opposite of the stereotypical African American male student-athlete. Most people probably think that these men are not serious students, who only take easy classes. Accounting is by no means an easy course. Also, most people would probably be surprised that he majored in accounting and then "wasted" the hard earned degree by going right into the NFL (002).
>
> I feel as though the young black student appears qualified, dignified, honored and respected. I think there is a widely known stereotype that African American men who play collegiate sports lack the intellect to attend certain universities . . . clearly, this young man proves otherwise (150).

Fifth is the theme of Role Models. Several respondents felt that the picture of the African American male student-athletes was a positive image of a role model. This theme may have emerged because it is lacking in mainstream views of African American male student-athletes; it is not yet commonplace for this academic image to be seen. It is a positive sign that there were responses from both black and white respondents that this image is one of a role model:

> *I feel that this man should be made as an example for not just black athletes but all. You should come to get your education and then play the sport second (219).*
>
> *The first thought that came to my mind was pride. This African American student probably felt extreme accomplishment on this day. As a part of a minority group, and an oppressed race, he is acting as a representative for his entire race. He is probably thinking that he or any other African American can conquer any goal he or she strives for (123).*

Discussion

Much research has dealt with the indicators of poor academic performance of African American males (Sellers, 1992). This research has been valuable in evaluating the factors contributing to this academic inadequacy. However, research is lacking on the question of what to do about this inadequacy. If the problems that existed thirty years ago remain today, what must be done to break the cycle of academic failure for African American male student-athletes? Much of the current research evaluates attitudes and perceptions of white and African American students toward student-athletes and graduation, in an attempt to decipher if these attitudes may be influenced to become more positive toward an academic image for student-athletes, especially African American male student-athletes. Engaging this image will promote academically and athletically sound student-athletes.

Media hype and sociocultural conditioning often contribute to the dreams of many black men to be successful in sport and not in academics (Spigner, 1995). The media and images of the African American male athlete play a critical role in addressing these academic issues. Influencing the attitudes of major constituents involved in intercollegiate athletics is key to eliciting new academic images of African American student-athletes. Increasing the frequency of graduation is a recommendation for motivating this attitude change.

In the book *Cognitive Responses in Persuasion* (Petty, Ostrom, and Brock, 1981), the authors discuss that "the cognitive response approach postulates that when people receive persuasive communications, they will attempt to relate the new information to their existing knowledge about the topic" (p. 13). In doing so, the person may use cognitive material that is not in the communication itself. These self-generated cognitions may agree, disagree, or be irrelevant with what the source proposes (Petty, Ostrom, and Brock, 1981). This research attempts to evaluate attitudes and perceptions concerning African American male student-athletes, and to provide solutions that in effect change negative attitudes and perceptions. To understand cognitive response persuasion, one must understand the key components: attitude and persuasion.

The word attitude refers to a "general orientation toward something" (Petty et al. 1981). Sociologist Herbert Spencer was the first to use the word attitude as a mental concept (i.e., having the right attitude) in his book *First Principles* in 1862 (Petty et al. 1981). Charles Darwin elevated the word attitude in his work *Expressions of the Emotions in Man and Animals* (cited in Petty et al. 1981) by referring to the word as a motor concept (e.g., a scowling face meaning hostility).

Darwin defined attitude as a "biological mobilization to respond" (Petty et al., 1981). Over time, researchers have moved toward defining attitude as less physiological than cognitive, and have developed measurement tools for attitudes to satisfy empirical science. The first effort to sample public attitudes was done by Robert and Helen Lynd in 1929 when they published *Middletown*, which examined life in Muncie, Indiana (Petty et al. 1981). Petty et al. (1981) further contend that "by World War II, the cognitive conception of attitude was well entrenched in American scientific and lay vocabularies" (p. 10).

As the concept of attitude was created, research began to focus on attitude change. Several theories approach attitude change based on the concept of persuasion, including Learning Theory, Perceptual Theory, Functional Theory and Consistency Theory (Petty et al., 1981). For our purposes, Perceptual Theory is the most applicable.

Petty et al. (1981) describe Perceptual Theory as one that "emphasizes the meaning that the persuasive communication has for the subject" (p. 11). In order to have an indication of the attitude that will arise from the communication, one must understand the person's perception of it (Petty et al. 1981). Perception has two general effects on attitude change: selectivity of perception and frame of reference. Selectivity of perception evaluates the portion of the "objective world" that a person is paying attention to (Petty et al., 1981). Frame of reference examines context that may influence a person's perception. Visual stimulus is a prevalent form of image exposure and can be used to elicit more positive academic perceptions of African American male student-athletes. Negotiating any change in attitude toward this population will call for the use of visual interaction and experiences.

There is growing interest in the use of visual experiences when studying social and cultural realities. Images have become a means of circulating signs, symbols, and information (Curry, 1986; Fischman, 2001). Fischman (2001) contends that understanding visual culture will ultimately reveal relationships with the perception and reception of images regarding cultural, social, and economic conditions of the consumers and producers of visual culture (Fischman, 2001).

SOLUTIONS: HOW DO WE INCREASE THE FREQUENCY OF THE ACADEMIC MESSAGE?

Several forms of media promote images of African American male student-athletes. This research attempts to target the message promoted at the college campus level: athletic media guides made by the universities. These guides detail the experiences of student-athletes while attending their respective universities. However, academic messages are lacking and completely absent in some cases, giving the impression that studies do not play a prevalent role in the student-athlete experience. How can it be that intercollegiate athletic media guides deny the "student" portion of the "student-athlete" experience? To market the academic message to incoming recruits, boosters, general students, and society as a whole, media guides must take a more proactive approach of incorporating academics as integral to the student-athlete experience.

A preliminary textual analysis of Division I media guides found a paucity of academic messages. The following are a few examples of the academic messages presented in these media guides.

University of Mississippi features a photograph from the graduation ceremony of three of their student-athletes, team captains Deuce McAllister, Romaro Miller, and Shane Elam, with head football coach David Cutcliff and Chancellor Robert Khayat. The caption notes that 79 percent of Ole Miss's football players graduate. This picture illustrates the commitment of the student-athlete, the coach, and the administration to the promotion of academics as well as athletics.

A photograph in West Virginia University's media guide promotes the message of black masculinity with a representation of athleticism and academics. Four Mountaineer football players—Antwan Lake, Chris Edmonds, Terry Dixon, and David Carter—are shown in their caps and gowns; two are wearing ceremonial stoles from black fraternities, an image which promotes the fact that student-athletes are engaged in other aspects of college life and can balance them with the commitment to athletics.

The media guide for the University of Michigan's athletic department presents two photographs of Anthony Thomas, a star running back at Michigan and a current NFL player. The companion photographs, one taken at graduation and the other an action shot from the football field, promote both the athletic and academic message in the same context that brings the concept of scholar-baller to life.

Student-athletes utilizing an academic resource center are key in the message that promotes student-athletes engaged academically and show that the university is committed to providing them with the resources that they need to succeed.

These few examples of academic messages must be promoted more often in athletic media guides. Positive academic images of student-athletes in no way detract from the athletic prowess of these student-athletes. Promoting the academic message should only strengthen the prowess of an athletic reputation. There should be no question that the exclusion of positive and more diverse images is beneficial to the success of student-athletes, especially African Americans. Without the introduction of positive academic images, African American student-athletes will continue to suffer the lowest GPAs and graduation rates.

Two qualitative telephone interviews were also conducted with academic administrators to elicit thoughts and attitudes on the perceived issue of "baller syndrome" for African American male student-athletes. These interviews addressed the following issues: What are the effects of "baller syndrome"? What do consideration of self and low expectations have on student-athletes' academic performance? What are the effects of the "scholar-baller" notion when presented to student-athletes? What role should academic administrators play in promoting the academic message for student-athletes, the general public, and other campus constituents (faculty, students, university administration, athletic department administration, and coaching staff[s])?

Jean Boyd is the Manager for Student Services and Football Academic Development at Arizona State University. Boyd believes that the creation of the baller image stems from early-age socialization in predominantly inner-city African American communities (author interview, 2002). Boyd cites Hoberman's (1997) work that discussed how these young African American youth grow up watching the evening news where the only black faces are athletes, entertainers, or criminals. Boyd felt that the reinforcement of the baller image comes from student-athletes viewing themselves as ballers first and foremost. This reinforcement occurs in class, walking on campus, even going to the grocery store, because they receive acknowledgement and prestige for their athletic abilities.

Boyd feels that his role as a sports administrator is to "brand the concept" of the scholar-baller, and that this branding must occur during the recruitment process so that student-athletes are aware of the expectations. Boyd is animated in his efforts to translate competition on the field to competition in the classroom, to capitalize on the strengths of student-athletes who have developed into fierce competitors. Some of the ways Boyd "brands" scholar-ballers are through a scholar-baller board in the athletic department highlighting all student-athletes with a GPA of 3.0 or above. He also sends personal letters congratulating these student-athletes. There is also an end-of-the-year celebration to honor those students where each receives a T-shirt with a scholar-baller image. Boyd strongly agrees that visual acknowledgement is very important in branding the scholar-baller image and message. He stated, "Once they [student-athletes] understand the paradigm, they own it." Mr. Boyd shared a story that ended with a student-athlete asking, "What can I do to be one [a scholar-baller]?"

Boyd believes that the effects of the scholar-baller image on the student-athlete is that they mentally connect competition to another area; classes have more meaning and scholar-baller terminology begins to be used in the athlete peer subculture.

Dr. Harry McLaughlin is the Director of Academic Services for the Division of Kinesiology at the University of Michigan. Dr. McLaughlin believes that the baller image is presented to black male student-athletes at ages four or five based on what they see at home. He says that the baller image is reinforced when coaches and universities begin taking an interest in the student-athletes. The message consumed by these student-athletes is that someone outside of the home is taking an interest in their athletic abilities alone.

Dr. McLaughlin suggests that this baller notion is reinforced on campus because there is no reward system in place for student-athletes who excel academically. They also have to commit so much structured time to athletics that often they are exhausted and miss classes, excluding them from academics and campus culture.

Dr. McLaughlin alluded to structural inadequacies in terms of addressing the persistent academic problems of black male student-athletes. Often, athletic departments throw money at a problem without any viable solutions. They spend time getting students to maintain average grades and attend class "just enough." The athletic department is spending money trying to get the minimum requirements for eligibility, and nothing more. This "stand-alone" structure removes student-athletes from campus. Further, this allows the university president to become apathetic about the academic performance of student-athletes. McLaughlin states, "No president says he doesn't care [about academic performance of student-athletes], but do they do anything about the problem?"

Further, student-athletes become scapegoats for problems on campus for which the university itself shares the blame. Faculty and university administrators often blame lack of motivation on the part of the student-athlete as the cause of the breakdown in academic performance. Dr. McLaughlin calls this elitist mentality a system that perpetuates and rewards stereotypes. In order to overcome this mentality, student-athletes must work through these stereotypes.

Dr. McLaughlin feels that to improve the academic performance of student-athletes, the culture of athletics must change. This change involves images perpetuated by the coaching staff, structural academic support services, and interactions with faculty. Dr. McLaughlin shared a story about his own experience with faculty interaction as a student-athlete. He was nervous to attend office hours of his professors and would actually stand outside the office and debate going in. As both a student and an athlete, he did not feel comfortable with the faculty-student interaction. This is a common problem that needs to be addressed in order to improve the academics of all students.

It is evident that, in order to increase the frequency of the academic message and engage the concept of scholar-baller, universities and athletic departments must be willing to represent the complete life of a student-athlete. Intercollegiate media guides are only one of many forms of exposure that student-athletes have during their college careers. Other sources of exposure should be examined for their quality and quantity of promoting the academic message for the scholar-baller.

FUTURE RESEARCH AND LIMITATIONS

The main limitation of this research is that the comparison group of African Americans was small (N = 18). Therefore, some effects may not have been found statistically significant. Increasing the sample size would reduce the degree of error and increase the likelihood of finding actual effects.

Future research needs to address this issue, possibly including over-sampling of African Americans in order to have an equal number of participants in the white and African American groups. Also, future research should examine through random design the perceptions of both students and student-athletes at small and large institutions. Another stimulus with the same visual-elicitation approach may cultivate other interesting responses.

References

Adler, P. and Adler, P. (1987). Role conflict and identity salience: College athletics and the academic role. *The Social Science Journal*, 24 (4), 443–455.

Allport, G. (1954). *The nature of prejudice*. Garden City, New York: Doubleday Anchor Books.

Andrews, V. (1997). African American player codes on celebration, taunting and sportsmanlike conduct. *Journal of African American Men*, 2 (2/3), pp. 57–92.

Baucom, C. and Lantz, C. (2001). Faculty attitudes toward male Division II student-athletes. *Journal of Sport Behavior*, 24 (3), pp. 265–274.

Becker, H. (1963). *Outsiders: Studies in the sociology of deviance*. New York: The Free Press.

Benson, K. F. (2000). Constructing academic inadequacy: African American athletes' stories of schooling. *The Journal of Higher Education*, 71 (2), p. 1–10.

Brooks, D. and Althouse, R. (eds.) (2000). *Racism in college athletics: the African American athlete's experience*. Morgantown, WV: Fitness Information Technology.

Boyd, Jean. Author interview, May 8th, 2002.

Boyd, T. and Shropshire, K. (2000). *America above the rim: Basketball Jones*. New York: New York University Press.

Cauthen, N. R., Robinson, I. E., and Krauss, H. H. (1971). Stereotypes: A review of the literature 1926–1968. *Journal of Social Psychology*, 84, 103–125.

Chavous, T. (2000). The relationships among racial identity, perceived ethnic fit, and organizational involvement for African American students at a predominantly white university. *Journal of Black Psychology*, 26 (1), 79–100.

Childs, E. (1999). Images of the black athlete: Intersection of race, sexuality, and sports. *Journal of African American Men*, 4 (2).

Coakley, J. (2001). *Sport in society: Issues and controversies*. Boston, MA: McGraw Press.

Comeaux, E. and Harrison, C. K. (in press). Labels of African American ballers: A historical and contemporary investigation of African American male youth's depletion from America's favorite pastime, 1885–2000. *Journal of American Culture*.

Curry, T. (1986). A visual method of studying sports: The photo-elicitation interview. *Sociology of Sport Journal*, 3, 204–216.

Dates, J. and Barlow, W. (1993). *Split Image: African Americans in the mass media.* Washington, D.C.: Howard University Press.

Davis, T. (1995). The myth of the Superspade: The persistence of racism in college athletics. *Fordham Urban Law Journal,* XXII (3).

Davis, T. (1999). Racism in athletics: Subtle yet persistent. Paper presented at the Ben J. Altheimer Symposium: Racial Equity in the Twenty-First Century, Feb. 26–27, 1999.

Duderstadt, J. (2000). *Intercollegiate athletics and the American university.* Ann Arbor, MI: University of Michigan Press.

Dyson, M. E. (1993). *Reflecting black: African American cultural criticism.* Minneapolis, MN: University of Minnesota Press.

Edwards, H. (1971). The sources of black athletic superiority. *Black Scholar,* 33–41.

Edwards, H. (1973). The black athletes: 20th Century gladiators for white America. *Psychology Today,* 43–52.

Edwards, H. (1979). Sport within the veil: The triumphs, tragedies, and challenges of Afro-American involvement. *Annals of the Academy.*

Edwards, H. (1989). Racism in sports. Lecture given at the University of Michigan, Ann Arbor.

Ellickson, K. (April 1990). Do sports sap energy? *USA Today* 118, 12–13.

Engstrom, C. and Sedlacek, W. (1991). A study of prejudice toward college student athletes. *Journal of Counseling and Development,* 70, 189–193.

Fischman, G. (2001). Reflections about images, visual culture, and educational research. *Research News and Comment,* 28–33.

Gates, H. L. (1996). Thirteen ways of looking at a black man. In J. Arthur and A. Shapiro (Eds.), *Color class identity: The new politics of race* (11–23). Boulder, CO: Westview Press.

Goffman, E. (1959). *The presentation of self in everyday life.* University of Edinburgh Social Sciences Research Centre. Garden City, NY: Anchor Books.

Goffman, E. (1971, 1963). *Stigma: Notes of a spoiled identity.* Englewood Cliffs, NJ: Prentice Hall.

Gonzalez, G. L. and Jackson, N. (2001). Perceptions of success in professional baseball as determined by race/ethnicity: A photo-elicitation study. Paper presented at the North American Society for the Sociology of Sport Annual Meeting in San Antonio, TX.

Hallinan, C. J. and Snyder, E. E. (1987). Forced disengagement and the college athlete. *Arena Review,* 11, 28–34.

Harris, O. (1997). The role of sport in the black community. *Sociological Focus,* 30, 311–319.

Harris, O. (2000). *Racism in college athletics. African American predominance in sport.* Morgantown, West Virginia: Fitness Information Technology.

Harris, W. and Duhon, G. (eds.) (1999). *The African American perspective of barriers to success.* Lewiston, ME: The Edwin Mellen Press.

Harrison, C. K. (in review). Black issues in higher education's Arthur Ashe Awards (1995–2000): Invisible men and women (Scholars and Ballers).

Harrison, C. K. (in review). Images and perceptions of the revenue sport participant as college graduates in NCAA Division I athletics: A visual elicitation with university students.

Harrison, C. K. (1998). Themes that thread through society: Racism and athletic manifestation in the African American community. *Race Ethnicity and Education*, 1(1), 63–74.

Harrison, C. K. and Lampman, B. (2001). The image of Paul Robeson: Role model for the student and athlete. *Rethinking History*, 5(1), 117–130.

Hartmann, D. (2000). Rethinking the relationships between sport and race in American culture: Golden ghettos and contested terrain. *Sociology of Sport Journal*, 17, 229–253.

Hawkins, B. (1998). The dominant images of black men in America: The representation of O. J. Simpson. In G. Sailes (ed.), *African Americans in sport*. New Brunswick, NJ: Transaction Publishers.

Hoberman, J. (1997). *Darwin's athletes: How sport has damaged black America and preserved the myth of race*. Boston, MA: Houghton Mifflin.

King, R. C. and Springwood, C. (2001). *Beyond the cheers: Race as a spectacle in college sport*. New York: State University Press of New York.

Kirk, W. and Kirk, S. (eds.) (1993). *Student athletes: Shattering the myths and sharing the realities*. Alexandria, VA: American Counseling Association.

Knight Commission Report (2001).

Lapchick, K. E. and Slaughter, J. B. (1989). *The rules of the game: Ethics in college sports*. New York, NY: Macmillan.

McLaughlin, H. Author interview, May 10, 2002.

Myers, J. (1991 December 16). What's the difference? Studies inconclusive. *USA Today*.

Ogbu, J. U., and Matute-Bianchi, M. A. (1986). Understanding socio-cultural factors: Knowledge, identity, and social adjustment. In California State Department of Education, Bilingual Education Office, Beyond language: Social and cultural factors in schooling. Sacramento, CA: California State University Evaluation, Dissemination and Assessment Center.

Patton, M. Q. (1990). *Qualitative evaluation and research methods*. Newborn Park, CA: Sage.

Petty, R., Ostrom, T., and Brock, T. (eds.) (1981). *Cognitive responses in persuasion*. Hillsdale, NJ: Lawrence Erlbaum Associates.

Polite, V. and Davis, J. (eds.) (1999). *African American males in school and society*. New York: Teachers College Press.

Sailes, G. (1990). *Facts and figures on the black athlete: A reader*. Bloomington, IN: Indiana University Press.

Sellers, R. (1992). Racial differences in the predictors for academic achievement of student-athletes in Division I revenue producing sports. *Sociology of Sport Journal*, 9, 48–59.

Snyder, E. E., and Kane, M. J. (1990). Photo-elicitation: A methodological technique for studying sport. *Journal of Sport Management*, 4, 21–30.

Sperber, M. (1991). Why the NCAA can't reform college athletics. *Academe*, 77, 13–20.

Spigner, C. (1995). African American student-athletes: Academic support or institutionalized racism? *Education*, 114 (1).

Steele, C. M. (1997). A threat in the air: How stereotypes shape intellectual identity and performance. *American Psychologist*, 52, 613–629.

Stone, J. (2000). Stereotype threat effects on the performance of black and white athletes. Paper presented at the North American Society for the Sociology of Sport Annual Meeting in Colorado Springs, CO.

Tashakkori, A. and Teddlie, C. (1998). *Mixed Methodology: Combining qualitative and quantitative approaches*. London, UK: Sage Publications.

Vontress, C. E. (1971). Racial difference: Impediments to rapport. *Journal of Counseling Psychology*, 18, 7–13.

White, J. and Cones III, J. (1999). *Black man emerging: A black masculine coping and expressive style*. New York: Routledge.

Wilson, W. J. (1996). *When work disappears: The world of the new urban poor*. New York: Knopf.

CONTRIBUTORS

SCOTT BROOKS is an assistant professor of sociology at the University of California–Riverside. He studies black urban living as well as gender and race in sports and popular culture. He is currently working on a manuscript titled "The I in Team" which reports on young black male experiences in an inner city and the importance of basketball for their social status and masculinity. He is also co-editor and contributor to the *Annals* (August 2004) special volume on ethnography.

JOHN M. CARROLL is professor of history at Lamar University. He has published several books including *Red Grange and the Rise of Modern Football*, University of Illinois Press, 1999, and *Fritz Pollard: Pioneer in Racial Advancement*, University of Illinois Press, 1992. Recently he was a consultant and appeared on an ESPN special examining the early history of the National Football League. Currently he is working on a biography of Jim Brown.

GERALD R. GEMS is professor and chair of the Department of Health and Physical Education at North Central College in Illinois. He is the author of some ninety publications including his most recent book *For Pride, Profit, and Patriarchy: Football and the Incorporation of American Cultural Values*. He is the president-elect of the North American Society of Sport History and book review editor for the *Journal of Sport History*.

C. KEITH HARRISON established the Paul Robeson Research Center for Academic and Athletic Prowess at the University of Michigan in 1998 while on the faculty in sport management. He currently teaches at Arizona State University in the Division of Educational Leadership and Policy Studies and has published numerous peer-review articles and book chapters on student-athletes, masculinity and sport, and images of intercollegiate athletics in American higher education. The Black

Coaches Association (BCA) awarded Harrison a three-year grant to study the lack of diversity in the hiring process of Division IA and IAA head football coaches.

RITA LIBERTI is assistant professor of kinesiology and physical education at California State University, Hayward. Her published articles include "Black Feminist Theory and Women's Sport History"; "Exploring the Place and Significance of Physical Education at Black Colleges and Universities During the Late Nineteenth and Early Twentieth Centuries"; and "African American Womanhood and Competitive Basketball at Bennett College, 1928–1942."

MICHAEL E. LOMAX is assistant professor in the Department of Physical Education and Sport Studies at the University of Georgia. His published articles include "Black Entrepreneurship in the National Pastime: The Rise of Semiprofessional Baseball in Black Chicago, 1890–1915"; "If We Were White: Portrayals of Black and Cuban Players in Organized Baseball, 1880–1920"; and "Black Baseball's First Rivalry: The Cuban Giants and the Gorhams of New York and the Birth of the Colored Championship."

PATRICK B. MILLER is associate professor of history at Northeastern Illinois University. He is the author of *The Civil Rights Movement Revisited: Critical Perspectives on the Struggle for Racial Equality in the United States*, Transaction Press, 2001; *The Sporting World of the Modern South*, University of Illinois Press, 2002; and several scholarly articles. He appeared on ESPN's *Sports Century* in June 1998 and was consultant for the April 1994 PBS documentary *Safe at Home Plate*, about Negro League baseball in the South.

KENNETH L. SHROPSHIRE is professor of legal studies and real estate in the Wharton School of Business at the University of Pennsylvania. He has published several books including *The Business of Sports Agenda*, University of Pennsylvania Press, 2002; *In Black and White: Race and Sports in America*, New York University Press, 1996; and *The Sports Franchise Game: Cities in Pursuit of Sports Franchises, Events, Stadiums, and Arenas*, University of Pennsylvania Press, 1995. In January 1996 he testified before the Senate Judiciary Committee regarding professional sports franchise relocations. He has appeared on ESPN in December 2000 on its *Outside the Lines*, discussing "Marketing the Hip-Hop Athlete."

EARL SMITH is professor and chair of the Department of Sociology and director of the American Ethnic Studies Program at Wake Forest University. He is the author of several publications, including *A Comparative Study of Occupational Stress in African American and White University Faculty*, E. Mellen Press, 1992, and with Joyce Tang co-edited *Women and Minorities in American Professions*, published by State University of New York Press, 1996. Currently he is working on a book on African American female athletes. He is president of the North American Society for the Sociology of Sport.

ALICIA VALDEZ is the Director of Brand Management for the Detroit Pistons (NBA) and Detroit Shock (WNBA) at the Palace of Auburn Hills. She attended the sport management graduate program at the University of Michigan where her master's thesis was "Sport Management and Higher Education: An Investigation of the Cultural Images of Black Male Sport Participants in Basketball and Football That Construct and Transform the Athlete to Student-Athlete."

INDEX

Printed in the United States
87611LV00005B/157/A